Understanding Financial Information

Dr. Janice Cobb, Ed.D, CPA

innovativeink
PUBLISHING

Cover image Shutterstock.com

innovativeink PUBLISHING

www.innovativeinkpublishing.com
Send all inquiries to:
4050 Westmark Drive
Dubuque, IA 52004-1840

Print ISBN: 979-8-3197-1164-9

Published in the United States of America

Table of Contents

1. Accounting and Reporting Guidance

Accounting guidance was first provided by the **Committee on Accounting Procedure (CAP)** of the **American Institute of Accountants (AIA)** which was subsequently renamed the **American Institute of Certified Public Accountants (AICPA).**

The AICPA is the current national professional organization of accountants. The CAP issued 51 *Accounting Research Bulletins* (ARBs) between 1938 and 1958 that provided guidance for specific accounting and reporting issues.

The **Accounting Principles Board (APB)** replaced the CAP in 1959. The APB issued 31 *Accounting Principles Board Opinions* (Opinions) between 1959 and 1973. Members of the Accounting Principles Board were voluntary, part-time, lacked independence, and did not have the time to devote to issuing timely guidance.

The **Financial Accounting Standards Board (FASB)** replaced the APB in 1973 to provide unbiased and dedicated effort to addressing financial accounting and reporting issues.

FASB is the current independent non-governmental organization that provides accounting and reporting guidance in the United States. FASB consists of seven full-time voting board members and a large staff of accountants to research accounting issues. Audit partners, corporate accountants, educators, financial analysts, and capital investment advisors (among others) serve as FASB voting members.

The goal of the FASB is to provide accounting guidance that results in useful financial information. New business transactions require new accounting guidance. Guidance that has been followed for many years often needs revision to report the current economic impact of transactions.

FASB issues accounting standards after consulting accounting and finance professionals.
A formal process occurs as follows:

- The investment or accounting community identifies a reporting issue and makes a request for consideration to the FASB.
- The FASB Chairman adds the issue to the agenda.
- FASB staff research the issue and identify associated issues.
- The Board deliberates the various issues identified at one or more public meetings.
- The Board issues a *Discussion Draft* or an *Exposure Draft* to the business community for comments.
- FASB receives and incorporates comments into a revised draft.
- The process of comments and revision continues until proposed guidance is **generally accepted** by most users of financial statements involved in the process.
- The FASB votes on and approves new guidance.
- The Board issues revised accounting guidance that states the amendment to GAAP.

A detail discussion of the issues and projects FASB is currently addressing is available on their website at www.fasb.org. The total body of guidance accountants follow is referred to as **generally accepted accounting principles** (GAAP).

Current GAAP is organized and numbered according to **Accounting Standard Codification Topics** (ASC) as follows:

Topic	Numbered
General Principles	100 - 199
Presentation	200 - 299
Assets	300 - 399
Liabilities	400 - 499
Equity	500 - 599
Revenues	600 - 699
Expenses	700 - 799
Broad Transactions	800 - 899
Industry	900 - 999

The **Securities Exchange Commission** (SEC) is the government entity that regulates the information public companies are required to provide to investors and creditors. The SEC was established just after the stock market crash of 1929 to ensure public companies provide reliable financial information. The SEC has delegated the authority to issue accounting guidance to the FASB; however, the SEC also issues accounting guidance when necessary (called Staff Accounting Bulletins and Financial Reporting Releases). Public companies that violate SEC reporting requirements violate the law.

Privately held companies are not required to follow GAAP. However, privately held companies that do not follow GAAP find it very difficult to obtain money from outsiders. Investors and lenders who allocate capital generally do not have confidence in financial information that is not prepared in accordance with GAAP.

Public Accounting Firms (the Auditor)

Public accounting firms (auditors) review and issue an opinion on financial statements and footnotes before the financial information is provided to the general public (**audit**). The **auditor's report** states whether or not the financial statements are fairly presented in accordance with GAAP. **Fairly presented** means a user of the financial information **would not be misled** when relying on the information to make a financial decision. Fairly presented does not mean the financial information is 100% accurate. Financial statements may contain minor errors that do not significantly change the interpretation of the financial information provided.

All **public companies** must provide audited financial information. Investors and creditors often require **private companies** to be audited in order to have a higher level of confidence in the information provided by the financial statements and footnotes.

The **Public Company Accounting Oversight Board** (PCAOB) was established by Congress as part of Public Company Accounting Reform and Investor Protection Act of 2002. The act is referred to as Sarbanes Oxley (SOX). SOX requires company management to establish and document internal controls designed to ensure the integrity of financial data. Managers of public companies are required to sign off on the adequacy of accounting internal controls. Auditors are required to review and report on the adequacy of accounting internal controls.

The PCAOB establishes standards that auditors must follow and conducts reviews to "audit the auditors" procedures. The PCAOB was established to bring consistency and credibility to the audit process after several instances of erroneous financial statements were issued with a clean opinion.

International Financial Reporting Standards

Accounting principles and guidelines around the world differ. Many countries have their own financial accounting guidelines an organization similar to FASB provides. Other countries follow accounting guidance provided by the **International Accounting Standards Board** (IASB), an organization that is attempting to standardize accounting guidance around the world. The IASB has issued over 40 **International Financial Reporting Standards** (IFRS.)

Many argue that one set of financial accounting standards used world-wide would improve comparability and facilitate access to global capital markets. Others argue that the U.S. needs accounting standards that specifically address the economic issues of the U.S. business environment. Those opposed to a common set of standards argue that differences in enforcement could make the financial statements appear more comparable than they really are.

Accounting Concepts

The Statements of Financial Accounting Concepts (SFAC) provide the following:

- The **objective of financial reporting:**
  To provide financial information that is useful to capital providers
    - ✓ about the reporting entity
    - ✓ useful to existing and potential investors and creditors
    - ✓ useful for making decisions about allocating resources

- The definitions of the **elements:** asset, liability, equity, investments by owners, distributions to owners, revenues, expenses, gains, losses, comprehensive income.

- The **qualitative characteristics, constraints, recognition, measurement and disclosure concepts** users can rely on when using financial information to make decisions.

Recognition of Elements on the Financial Statements
According to *Statements of Financial Accounting Concepts Statement 5*, an item should be recognized on the basic financial statements when it meets all of the following four criteria (subject to cost/benefit and materiality:

Definition: The item meets the definition of an element of financial statements.
Measurability: The item can be measured with sufficient reliability.
Relevance: The information is capable of making a difference in a decision.
Reliability: The information is true and can be relied upon.

Conceptual Framework Overview

Recognition, Measurement, and Disclosure Concepts

- ➢ Assumptions
    - Economic entity
    - Periodicity
    - Going concern
    - Monetary unit

- ➢ Principles
    - Revenue recognition
    - Expense recognition
    - Measurement (mixed attribute)
    - Full disclosure

- ➢ Constraints
    - Cost effectiveness

Qualitative Characteristics

- Relevance
  - Predictive value
  - Confirmatory value
  - Materiality

- Faithful Representation / Reliable
  - Completeness
  - Neutrality
  - Free from error

- Enhancing
  - Comparability
  - Verifiability
  - Timeliness
  - Understandability

Recognition, Measurement, and Disclosure Concepts

The following assumptions can be made by users when reading the financial statements:

Economic Entity Assumption

- Each business is its own legal entity and only transactions of the entity are reported on the financial statements.

- The activities of the business must be reported separately from activities of owners.

- Owners' personal transactions are not included on the company's financial statements.

Periodicity Assumption

- Financial statements report the economic activities of a business in separate periods of time. The period of time is usually a month, quarter, or year.

Going Concern Assumption

- Users may assume a company will remain in business, assets will be used, and liabilities will be repaid as part of future ongoing business unless stated otherwise. A going concern warning must be presented if it is highly unlikely the company will continue to do business.

- A company's management team and the auditors generally make this determination.

Monetary Unit Assumption

- Economic activity is expressed in nominal units of money (dollars.)
- Accountants assume the dollar is reasonably stable over time and amounts are not adjusted for inflation or deflation. The rate of inflation in the United States has historically been too low to impact decisions made by investors and creditors.

Accountants conform to the following <u>principles</u> when presenting financial information:

Revenue Recognition

Revenue is recognized when goods or services are transferred to customers (customer controls) at the amount the company expects to be entitled to receive in exchange for the goods or services.
No revenue is recognized if receipt of payment is not <u>probable</u>.

These criteria help to make sure a company doesn't record revenue before it has performed all of the obligation to the buyer and the buyer has the ability to pay.

Reporting revenue on the income statement also results in an increase to an asset or a decrease to unearned (deferred) revenue in the same period.

Expense Recognition

- Expenses must be recorded and reported in the same period the revenue is generated in order to report earnings for a specific period of time.
- Expenses are not always incurred directly to support specific revenue.

Acceptable methods used to record expenses are as follows:

- ***Exact Cause and Effect Relationship:*** The expense occurs as part of the revenue process. Examples: cost of goods sold and sales commission as a percent of sales
- ***Associate the Expense with Revenues in the Same Time Period:*** The expense occurs during the same time period the revenue is generated. Examples: interest expense, rent expense, and salary expense
- ***Systematic and Rational Allocation over time:*** The cost of using long-term assets is allocated to each period assets are used. Example: depreciation and amortization expense
- ***In the Period Incurred:*** No <u>direct</u> connection to the specific revenues earned during the period. Example: Advertising expenses, research and development expenses

Measurement

All items presented on the financial statements must be presented with an amount. The chosen measurement should provide the greatest relevance and reliability. Companies will use a combination of the following measurement techniques provided by SFAC 5:

- ***Historical Cost:*** Assets are initially reported at historical cost (the amount paid.)
  - Historical cost can be verified and is reliable.
  - For liabilities, the "cost" is the value of the asset received in exchange for the liability.
  - Cost is based on an exchange between independent parties

- ***Net Realizable Value***: the net amount of cash the asset is expected to convert into during normal business operations

- ***Current Cost:*** the cost to replace the asset

- ***Present Value of Future Cash Flows:*** approximation of fair value given a specific rate of interest

- ***Fair Value:***
  - Market approach: valued of instruments traded on a market exchange
  - Income approach: the present value of earnings or cash flows
  - Cost approach: the cost of replacing the asset (buy or reproduce)

Full Disclosure

All information that would influence a user's decision must be reported on the financial statements or stated in the footnotes. Footnotes must be provided with financial statements. FASB provides general guidance on the type and detail of information that must be disclosed in the footnotes.

Common footnote disclosures that are important for users to take notice of are as follows:

- ***Subsequent Event Disclosures:*** Subsequent events are significant events that occur after the company's year-end and before the financial statements and footnotes are released to the public. Examples of subsequent events are significant debt issuances, losses from natural disasters, and mergers or acquisitions.

- ***Related Party Disclosures:*** Related parties are owners, management, families of owners and management, affiliated companies and other parties that may have influence on the company. Users should be aware of related party transactions because favorable treatment may occur or the economic substance may differ from the legal form in transactions with related parties.

- ***Irregularities and Illegal Acts:*** Intentional mistakes in reported financial information and other violations of the law.

Cost Effectiveness

Preparing and presenting financial information has a cost. Accountants have agreed that the benefit of providing information must exceed the cost of gathering and presenting information.

An example of presenting information that has a cost higher than the benefit would be listing the names of every customer of a company. Preparing and printing the names of all customers is costly and has no benefit to investors and creditors. Companies are required to disclose when more than one customer accounts for 10% or more of total sales because this information is necessary to assess risk of continued earnings.

Qualitative Characteristics

Relevance

Financial information presented must be capable of making a difference in a decision as evidenced by the following:

- Assisting the user in predicting future performance **(predictive value)**
- Assisting the user in evaluating past performance **(feedback/confirmatory value)**
- Information would affect a users' decision is not omitted or misstated. **(materiality)**

More on Materiality

GAAP requires that all information with an amount large enough to influence the judgment of a reasonable person must be presented either on the financial statements or in the footnotes. Material information is always relevant; both refer to information that makes a difference in a decision. Materiality is different from relevance because it refers specifically to the **amount** presented. A transaction with a value that is not large enough to matter is not required to be reported and accounted for in accordance with GAAP.

The following examples illustrate materiality:

1) A company with total assets of $100 million could have an accounting error of $10,000 on the balance sheet. The amount of $10,000 is not a material amount.

2) Earnings per share is reported at $2.10. Investors are expecting earnings per share to be $2.11. One cent is material to investors because the fact that the company did not meet expectations could influence the decision of an investor.

Materiality is generally determined based on how the amount compares to total assets or net income on a percentage basis. As a general rule, a typical investor or creditor is likely to be impacted by an error related to an amount:

- on the balance sheet that is 5 % or more of the reported total assets
- on the income statement that is 3 % or more of total net income.

Financial information is material if omitting it or misstating it could impact a user's decision. Whether an amount is material is subject to the judgment of the accountant and the auditor.

Faithful Representation / Reliable

Users of financial information must be able to rely on and have confidence in the information. Reliable financial information consists of the following:

1) Represents the economic position as it really is **(faithful representation)**
The financial information is **complete** and **free from material error.**

2) Presented in a manner that would not sway the user's opinion **(neutrality/conservatism)**

Relevance versus Reliability

The accountant often must determine whether relevance or reliability is more important to the user. Recording assets at historical cost is reliable; however, it is not relevant if the fair market value has changed significantly since the asset was purchased. Reporting assets at fair market value is relevant; however, it is subjective and not always reliable.

United States GAAP generally holds that reliability is more important than relevance when reporting asset values.

Accounting estimates are rarely accurate. However, United States GAAP generally supports that it is more important for transactions to be recorded timely than to wait until the actual amount is known.

Comparability

Comparability allows users to identify similarities and differences from one year to the next (for a single company) and from one company to another (when comparing more than one company.)

Comparability is accomplished by using

- standard formats
- common account names
- and comparable valuation methods (i.e. historical cost or fair market value.)

Accounting methods are disclosed in the footnotes to allow users to identify any inconsistencies between companies. A public company is required to present two years of information on the balance sheet and three years of information on the other three financial statements.

Consistency

FASB often provides a choice of methods to use when accounting for transactions. Accountants cannot change a method of accounting unless there is a significant change in the way the business operates that justifies the change.

Examples of an acceptable reason for changing a method is the acquisition of another company and a change is made for consistency in the new company and new guidance is provided by FASB. A description of methods used by the company and the impact of all material changes in methods must be stated in the footnotes.

Verifiability

Verifiability is met when independent knowledgeable business people reach the same conclusion about whether or not the information is an accurate representation of financial results.

- Some items and values can be directly verified with documentation of the exchange.
- Other items and values are estimated and projections and models are reviewed for reasonableness.

Timeliness

Information is timely if it is provided periodically and is available to users in time to be used to make decisions.

Understandability

Financial information is understandable when users are able to comprehend the information in the context of the decision being made.

- Users are assumed to have a reasonable understanding of business transactions.

The Fair Value Option

GAAP provides the option to report some or all of the ***financial** assets and **financial** liabilities* at fair market value. Financial assets and financial liabilities convert directly into known amounts of cash. Examples of financial assets and liabilities are notes receivable, investments, derivatives, notes payable, and other long-term liabilities.

Financial assets and financial liabilities selected to be reported at fair market value report changes in fair market value for the current period as a gain or loss on the income statement.

FASB provided the fair value option to companies to allow for consistency with other investments and derivatives required to be reported at fair market value. Companies are allowed to select the types of financial assets or liabilities they report at fair market value.

A company may not switch back to reporting the selected items at historical cost once the fair value option is elected.

Three levels of fair value:

Level 1: Quoted prices in active markets

Level 2: Based on direct or indirect observable inputs – similar assets or liabilities

Level 3: Unobservable inputs – best information available to project future cash flows

2. The Balance Sheet

Owners of a business must first obtain capital to fund the operations of the business. The original founders of a corporation and others contribute capital in exchange for shares of ownership **(investors).** The business may also borrow funds from banks or other investors **(creditors).**

Stock and capital report the total amount of cash owners paid the company for shares of ownership.

Example 1: Initial owners contributed $75,000 and investors paid $25,000 at a later date in exchange for ownership shares. No distinction is made on the balance sheet between initial owners and subsequent owners.

Assets:		Liabilities:	
Cash	$100,000		
		Shareholders' Equity:	
		Stock and Capital	$100,000
Total Assets	$100,000	Total Liabilities & Shareholders' Equity	$100,000

Stock and capital report funds received from investors in exchange for ownership.

- **Advantage** of stock issuance: the company does not have to repay the funds or pay interest on the funds.
- **Disadvantage** of stock issuance: each existing owner's share of profits, total market value, and voting power decreases because the company has more owners.

Companies may also **borrow** money from various lenders (creditors) for operations or to purchase assets. The company and the lender negotiate the cost of interest and the terms of repayment.

- **Advantage** of debt: current owners do not have to share with additional new owners.
- **Disadvantage** of debt: the company must repay the debt plus interest expense that reduces earnings.

Debt is typically not a problem if the company:

- earns more using the money than the cost to use the money
- generates enough profit to repay the amount borrowed.

A **liability** is an amount that a company must repay in the future. A liability a company reports on the balance sheet must have **all** three of the following characteristics:

1) Is owed to an outside party.
2) Is a result of a past transaction (received something in exchange for the debt).
3) Expect to repay the amount.

The following account names companies report as a liability on the balance sheet indicates the type and purpose of the debt.

Accounts Payable

Accounts payable reports amounts owed to suppliers who repeatedly provide goods and services to a company. The company agrees to pay the supplier at a later date without interest.

Accounts payable increases when the company receives goods or services **"on account".** The company receives an invoice (bill) and normally has 30 days to pay amounts owed, without interest.

Accounts payable decreases when the company pays the supplier the amount owed.

Commercial Paper

Commercial paper reports amounts owed to investors the company intends to repay in less than a year. Investors loan short-term only to very large companies with strong credit ratings. Interest costs on funds borrowed for a short period of time are typically very low.

A company normally repays the investor after borrowing from another investor and does not use cash on hand to repay amounts owed.

Notes Payable

Short-term notes payable reports mounts owed to banks and other financing companies the company expects to repay **within one year or less.**

Long-term notes payable reports amounts owed to banks and other financing companies the company expects to repay sometime **after one year.**

Periodic payments to repay notes payable include interest for the period and a portion of the principal owed.

Long-term Debt

Long-term debt reports amounts owed to banks, finance companies, or investors. Long-term debt and long-term notes payable mean the same thing. Companies provide the detail terms of the debt in the footnotes.

Current Maturities of Long-term Debt or Current Maturities of Notes Payable

Companies report the portion of notes payable or long-term debt they must repay within one year as current maturities of long-term debt or current maturities of notes payable.

Companies that repay debt with **periodic payments** (monthly or quarterly) must report the portion of the debt due within the next year separate from the portion of debt due after one year.

An example is a five-year car loan repaid in monthly payments. The borrower must report principal payments due within the next twelve months as current maturities of long-term notes payable and principal payments due in the next two to five years as long-term notes payable.

Bonds Payable

Companies report borrowings from investors as bonds payable. The company pays interest according to the terms of the bond (monthly, quarterly, or annually) and repays the entire principal on a specified date in the future (maturity date).

Bonds payable is sometimes referred to as notes payable or long-term debt on the balance sheet. The footnotes provided the details of the debt.

Interest Payable (on Notes Payable, Long-term Debt, and Bonds Payable)

A company is charged interest on long-term borrowings. However, the liability reported on the balance sheet is the principal amount only and does not include interest. The company will separately report amounts owed for interest as “interest payable”.

Example 2 presents a balance sheet for a company that has obtained funds to establish the business. No borrowings have been repaid as of the balance sheet date.

Assets:		**Liabilities:**	
Cash	$500,000	Short-term Notes Payable	$ 50,000
		Current Maturities of Long-term Notes Payable	$ 30,000
		Total Current Liabilities	$ 80,000
		Long-term Notes Payable	$170,000
		Bonds Payable	$240,000
		Total Liabilities	$490,000
		Shareholders' Equity:	
		Stock and Capital	$ 10,000
Total Assets	$500,000	Total Liabilities & Shareholders' Equity	$500,000

This company obtained $500,000 in cash to operate the business from the following sources:

- **Short-term Notes Payable**: The company borrowed $50,000 from a ***bank or financing institution*** and must repay in one year or less

- **Notes Payable:** The Company borrowed $200,000 from ***banks or financing institution***
  - must repay $30,000 in one year or less ***(current maturities of long-term notes payable)***
  - must repay $170,000 after one year ***(long-term notes payable.)***

- **Bonds Payable:** The Company borrowed $240,000 from investors they must repay after one year.

- **Stock and Capital:** Investors contributed $10,000 to the company in exchange for ownership.

More on Long-term Borrowings

Large public companies and municipalities have the option of borrowing long-term from a bank or financing institution (note payable or long-term debt) or from investors (bonds payable).

The most important difference in the debt is the payment terms.

Notes Payable and Long-term Debt:
Period cash payments include principal and interest

Bonds Payable: Periodic cash payments include only interest
Principal is all repaid on the maturity date (at the end).

Bonds payable have lower annual cash outflows than notes payable and long-term debt.

Assets

Companies use funds obtained from investors (owners) and creditors (lenders) to purchase assets used to operate the business. The assets a company reports on the balance sheet must have **all three** of the following characteristics:

1) Provide probable future economic benefit.
   PFEB: exchange for cash or use to generate cash

2) Be owned or controlled by the company.

3) Be a result of a past transaction (an exchange has occurred).

A "cost" is a cash outflow. Companies either report a "cost" on the balance sheet as an asset or on the income statement as an expense.

A company may only report a cost as an **asset** when the cost provides **probable future economic benefit.** Assets a company uses to do business will eventually become an expense when the asset is used.

A company will report a cost on the income statement as an **expense** when a cost does not provide probable future economic benefit (generally because the benefit was fully received in the current period.)

- A consistent payment for the same service is an indication of no probable future economic benefit.

Accountants use **common names for assets** so that financial statement users understand the items the company uses to conduct business.

Cash

Cash is money or any instrument that banks will accept for deposit in a company's bank. Cash includes checks, money orders and bank drafts.

Cash Equivalents

Cash equivalents are financial instruments the company expects to convert to cash within a year or less with **no risk of loss of principal**. Market values generally do not change if interest rates change.

Cash equivalents include certificates of deposit, treasury bills and commercial paper.
A certificate of deposit is money loaned to a bank. Treasury bills report money loaned to the government.

Investments and Marketable Securities

A company reports an investment (or marketable security) when it uses excess cash to purchase a financial instrument (typically stocks or bonds) to earn a return. A company that makes an investment in stock becomes an owner of another company. A company becomes the lender (creditor) to another entity when it makes an investment in a bond.

- **Investments:** Generally non-liquid private
- **Marketable Securities:** Generally traded on a public exchange

Investments decrease when a company sells the investment and receives cash.

The placement on the balance sheet reports how long a company intends to hold the investment:

Short-term (current): the company intends to hold the investment one year or less

Long-term (noncurrent): the company intends to hold the investment more than one year

Investments and marketable securities carry a risk of loss of the invested amount.

Inventory

Companies report items **held only for sale to customers** as inventory.

Inventory increases when a company purchases or manufactures goods to sell to customers. Inventory decreases when a company provides goods to customers.

Supplies

Companies report items **used in day to day operations** they consistently replace as supplies. Supplies may include office supplies, paper products, glue, screws, etc.

Prepaid Expenses

A company reports prepaid expenses when the company pays in advance for services the company will receive in future periods.

Prepaid expenses decrease when the company receives the service, often as time passes. The most common prepaid expenses include insurance, rent, and advertising.

Examples:

> On January 1, the company paid for six months of insurance coverage. The insurance coverage is "prepaid" for the time in the next six months that has not yet passed. As time passes, the prepaid becomes insurance expense.
>
> On January 1, the company paid for rent for the month of January. Rent is "prepaid" for the days in January that have not yet passed. The prepaid becomes rent expense as the month passes.

Notes Receivable and Financing Receivables

Companies report notes receivable when it loans money to another entity in exchange for periodic payment of principal and interest. The company charges the borrower interest and earns interest revenue (income).

Companies report financing receivables when it finances the sale of goods to customers. Customers agree to pay for the goods or services over a period of time with interest.

Notes or financing receivables include only the principle amount and does not include interest. Interest earned is reported separately as **interest receivable** until the borrower pays the interest.

Companies report notes and financing receivables as **short-term or current** (one year or less) or **long-term or noncurrent** (more than one year) depending on when the company expects repayment.

Property, Plant and Equipment

Companies report physical items currently **used long-term** to provide goods or services to customers as property, plant, and equipment. Property, plant, and equipment include land, buildings, leasehold improvements, equipment, furniture and fixtures, computers, vehicles, etc.

Intangible Assets

Intangible assets have **no** physical substance and represent an exclusive right. Examples of different types of intangible assets follow:

- ***Trademarks*** give the exclusive right from the U.S. Government to use a symbol or name.
- ***Copyrights*** give the exclusive right from the U.S. Government to reproduce written work.
- ***Patents*** give the exclusive right from the U.S. Government to use a new innovation.
- ***Franchise*** gives the company the exclusive right to sell a specific branded product from the owner of a branded business.
- ***Goodwill*** is the amount a company paid to acquire 100% of another company that was above the fair market value of the net assets acquired. Goodwill represents the expected future cash flows related to a good management team, a good location, and name brand recognition. Companies pay for goodwill because the business is established and has the ability to generate more future cash flows than the separate individual assets.

  The amount paid for the entire company
  \- The fair market value of net assets acquired
  = Goodwill

  Companies only report purchased goodwill on the balance sheet. Internally generated goodwill is not reported on the balance sheet because no exchange occurs and a reliable value is difficult to determine.

Example 3 illustrates how a company values and reports goodwill on the balance sheet. Bop, Inc. purchases Yip, Inc. for $500,000 cash. The fair market value of the identifiable assets acquired in the purchase is $220,000. Bop, Inc. agreed to repay $100,000 owed by Yip, Inc.

	The amount paid for the entire company	$500,000
+	The amount of liabilities assumed in the purchase	$100,000
-	The fair market value of assets purchased	($220,000)
=	Goodwill	$380,000

The balance sheet for Bop, Inc. will report $500,000 less cash, $220,000 of Yip's assets (such as inventory, equipment, trademarks, etc.), goodwill for $380,000, and liabilities of $100,000.

Other Long-term Assets

Companies report assets held for more than one year which do not fit into other asset categories as other long-term assets. Other long-term assets include property and equipment the company is not currently using, long-term prepaid expenses, and the cash value of life insurance policies.

Shareholders' Equity

Shareholders' equity begins when investors give capital to the company in exchange for shares of ownership. Additional equity accounts report the results of activity directly with owners.

The shareholders' equity of a company is very similar to the equity of a homeowner. A $100,000 house purchased with a loan in the amount of $85,000 and a cash down payment of $15,000 from the owner is reported on a balance sheet as follows:

Assets:		Liabilities:	
House	$100,000 (cost)	Notes Payable	$85,000 (borrowed)
		Shareholders' Equity:	
		Stock and Capital	$15,000 (owners)

The $100,000 cost of the house less the amount of $85,000 owed is the $15,000 "equity" in the home. In the same way, a company's Shareholders' equity is the net of the total assets and total liabilities of the company.

Shareholders' equity initially consists of:

1) Ownership of Stock and Capital
2) Earnings the company keeps to reinvest

Stock and Capital

A company that sells shares of ownership to investors reports cash received in exchange for ownership on the balance sheet as **stock and capital.** Companies typically report stock and capital as two separate lines on the balance sheet. The value for **stock** on the balance sheet is the **par value** of one share multiplied by the total number of shares issued to investors.

"Capital" is also reported as capital in excess of par, paid in capital, additional paid in capital or contributed capital. Common stock plus capital is the total amount received from owners.

Par value is:

- the per share amount stated in the Articles of Incorporation.
- the legal amounts owners are responsible to pay if the company can't pay debts.
- typically set at a very small amount to keep owner's liability minimal
- not the fair market value of the stock.

Example 4 illustrates how the balance sheet reports funds received from owners in exchange for shares of ownership.

The company issued 5,000 shares of common stock with a par value of $0.10 per share in exchange for $10,000.

The balance sheet will report the following:

Stock	$ 500	5,000 shares x $0.10 par value
Capital	$ 9,500	

First determine the par value of the stock. Second, capital is the difference in $10,000 total cash received and $500 total par value of the issued shares of stock.

Corporations issue (sell to investors) **common stock** or **preferred stock.**

Characteristics of ***preferred stock***:

- Investors have no voting rights.
- Preferred stock investors expect to receive a dividend at the stated rate
- The fair market value of preferred stock increases and decreased with changes in market interest rates.

Characteristics of ***common stock***:

- Investors have voting rights.
- Investors desire fair market value appreciation or the ability to influence operations.
- The fair market value of common stock generally increases as earnings increases.

Treasury Stock

Treasury stock is common stock the company itself temporarily owns. Companies purchase their own stock to demonstrate confidence in future performance, to reduce the number of outstanding shares held by outside owners, or to provide to employees at a later date.

Treasury stock is common stock that is reported separately because the company owns those shares of common stock.

Common Shares	100,000	Total shares issued to all owners
- Treasury Shares	(5,000)	Company owned shares
= Outstanding Shares	95,000	Shares owned by outside owners

Companies report **treasury shares as negative** because outside ownership decreases when the company repurchases the stock. The reported value is the amount the company paid to purchase its own common stock.

Total Shareholders' equity represents the amount owned by **owners outside the company**.

A corporation must report the number of ownership shares authorized, issued, and outstanding on the balance sheet.

Authorized: The maximum number of shares a corporation can issue.
The Board of Directors can easily change authorized shares.

Issued: The total shares sold to date

Outstanding: The total shares owned by stockholders other than the company
(Outstanding Shares = Issued Shares - Treasury Shares*)

Retained Earnings

Retained earnings is the company's total cumulative earnings less all dividends returned to shareholders since the first day of operations.

The amount reported on the balance sheet for retained earnings is:

Retained Earnings, at the beginning of the year (prior year ending balance)
\+ Current year earnings (losses) reported on the income statement
\- Dividends declared to stockholders during the current year
= Retained Earnings, at the end of the year (reported on the balance sheet)

<u>Dividends</u>

The Board of Directors <u>must</u> authorize all dividends paid to shareholders. Dividends have three important dates.

- The Board of Directors announces the promise to pay owners on the ***declaration date.***
- The owner of each share of stock on the ***record date*** will receive the dividend.
  The company compiles a list of owners on the record date (shareholders of record).
- The company pays shareholders of record on the ***payment date***.

Other things to note about dividends:

- Companies generally pay dividends approximately ten to forty-five days after the dividend is declared. The balance sheet reports a dividend payable until the company pays the dividend.
- Companies pay dividends to preferred stockholders before common shareholders.
- Dividends are considered a return of investment to owners
  - Dividends directly reduce retained earnings.
  - A dividend is NOT an expense on the income statement.

A company has no obligation to pay dividends to shareholders. The Board of Directors may decide the company should keep the funds for other purposes.

<u>Other Comprehensive Income</u>

Other comprehensive income consists of gains or losses not (or not yet) reported on the income statement. Other comprehensive income item gains and losses are reported as part of shareholders' equity until the time comes to report the amount on the income statement (according to accounting rules).

Currently, other comprehensive income gains and losses are limited to:

- foreign currency gains and losses
- gains and losses on certain long-term investments
- gains and losses on derivatives
- employee pension related gains and losses

The above items are not reported on the income statement because management cannot control market factors. Accountants and finance professionals believe the income statement should reflect the economic results of management performance.

The Classified Balance Sheet

GAAP requires companies to report a classified balance sheet. The classified balance sheet lists and subtotals groups of assets and liabilities based on **liquidity**. Liquidity refers to how soon the company expects to convert an asset to cash or pay liabilities.

Short-term or current is one year or less

Long-term or noncurrent is more than one year.

The classified balance sheet presents the following categories:

Current Assets include all assets the company expects to use or exchange for cash within one year or less.

Property, plant and equipment includes all physical assets the company expects to use to operate the business for more than one year.

Intangible assets include all non-physical assets the company expects to use for more than one year.

Current liabilities include all amounts the company expects to pay within one year or less.

Long-term Liabilities include all amounts the company expects to pay in more than one year.

A classified balance sheet provides the information necessary to perform financial analysis.

Example 5 presents a classified balance sheet of a company that has obtained money from investors and creditors and used the money to purchase items to operate the business.
This balance sheet reports the company's financial position <u>before</u> the company provides goods and services to customers.

ABC, Inc.
Balance Sheet
As of a Particular Date

Assets:	
Cash and Cash Equivalents	10,000
Inventory	42,000
Supplies	1,000
Prepaid Expenses	3,000
Short-term Investments	25,000
Total Current Assets	**81,000**
Long-term Investments	50,000
Long-term Notes Receivable	15,000
Property, Plant, and Equipment:	
Land	100,000
Buildings	300,000
Furniture and Fixtures	62,000
Equipment	95,000
Vehicles	43,000
Total Property, Plant, and Equipment	**600,000**
Intangible Assets	
Goodwill	88,000
Patents	12,000
Copyrights	6,000
Trademarks	11,000
Total Intangible Assets	**117,000**
Other Long-term Assets	16,000
Total Assets	**879,000**

Liabilities:	
Accounts Payable	9,000
Short-term Notes Payable	30,000
Current Maturities of Long-term Debt or Notes Payable	40,000
Total Current Liabilities	**79,000**
Long-term Debt (Notes Payable)	200,000
Bonds Payable	400,000
Total Liabilities	**679,000**
Shareholders' Equity:	
Common Stock and Capital	200,000
Total Shareholders' Equity	**200,000**
Total Liabilities & Shareholders' Equity	**879,000**

Total assets must equal total liabilities plus total shareholders' equity. Companies either owe for or own all assets used to operate the business. Total funds to purchase assets come from borrowings, or owners, or cash generated from operations.

All items reported on the balance sheet must meet the accounting definition of an asset, liability, or shareholders' equity.

The balance sheet does not state a company's transactions that changed assets and liabilities. The balance sheet states items used by the company to do business and amounts owed by the company **on a specified date.**

Companies initially report assets on the balance sheet at **historical cost**. Historical cost is the amount paid to acquire the asset on the date of the purchase plus amounts to be paid in the future.

Example 6 illustrates how a company determines historical cost. A company gave equipment valued at $12,000, gave cash of $20,000, and agreed to pay $8,000 over the next 5 years, and purchased a delivery truck.

The historical cost of the truck, $40,000, is the total exchanged for the asset.

($12,000 + $20,000 + $8,000 = $40,000)

GAAP requires companies to initially report assets on the balance sheet at historical cost because historical cost can be verified. Fair value amounts may be more useful for making financial decisions; however, fair market value is often a subjective opinion that may not be reliable (verifiable).

Companies do report investments that trade on an exchange at fair market value because fair market value is reliable and verifiable.

Another exception is that assets cannot be reported at cost if cost is higher than the expected probable future economic benefit of the asset (future cash flows).

For example: A machine that cost $100,000 is currently expected to produce products that can be sold for net cash of $80,000. The value reported for the machine cannot be higher than the probable future economic benefit. The machine is reported at on the balance sheet at $80,000.

Assets are never reported at an amount greater than historical cost.

3. Changes to the Balance Sheet

The balance sheet reports items the company uses to operate the business (assets), amounts owed (liabilities), and amounts owned by shareholders (equity), cumulative **as of a specific date**. Cumulative is the net of all increases and decreases from the first day of business.
GAAP requires companies to report balance sheet items and amounts as of two consecutive dates.

- ✓ Assets will either be exchanged for cash or used to operate the business to generate cash.
- ✓ Liabilities will be paid in the future.
- ✓ Shareholders' equity reports outside ownership of the company.

Companies report items on the balance sheet using a name that finance and accounting professionals uniformly understand. A common name used consistently to describe an item is referred to as an **account.** Chapter two discussed the accounts reported on the balance sheet.

The balance sheet does not report the transactions that change the amounts. Therefore, the financial statement user must know the types of transactions that occur to change the reported line items.

A **transaction** is an exchange of one item for another item. All businesses have the following common transactions:

- ✓ Assets increase with purchases and decrease with sales or use.
- ✓ Liabilities increase when the company borrows funds and decrease with repayment.
- ✓ Shareholders' equity changes when funds are exchanged between the company and the owners and with profits and losses.

Accounting is a double entry system because a minimum of two accounts will change with each transaction. A transaction is an exchange of one thing for another; therefore, at least two things must always change.

The Accounting Equation

The left side of the accounting equation contains items the company uses to operate the business and the right side of the equation represents how the company finances the assets (with debt, cash from owners, or generated by operations.)

Assets	=	**Liabilities**	+	**Shareholders' Equity**
Have		Owe		Own (includes earnings)

The accounting equation will always stay in balance when a transaction occurs.

Both sides of the equation do not have to change. Two accounts can change on one side of the equation that nets to zero and remains equal to the other side with no change.

Answer the following questions to determine which balance sheet accounts will change with each transaction:

Does the company have more or less? **Changes assets; which account?**

Does the company owe more or less? **Changes liabilities; which account?**

Was there an exchange that involved the owners? **Changes Shareholders' equity; which account?**

The balance sheet begins when the company borrows money or sells ownership to investors. The cash is used to purchase assets used to operate the business. The company either pays for the assets purchased in the same period (cash decreases), pays for the asset at a later date (liability), or uses a combination of both.

Four common transactions occur repeatedly that change the balance sheet.

1) Receive cash from investors (owners.)

Assets	**=**	**Liabilities**	**+**	**Shareholders' Equity**
Have more	=		+	Own more

2) Trade one asset for another asset (often paying cash for another asset.)

Assets	**=**	**Liabilities**	**+**	**Shareholders' Equity**
Have more	=		+	
and				
Have less				

3) Receive an asset and pay for the asset in the future (liability.)

Assets	**=**	**Liabilities**	**+**	**Shareholders' Equity**
Have more	=	Owe more	+	

4) Pay cash to reduce amounts owed (liability.)

Assets	**=**	**Liabilities**	**+**	**Shareholders' Equity**
Have less	=	Owe less	+	

Example 1 demonstrates how accountants use the three questions to identify the items that change on the balance sheet with each transaction. The accountant determines the account names that change, records the amount, and summarizes the total results of all transactions. The balance sheet reports all accounts that change with the final amounts.

Example 1: Pillow Soft, Inc. sells pillows to retailers. The company had the following business transactions during the first month of operations. Each transaction changes the balance sheet.

1. The company sold 100 shares of common stock for $2,000 per share for a total of $200,000 cash.

The company received cash and gave ownership to others outside the company.

1) Does the company have more or less? **More cash; $200,000**

2) Does the company owe more or less? **No**

3) Was there an exchange that involved the owners? **Yes,** the owners put money into the company in exchange for ownership;
More common stock; $200,000

2. Paid $6,000 to rent a warehouse and office facility for the next three months.

The right to use the facility for three months is a future economic benefit (asset.) One asset was traded for another asset.

1) Does the company have more or less? **Less cash; $6,000**
More prepaid rent; $6,000

2) Does the company owe more or less? **No**

3) Was there an exchange that involved the owners? **No**

3. Purchased warehouse equipment for $50,000 cash.

The company received warehouse equipment in exchange for cash. The warehouse equipment will be used to generate future economic benefit.

1) Does the company have more or less? **Less cash; $50,000**
More warehouse equipment; $50,000

2) Does the company owe more or less? **No**

3) Was there an exchange that involved the owners? **No**

4. Purchased office furniture for $15,000 cash.

The company received office furniture in exchange for cash.
The office furniture will be used to generate future economic benefit.

1) Does the company <u>have</u> more or less? **Less cash; $15,000**
More office furniture; $15,000

2) Does the company <u>owe</u> more or less? **No**

3) Was there an exchange that involved the owners? **No**

5. Purchased computer equipment for $18,000 cash.

The company received computer equipment in exchange for cash.
The computer equipment will be used to generate future economic benefit.

1) Does the company <u>have</u> more or less? **Less cash; $18,000**
More computer equipment; $18,000

2) Does the company <u>owe</u> more or less? **No**

3) Was there an exchange that involved the owners? **No**

6. Paid $12,000 cash for six months of future insurance coverage.

The company paid for insurance coverage before it receives the service.
The company paid for future economic benefit (an asset).

1) Does the company <u>have</u> more or less? **Less cash; $12,000**
More prepaid insurance; $12,000

2) Does the company <u>owe</u> more or less? **No**

3) Was there an exchange that involved the owners? **No**

7. Purchased goods to sell to customers for $60,000 on account (pay in 30 days.)

The company received inventory and agreed to pay the supplier in the future.

1) Does the company have more or less? **More inventory; $60,000**

2) Does the company owe more or less? **More accounts payable; $60,000**

3) Was there an exchange that involved the owners? **No**

8. Paid $300 for office supplies, on account.

The company owes the supplier for office supplied it will use to operate the business.

1) Does the company have more or less? **More office supplies; $300**

2) Does the company owe more or less? **More accounts payable; $300**

3) Was there an exchange that involved the owners? **No**

9. Borrowed $25,000 from the bank. $5,000 must be repaid at the end of every year for five years.

The company received cash and agreed to pay in the future.

1) Does the company have more or less? **More cash; $25,000**

2) Does the company owe more or less? **More notes payable;**
$5,000 is Current Maturities of Long-term Notes Payable;
$20,000 is Long-term Notes Payable

3) Was there an exchange that involved the owners? **No**

The accountant records the items that change with each transaction and prepares the balance sheet to show items and amounts the company **has** (assets), **owes** (liabilities), and **owns** (Shareholders' equity) at the end of the period. A simple spreadsheet can be used to record transactions. The balance sheet reports every account name that changes.

The spreadsheet on the next page illustrates how Pillow Soft, Inc.'s accountant recorded and summarized transactions.

Assets

	Cash	Inventory	Prepaid Rent	Prepaid Insurance	Office Supplies	Warehouse Equipment
1)	$200,000					
2)	($6,000)		$6,000			
3)	($50,000)					$50,000
4)	($15,000)					
5)	($18,000)					
6)	($12,000)			$12,000		
7)		$60,000				
8)					$300	
9)	$ 25,000					
Total	**$124,000**	**$60,000**	**$6,000**	**$12,000**	**$300**	**$50,000**

	Office Furniture	Computer Equipment	Accounts Payable	CM Notes Payable	L/T Notes Payable	Common Stock and Capital
1)						$200,000
2)						
3)						
4)	$15,000					
5)		$18,000				
6)						
7)			$60,000			
8)			$ 300			
9)				$5,000	$20,000	
Total	**$15,000**	**$18,000**	**$60,300**	**$5,000**	**$20,000**	**$200,000**

Assets	=	Liabilities	+	Equity
$285,300	=	$85,300	+	$200,000

Pillow Soft, Inc.'s classified balance sheet as of January 31st, will report the following:

Assets:		Liabilities:	
Cash	$124,000	Accounts Payable	$60,300
Inventory	60,000	Current Maturities of	
Prepaid Rent	6,000	Notes Payable	$ 5,000
Prepaid Insurance	12,000	Total Current Liabilities	$65,300
Office Supplies	300		
Total Current Assets	202,300	Long-term Notes Payable	$20,000
		Total Liabilities	$85,300
Property, Plant, & Equipment:		Shareholders' Equity:	
Warehouse Equipment	50,000		
Office Furniture	15,000	Common Stock	
Computer Equipment	18,000	and Capital	200,000
Total Prop., Plant, Equip.	83,000		
		Total Liabilities &	
Total Assets	$285,300	Shareholders' Equity	$285,300

The balance sheet reports that on January 31st, the company has:

- cash in the bank of $124,000.
- inventory at a cost of $60,000 that is expected to be sold to customers.
- paid $18,000 for rent and insurance before the space is used and the coverage is provided.
- office supplies that cost $300.
- warehouse equipment, office furniture and computer equipment at a total cost of $83,000 the company expects to use P,P,E for more than one year to operate the business.

Pillow Soft will use all **assets** (other than cash) to operate the business or will exchange the **asset** for cash.

Pillow Soft expects to pay all **liabilities** in the future. The company owes $60,300 to suppliers for repeat purchases on account payable within 30 days. Notes payable reports $25,000 owed to banks and financing institutions; $5,000 of the total amount owed will be repaid within the next year.

Shareholders' equity represents ownership by outside investors. Investors have contributed $200,000 to the company in exchange for ownership (common stock and capital).

The company does not have retained earnings until they begin to provide goods and services to customers.

4. The Income Statement

The income statement reports the economic earnings that result from a company's activity during a specific period of time. The income statement does not report the change in cash.

A business operates to provide goods or services to customers at a higher price to customers (revenues) than the cost to provide the goods or services (expenses.) A company's economic performance (net earnings) is the difference in the value provided to customers and the cost to provide the goods or services to the customer.

Revenue is reported on the income statement during the period it is **earned.**
Revenue is considered to be **earned** when the following two things occur:

1) The company provides goods or services to others and nothing more is owed to the customer.

and

2) The company is **entitled** to payment and **expects to receive** the payment.

Revenue is reported in the period a company **provides** goods or services to others, **not** the period **cash** is received from the customer.

A company must report **expenses** on the income statement during the period **incurred.**
An expense is **incurred** when the company:

1) **receives a service** it must pay for.

or

2) **uses an asset** other than cash to provide goods or services.

An expense is reported in the period a company **receives a service or uses an asset**, **not** when the company pays **cash** for the service or asset.

Companies also report gains and losses related to asset sales (other than inventory) on the income statement.

- **Gains** occur when a company sells an asset and receives <u>more</u> than the asset's net cost.
- **Losses** occur when a company sells an asset and receives <u>less</u> than the asset's net cost.

Companies report losses related to lawsuits, environmental cleanups, and natural disasters such as tornados, hurricanes or floods.

Example 1: An income statement for a business that provides lawn care services would report the following:

Lawn Care, Inc. **Income Statement** **For the Year Ended 12/31/20XX**	**The following happened during 20XX:**
Service Revenue	Lawn services provided to customers.
- Salary Expense	Employees provided services to the company.
- Gasoline Expense	Used the asset gasoline.
- Depreciation Expense	Used equipment to service customers.
- Business Insurance Expense	Received insurance coverage.
= Income from Operations	Earnings from daily operations.
+ Gain from Selling Investments	Investments were sold for > than reported value.
- Loss from Fire	The net cost of assets lost in a fire.
= Income Before Tax	Earnings before payments to the government.
- Income Tax Expense	The service received from the government.
= Net Income	Net earnings of the company for the year.

Important to Note:

All accounts and amounts reported on the income statement happened during the year ended December 31, 20XX (between January 1 and December 31, 20XX.)

The income statement **<u>reports activity</u>** and does **<u>not</u>** report the amount of **<u>cash</u>** collected or paid.

When cash is received or paid is not reported on the income statement (although cash may be exchanged in the same period as the activity occurs.)

A company reports revenues on the income statement when the company **provides goods or services during the period.**

Report revenue for the current period:

- Shipped pillows to customers.
- A heating and air conditioning company repaired a customer's air conditioning system.
- A paint and body shop repaired a customer's auto.
- Microsoft ships software to Dell Computer.
- Google provides a search click to a customer and an internet user clicks on the ad.
- A customer flies from Dallas to Orlando.

The company provided goods or services during the current period.

Do NOT report as revenue for the current period:

- Receive an order for pillows from customers.
- A heating and air conditioning company schedules a repair of a customer's air conditioning system.
- A paint and body shop is paid by an insurance company to repair a customer's auto and the repair will be done next month.
- Microsoft agrees to ship software to Dell Computer over the next three months.
- Google agrees to provide a search click for a customer and no clicks have occurred.
- A customer pays for a flight for next month.

The company did not provide goods or services to a customer.

Companies report expenses on the income statement when an **asset** (other than cash) is **used** or the company **receives a service <u>during the period</u>.**

Report an expense in the current period:

- Advertisements of the company's products appeared in a weekly magazine.
- Employees worked for the company during the period.
- The company is covered by an insurance company during the period.
- Used supplies during the period.
- Provided inventory to customers during the period.
- Used equipment during the period.

The company received a service or used an asset in the current period.

Do NOT report an expense in the current period:

- Paid for advertisements scheduled to be run next month in a weekly magazine.
- Hired employees that will begin work next period.
- Paid for insurance coverage to begin next period.
- Purchased supplies the company has not used.
- Purchased inventory that is in the warehouse (not sold).
- Purchased equipment the company has not used.

The company did not receive a service or use an asset in the current period.

Remember the following with respect to the income statement:

- ✓ The income statement generally reports two or three consecutive periods of time to allow trend analysis. A period of time is normally a month, a quarter, or a year.

- ✓ The income statement reports only activities during a reporting period.
  - The event (goods or services provided to customers, use an asset, or receive a service) must occur during the reporting period for the company to report activity on the income statement for that period.

- ✓ The income statement reports activities when they occur, **not** when cash is received or paid.
  - It is common for a company to receive cash in the same period the revenue is earned.
  - It is common for a company to pay cash in the same period the expense is incurred.
    - The **cash exchange is not the reason** the company reports the amount.
    - The income statement only **reports activity**

The income statement reports the following three activities for a specific period of time:

1) Goods or services were provided to the customer. **Revenue**

2) An asset (other than cash) was used **Expense**

3) The company receives a service*. **Expense**

* Companies report an asset when it receives goods until the company uses and no longer has the goods.

Example 2 gives several transactions and demonstrates how to use the three questions to determine if a transaction is reported on the current period income statement. This example also illustrates some of the common names reported on the income statement.

a. Received cash from owners in exchange for ownership.

1) Goods or service provided to customers? NO
2) Service received? NO
3) Asset other than cash used (up)? NO

Report nothing on the income statement.

b. Used lawn equipment to service customers.

1) Goods or service provided to customers? NO
2) Service received? NO
3) Asset other than cash used (up)? Yes, using a long-term asset is called depreciation

Depreciation expense is reported on the income statement.

c. Used gasoline.

1) Goods or service provided to customers? NO
   (Do not assume that a service was provided to use the gasoline.)
2) Service received? NO
3) Asset other than cash used (up)? YES, gasoline

Gasoline expense is reported on the income statement.

d. Cut lawns for customers.

1) Goods or service provided to customers? YES, lawn service revenue
2) Service received? NO
3) Asset other than cash used (up)? NO

Lawn service revenue is reported on the income statement.

e. Purchased supplies (weed eating twine, bags, grass squares).

1) Goods or service provided to customers? NO
2) Service received? NO
3) Asset other than cash used (up)? NO

Nothing is reported on the income statement until an asset is used.

Example 2 continued

f. Employees worked this period.

1) Goods or service provided to customers? NO
2) Service received? YES, employees worked for the company
3) Asset other than cash used (up)? NO

Salary expense or wages expense is reported on the income statement.

g. A radio station promoted the company in the current period.

1) Goods or service provided to customers? NO
2) Service received? YES, advertising
3) Asset other than cash used (up)? NO

Advertising expense is reported on the income statement.

h. Planted a new lawn for a customer.

1) Goods or service provided to customers? YES, lawn service revenue
2) Service received? NO
3) Asset other than cash used (up)? NO

Lawn service revenue is reported on the income statement.

i. Used supplies (grass squares).

1) Goods or service provided to customers? NO
2) Service received? NO
3) Asset other than cash used (up)? YES, supplies

Supplies expense is reported on the income statement.

j. An insurance company provided liability coverage to the company. The company paid for the coverage in the current month.

1) Goods or service provided to customers? NO
2) Service received? YES, insurance coverage
3) Asset other than cash used (up)? NO

Insurance expense is reported on the income statement.

Accrual Basis versus Cash Basis

A company's economic earnings for a period of time is the difference in the value of goods and services provided to customers and the cost to provide the same goods and services during the **same** period of time.

Accountants use the accrual basis of accounting. The "accrual basis" essentially means the income statement reports activities, not cash received and paid.

The **accrual basis income statement** reports:

Revenue when the company provides goods or services to customers

- Expenses when the company receives a service or uses an asset

= Earnings for the reporting period

Many small businesses use a cash basis income statement because it seems easier to track the cash paid and received. However, the change in cash is not a proper reflection of the economic earnings for a period of time.

Cash is not always received in the same period the company provides goods and services to customers.

Cash is not always paid in the same period the company receives the service or uses the asset.

The **cash basis income statement** reports:

Revenues when the company receives cash for providing goods or services.

- Expenses when the company pays cash for assets and services received.

= Change in cash for a period of time

Net change in cash is not a proper reflection of the economic earnings from activities of the business during the period. Therefore, the cash basis income statement is not in accordance with GAAP.

Example 3 compares the cash basis to the accrual basis of accounting.

On January 2, 20Y1, Canterbury Publishing sold three-year subscriptions of its quarterly publication, *Windy City Living*, to 2,500 subscribers. Customers paid the full subscription price of $300 (12 issues at $25 per issue) for all three years on January 2, 20Y1. The company purchased equipment that cost $500,000 on January 2, 20Y1 and expects to use the equipment for the next eight years. The company pays $60 annually for each subscriber to publish and distribute the magazines.

For the Year Ended December 31, 20Y1

	Cash Basis:		**Accrual Basis:**	
Sales:	$750,000	($300 x 2,500)	$250,000	(1 year only; $100 x 2,500)
Costs:				
Publishing/distribution	$150,000	($60 x 2,500)	$150,000	($60 x 2,500)
Equipment	$500,000		$ 62,500	(1 year only; $500,000 / 8 years)
Total Costs	$650,000		$212,500	
Net:	$100,000		$ 37,500	

The cash basis income statement reports the amount of cash received and the amount of cash paid during the year 20Y1.

- Customers pay for all magazines in the first year.
- The company paid for the equipment in the first year.
- The company pays publishing and distribution costs in the same year the company provides magazines to customers.
- The increase in cash is $100,000 at the end of the first year.

The accrual basis income statement reports the earnings from operating the business during 20Y1.

- Sales represent the value of magazines provided to customers during 20Y1 only.
- The company incurred the publishing and distribution costs to produce magazines sold during 20Y1 only.
- The expense for equipment is the estimated cost of using the equipment during 20Y1 only (one year out of the eight total years the equipment is expected to be used.)
- The activities that occurred during 20Y1 give the economic earnings for the year 20Y1.
- The company earned $37,500 from operations during 20Y1.

When the company receives or pays cash does not determine when the activity is reported on the accrual basis income statement.

Example 3 continued

For the Year Ended December 31, 20Y2

	Cash Basis:	Accrual Basis:	
Sales:	$ 0	$250,000	(1 year)
Costs:			
Publishing/distribution	$150,000	$150,000	(1 year)
Equipment	$ 0	$ 62,500	(1 year)
Total Costs	$150,000	$212,500	
Net:	($150,000)	$ 37,500	

For the Year Ended December 31, 20Y3

	Cash Basis:	Accrual Basis:	
Sales:	$ 0	$250,000	(1 year)
Costs:			
Publishing/distribution	$150,000	$150,000	(1 year)
Equipment	$ 0	$ 62,500	(1 year)
Total Costs	$150,000	$212,500	
Net:	($150,000)	$ 37,500	

The cash basis statement reports:

- No sales for 20Y2 and 20Y3 because customers paid all cash in 20Y1.
- No cost of using equipment because the equipment was paid for in 20Y1.
- Publishing and distribution costs paid in the period.
- "Net" is not the results of economic activities during 20Y2 and 20Y3.

The accrual basis statement reports:

- The value of magazines provided to customers during 20Y2 and 20Y3.
- The costs associated with providing the magazines during 20Y2 and 20Y3.
- The **earnings** that result from the 20Y2 and 20Y3 economic activity.

The business conducts the same activities each year. Therefore, it is reasonable that the business would earn the same amount each year from the same transactions.

Businesses must record and track changes in cash; however, it is misleading to measure the economic performance for a certain period of time using net cash.

Generally accepted accounting principles requires the accrual basis of accounting.

5. Discontinued Operations and Other

Discontinued operations occur when a company is no longer involved in operating any material portion of a segment of the business whose operations and cash flows can be clearly distinguished for financial reporting purposes.

Gains or losses on discontinued operations occur when a company **sells or disposes** of a **significant separate** part of the business.

A discontinued operation is reported when operations are **held for sale or is being disposed of** and **both** of the following situations exist:

1. The operations and cash flows of the component are or will be eliminated from the ongoing business.

2. The entity will not have any significant continuing involvement in the operations of the component after disposal.

A discontinued operations component must meet one of the following situations:

1. ***Elimination of a business component***
    - operations and cash flows can be clearly distinguished for operations and for financial reporting from the rest of the entity
        - a subsidiary
        - operating segment
        - reporting unit
        - groups of assets

2. ***Existence of a strategic shift***
    - major geographic area
    - major product line
    - major equity method investment
    - other major parts of an entity

A footnote disclosure is provided that provides a description of the component being discontinued, the type of assets and liabilities associated with the discontinued operations, the reason for discontinuing, and the expected manner of disposition.

Reporting Discontinued Operations

Earnings from discontinued operations are reported separately for all years presented. Users of financial statements should not include discontinued operations in projected future earnings.

Discontinued operations may be:

- held for sale and operated
- held for sale and no longer operated.
- sold by the end of the current year

Gains and losses are reported net of the tax impact on the income statement because these items are reported below the income tax expense line item. **Gains and losses from discontinued operations** are taxable and reported net of the tax impact.

Example 1: A company, with a tax rate of 35% earned $500,000 before income tax expense and before an extraordinary gain of $100,000 is reported as follows:

Income before income taxes	$500,000
Income tax expense	($175,000)
Income from continuing operations	$325,000
Discontinued Ops (net of tax expense of $35,000)	$ 65,000*
Net Income	$390,000

* The before tax amount of	$100,000
x 1 less the tax rate (1.00-0.35)	0.65 (or 65%)
= the after tax (net of tax) amount	$65,000

Companies with Discontinued Operations Report 3 Things:

1) **Income from Operations:** the net income from operations while available for sale

2) **Impairment Loss:** The loss recorded when the assets have a fair value less than cost

3) **Gain or Loss on the Sale:** The cash received from the sale less the net assets sold

Discontinued Operations Sold before Year-End

A gain or loss on sale of discontinued operations is generally reported separate from the results of operations in the period when the discontinued operations are sold:

Income from continuing operations:	$1,000
Discontinued Operations:	
Income from discontinued operations (net of tax $150)	$ 500
Gain /(loss) on sale (net of tax of $60)	$ 200
Net Income	$1,700

Discontinued Operations Held for Sale at Year-End

The results of operating the discontinued operations is reported when the operations are held for sale and the sale is expected in the future. A gain or loss on impairment is reported separately.

Income from continuing operations:	$1,000
Discontinued Operations:	
Loss from Discontinued Operations (net of tax $100)	($ 250)
Impairment Gain/(Loss) (net of tax of $200)	($ 600)
Net Income / (Loss)	$ 150

The assets and liabilities that are held for sale are reported separately on the balance sheet on one line item called **"net assets held for sale"** at the lower of their book values or fair market value less the cost to sell.

The types of assets and liabilities held for sale are disclosed in the footnotes.

- Assets held for sale are not depreciated.

Earnings per Share

Companies are required to report earnings per share (EPS) on the income statement. Earnings per share represents the earnings of one share of common stock.

$$\frac{\text{Net Income} - \text{Preferred Stock Dividends}}{\text{Weighted Average Number of Common Shares Outstanding}} = \text{Earnings per Share}$$

Earnings per share is related to common shares. Dividends paid to preferred stockholders are subtracted from net income because this part of earnings is not available to common stockholders. Earnings per share is presented two different ways: basic and diluted.

> **Basic EPS** uses the weighted average number of common shares currently outstanding. Outstanding shares are owned by outside stockholders (not the company).

> **Diluted EPS** uses the weighted average number of common shares that could be outstanding given all the financial instruments currently issued that could be exchanged for common shares are exchanged for common shares.

Example 2 illustrates the difference the number of shares used in Basic EPS and Diluted EPS.

Actual weighted average number of shares outstanding:	100,000	Used in Basic EPS
Stock options issued that can be exercised and converted into common stock in the future:	10,000	
Debt that could be repaid with the issuance of common stock rather than cash:	15,000	
Total common stock shares that could be outstanding	125,000	Used in Diluted EPS

Financial instruments that can be exchanged for common shares are stock options and warrants to purchase the stock at a set price, debt convertible into common stock, and preferred stock convertible into common stock.

Diluted EPS is the "worst case scenario" of how low EPS could go given current obligations and net income remains the same.

Earnings per share is often used by investors to determine the market value of one share of common stock. An investor may multiply earnings per share by an expected growth percentage to determine an estimated fair market value (price) for one share.

Separate earnings per share must be reported for each of the following line item amounts reported on the income statement:

1. Income from continuing operations
2. Discontinued operations
3. Net Income

The amount reported for each line item is divided by the weighted average common shares outstanding to compute an EPS for each category.

Comprehensive Income

In an effort to compromise, some items that could be included in net earnings are reported directly to stockholder's equity as other comprehensive income (OCI). The following four types of gains and losses are reported as part of OCI:

1. Unrealized gains/losses from holding some types of long-term investments
2. Gains/losses related to employee benefit plans
3. Gains/losses on derivatives
4. Gains/losses on foreign currency

OCI gains and losses are not included in net income in the period they occur because management contends they cannot control and should not be held accountable for the gains or losses.

The gains and losses are recorded directly to OCI and reported as part of stockholder's equity on the balance sheet. Some items remain in OCI and other items are included in income in future periods depending on the accounting requirements related to each item.

IFRS also includes adjustments to fair market value on property, plant, and equipment and intangible assets in OCI. This is referred to as a fair value revaluation. GAAP does not allow long-term assets to be adjusted to fair market value.

Items included in comprehensive income can be reported in either of the following two ways:

1. At the bottom of the income statement after "net income".
2. A separate statement of comprehensive income.

6. Income Statement Part 2

The income statement reports the value of goods and services provided to customers and the cost to provide to customers during a specific time period (accrual basis). The income statement does not report the amount of cash received or paid.

Generally accepted accounting principles require the accrual basis of accounting because it best represents the results of the economic events that occurred during the period (earnings).

The accrual basis income statement reports the following during a period of time:

- **Revenues**
  - Goods or services provided to others during the period.
- **Expenses**
  - Services the company receives during the period.
  - The value of assets the company used (other than cash) to provide goods or services to others during the period.
- **Gains and Losses**
  - The difference in the cash received from selling (or disposing of) an asset and the reported value of the asset sold on the balance sheet.

    Gains: the company receives more cash than the amount on the balance sheet at the time of sale.

    Loss: the company receives less cash than the amount on the balance sheet at the time of sale.

The income statement reports **revenues** for the value the company expects to receive for providing goods or services to customers during the period. A company must be entitled to and expect to receive cash at some point.

The income statement reports **expenses** in the period a company receives a service or uses an asset to provide goods or services to customers. A company does not always pay cash in the period the expense is reported; however, a company will pay all expenses at some point.

The income statement reports expenses in the period a company receives a service. Common expense accounts and related services:

Expense Account:	Service provided to the company:
Utilities expense	Electricity, water, and other utilities
Salaries or wage expense	Employees worked
Insurance expense	Coverage for liability, property damage, etc.
Rent expense	Use an asset owned by another company
Advertising expense	Promote to potential customers
Interest expense	Use of another entity's money

A company may pay for the service in the same period the service is received, or the payment may occur before (prepaid) or after (liability) the service is received.

- Cash payment is not the reason an expense is reported on the income statement.
- The expense is reported in the period the company receives the service.

An expense occurs when the company uses items (other than cash) to provide goods or services to customers.

- Companies use supplies, prepaid expenses, inventory, property, plant, and equipment, and intangible assets to operate its business.
- The cost of the asset used is removed from the balance sheet and reported on the income statement as an expense in the period the company uses the asset to generate revenue.

Companies use current assets (inventory, supplies, prepaid expenses) and no longer have them available to use. Long-term assets (property, plant, and equipment and intangibles) the company uses remain available for future use. A long-term asset is reported on the balance sheet as long as it is still available for use.

The name of the expense indicates the asset used.

Inventory and Cost of Goods Sold

Inventory is purchased to sell to customers. **Cost of goods sold** is reported on the income statement in the period inventory is provided to the customer.

Supplies and Supplies Expense

Companies purchase and use supplies repeatedly to operate the day to day business. The balance sheet reports the supplies as an asset. Supplies decrease and **supplies expense** is reported on the income statement when the company uses the supplies to generate revenues.

Prepaid Expenses and Expense (Insurance, Rent, Advertising)

The balance sheet reports prepaid expenses when the company pays for a service before the service is company receives the service. Companies typically prepay time-based services (insurance, rent and advertising). As time passes, the company receives the service and the future benefit is no longer available. The cost of the prepaid expense leaves the balance sheet and the company reports an expense on the income statement in the period the service is received.

Property, Plant, and Equipment and Depreciation Expense

Property, plant, and equipment is reported on the balance sheet at historical cost. A portion of the cost of each asset is reported as ***depreciation expense*** on the income statement each year the asset is used. Companies report depreciation expense for assets they replace. Land is not expensed because companies do not replace land.

Accountants estimate the cost of using an asset each period by spreading the ***net cost*** over the total estimated time (years) the company expects to use the asset. The total ***net depreciable cost*** is equal to historical cost less residual value. ***Residual value*** is the amount the company expects to receive when the company sells the asset.

The ***straight-line method*** is one method used to report an expense in each year the plant and equipment is used.

$$\frac{\text{Historical Cost} - \text{Residual Value}}{\text{Estimated Useful Life in Years}} = \text{Annual Depreciation Expense}$$

The formula above is for the straight-line method which reports an equal amount of expense each year the company uses the asset. Chapter 11 discusses other common methods of determining depreciation expense for a period of time.

The balance sheet reports long-term assets at historical cost. **Accumulated depreciation,** a negative "contra" asset account, reports the decrease in the probable future economic benefit of property, plant, and equipment as the company uses the asset. The value of accumulated depreciation is the cumulative cost for all prior periods the company has used the asset.

Equipment
- Accumulated Depreciation
Equipment, net

The balance sheet reports property, plant and equipment and accumulated depreciation at a net cost. The net cost represents the portion of the cost that has not yet been expensed. The "net cost" is also referred to as **book value**. **"Net" does not represent fair market value.**

Example 1 illustrates how the financial statements report property, plant, and equipment and the cost of using property, plant, and equipment.

A company pays $50,000 for a machine they expect to use for ten years and sell it for $10,000 at the end of ten years. The estimated expense for each year the company expects to use the machine is expected to be:

$$\frac{\$50{,}000 - \$10{,}000}{10 \text{ years}} = \$4{,}000 \text{ expense each year for 10 years}$$

The balance sheet at the end of the year and the income statement for the year will report the following for the first three years:

Balance Sheet:	**End of Year 1**	**End of Year 2**	**End of Year 3**
Machine (1)	$ 50,000	$50,000	$50,000
- Accumulated Depreciation (2)	($ 4,000)	($ 8,000)	($12,000)
= Property, Plant & Equipment, net (3)	$ 46,000	$42,000	$38,000

Income Statement:	**Year 1**	**Year 2**	**Year 3**
Depreciation Expense (4)	$4,000	$4,000	$4,000

(1) The cost of the machine does not change and remains at the historical cost of $50,000.

(2) Accumulated depreciation is the total cumulative amount of depreciation expense for all years the machine has been used to date. Therefore, accumulated depreciation increases each year the asset is used.

(3) Property, Plant & Equipment, **net** decreases each year the asset is used. The **net amount** is the cost the company will **expense in future years.**

(4) Depreciation expense on the income statement is the estimated cost of using the machine for one year (period) only.

Important: The balance sheet does not attempt to report the fair market value of long-term assets. The net amount is the cost the company expects to expense over time in the future.

Using Intangible Assets

A company must also expense the cost of using intangible assets over the time the company expects to use the asset. The income statement reports an expense each year the company receives benefit from exercising their exclusive right to use the intangible asset.

Companies report intangible assets similar to property, plant, and equipment. An intangible asset is always reported at historical cost. **Accumulation amortization** is the "contra" asset account used to report a decrease to an intangible asset. **Amortization expense** is the cost of using an intangible asset. Amortization expense is computed using the straight-line method.

Example 2 illustrates how the financial statements report intangible assets.

The Company paid $30,000 for a patent they expect to use to produce revenue for 10 years. The estimated amortization expense for each year is computed as:

$$\frac{\$30{,}000 - \$0}{10 \text{ years}} = \$3{,}000 \text{ estimated amortization expense each year}$$

The balance sheet and income statement will report the following for the first three years:

Balance Sheet:	**End of Year 1**	**End of Year 2**	**End of Year 3**
Patent (1)	$30,000	$30,000	$30,000
- Accumulated Amortization (2)	($ 3,000)	($ 6,000)	($ 9,000)
Patent, net (3)	$27,000	$24,000	$21,000

Income Statement:	**Year 1**	**Year 2**	**Year 3**
Amortization Expense(4)	$3,000	$3,000	$3,000

(1) The patent is always reported at the historical cost of $30,000.

(2) Accumulated amortization is the total cumulative amount of amortization expense for all the years the company has used the patent.

(3) Patent, **net** decreases each year the company uses the asset. The **net amount** is the cost the company expects to **expense in future years. "Net" cost does not report fair market value.**

(4) Amortization expense is the estimated cost of using the patent for one year only.

Companies expense intangible assets with a limited life over the time the company intends to use the asset to generate revenue.

Companies do not report amortization expense for goodwill and other intangible assets that have an unlimited life.

Common formats used for the income statement

1) Companies that sell goods use a <u>multi-step</u> income statement.

Multi-step income statement:

Sales
\- Cost of Goods Sold
= Gross Profit
\- Operating Expenses:
General and Administrative
Selling and Marketing
Research & Development
Restructuring
= Operating Income
\+ - Other Revenues and Expenses:
Interest Income or Expense
Rent Income
Gains or Losses on Sale of Assets or Unusual Events
= Income Before Taxes
\- Income Tax Expense
= Income from Continuing Operations
\+ - Gain or Loss on Discontinued Operations
= Net Income

Key sections and line items on the multi-step income statement follow:

- ***Gross Profit:*** Earnings from selling goods only
- ***Operating Expenses:*** Services received and assets used to provide goods and services to customers
- ***Other Revenues/Expenses/Gains/Losses:*** Transactions unrelated to the primary day to day business of providing goods and services to customers.
- ***Income from Continuing Operations:*** Earnings expected to continue in future years.
- ***Discontinued Operations:*** Results of operations related to a major segment of the company it does not plan to operate in the future.

The Securities Exchange Commission provides guidelines related to the level of detail public companies must report on the income statement. A company has flexibility on the details it provides given the company provides all relevant information.

Income Statement Terms

Sales is the price of goods and services the company provided to customers and expects to receive.

Cost of goods sold is the cost the company paid to acquire or manufacture goods sold to customers. The cost of goods includes all material costs, labor costs, and costs to operate the manufacturing facility when the company manufactures goods.

Gross profit is the sales price less the cost of goods sold during the period. Gross profit is earnings from selling inventory only.

Operating expenses directly relate to primary day to day business operations with customers. Companies report operating expenses in the categories of:

- ***Selling and Marketing***: expenses related to acquiring new customers
  (advertising, shipping, sales people salaries, etc.)
- ***General and Administrative***: expenses related to managing the organization
  (accounting salaries, corporate office rent, business insurance, etc.)
- ***Research & Development***: expenses related to developing new products
- ***Restructuring of Operations***: expenses incurred to reduce future operating expenses; the company continues to operate the segment.
  (consolidate facilities, lay off employees, close stores, etc.)

Operating income is earnings from the primary day to day business with customers (expected to continue in the future).

Other revenues and expenses (also called non-operating) result from transactions that are **not** part of the primary day to day business with customers. Examples of other revenues and expenses follow:

Interest expense ⟶ the cost of borrowing money
Gains or losses ⟶ the results from selling assets
Rent income ⟶ earned from leasing excess space to others
Interest income ⟶ earned from investing excess cash
Dividend income ⟶ earned from investing excess cash
Unusual gains and losses ⟶ lawsuits, theft, fire or natural disasters

Income tax expense is the amount the company will pay federal and state governments based on a percent of current period earnings. Income tax expense is reported separately below operating income because management has minimal control over this large expense.

Total income tax expense is based on a percentage of income before tax set by the internal revenue service (IRS.) For example, income tax expense reported for a company with income before tax of $100,000 when the IRS rate is 35% is:

Income Before Tax	$100,000
x IRS %	35%
= Income Tax Expense	$ 35,000

A detail discussion of income tax expense is beyond the scope of this book. Income tax expense for large companies may not be quite this simple due to complex IRS rules that change the amount the company owes to the IRS.

Income from continuing operations is the earnings from activity the company expects to continue in future periods. Investors use income from continuing operations to project future earnings.

Gains and Losses from Discontinued Operations occurs when a company sells or disposes of a major separate segment of the business.

The IRS taxes gains and allows deductions for losses from discontinued operations. However, gains and losses are reported net of the tax impact because it is reported below the income tax expense line item on the income statement.

For example, a $100,000 gain for a company with a 35% tax rate will report the net of tax amount of $65,000:

	Gain	Loss
Before tax amount	$100,000	($100,000)
x 1 – tax rate	x 65%	x 65%
= Net of tax amount	$65,000	($65,000)

Net income is the total economic earnings a business generates during the period.

2) Service companies that do not sell goods use a single step income statement.

A single step income statement reports subtotals for all revenue and all operating expenses.

Single-step Income Statement	**Multi-step Income Statement**
Software Revenue	Sales
+ Service Revenue	- Cost of Goods Sold
= Total Revenue	= Gross Profit
- General and Administrative	
- Selling and Marketing	
- Research & Development	
- Restructuring	
Total Operating Expenses	Same as single step
= Operating Income	
+ - Other Revenues and Expenses:	
Interest Income or Expense	
Rent Income	
Gains or losses on sales of assets or unusual events	
= Income Before Tax	
- Income Tax Expense	
= Income from Continuing Operations	
+ - Gain or Loss on Discontinued Operations	
= Net Income	

Notice the following:

- The single step income statement does not report gross profit. A company that uses a single step income statement does not sell a significant amount of goods.
- The multi-step and the single step income statement report the same line items below total revenue and gross profit.

All companies use the same format to report activity related to operating expenses, operating income, income tax expense, income from continuing operations, discontinued operations, and net income.

Companies that sell both goods and services may use a mixture of the multi-step and single-step format.

7. Balance Sheet & Income Statement Relationship

Companies report revenues and expenses on the income statement in the period earned or incurred, NOT when cash is paid or received. The balance sheet reports accounts that indicate if and when the cash exchange occurred.

Revenues

The income statement reports revenues on the income statement in the period the company provides goods and services. A change to the balance sheet always occurs with revenue.

2 Things: 1st Report the **revenue,**

and

2nd One **balance sheet account** also changes

- **unearned revenue** decreases
  (when cash is received in a prior period)
- **cash** increases (when cash is received in the same period)
- **receivable** increases (when cash is received in a future period)

Unearned Revenue (also called deferred revenue)

The balance sheet reports unearned revenue when a company receives cash in a period **before** it provides goods or services to the customer. The company owes the customer until it provides the goods or services..

- Unearned revenue is a liability.
- Unearned revenue leaves the balance sheet and becomes revenue on the income statement in the period the company provides the goods or services to the customer.

  Examples of unearned revenues:
  - A customer pays in order to guarantee the future shipment of goods.
  - A customer pays for a 3-year service contract at the beginning of the first year.
  - A customer pays for a gift card to purchase goods in the future.

Receivables

Companies report receivables on the balance sheet when the company expects the customer to pay in a **period after** the company provides goods or services. A receivable means the customer owes the company. Customers normally pay in 30 to 90 days.

Common types of receivables:

Accounts Receivable:	Customers owe the company for goods or services.
Credit Card Receivable:	Customers paid for goods or services with a credit card and the bank that issued the card will pay the company.
Interest Receivable:	Other entities owe the company for using the company's money.
Rent Receivable:	Other entities owe the company for the use of excess space.
Dividend Receivable:	Other entities owe the company for earnings on its investments.

Receivables report the cash the company expects to received in future periods.

Expenses

The income statement reports an expense in the period the company receives a service. A change to the balance sheet also occurs with the expense.

2 Things: 1st Report the **expense**

and

2nd One **balance sheet account** also changes

- **prepaid expense** decreases (if paid in a prior period)
- **cash** decreases (if paid in the current period)
- **payable** increases (if paid in a future period)
- **accrued liabilities** increases (if paid in a future period)

Prepaid expense

The balance sheet reports a prepaid expense when a company pays cash for services in a period **before** the company receives the service. Companies typically prepay insurance, rent, and advertising.

The asset prepaid expense moves from the balance sheet and is reported on the income statement as an expense when the company receives the service.

Companies use a variety of current liability account names to report amounts it owes for services received. Common current liabilities follow:

Accounts payable

The balance sheet reports accounts payable to suppliers that provide repeat services with the expectation of payment in approximately 30-60 days. Accounts payable includes amounts owed for credit cards and invoices that come in the mail.

"________________" payable

Companies may report large amounts owed for specific types of services separately on the balance sheet. A "payable" indicates the company received the service and cash will be paid in a future period. The company has committed to pay and normally does not receive an invoice.

The name of the payable describes the service received. For example:

- salaries and wages payable
- rent payable
- interest payable
- income taxes payable.

Alternatively, a company may report a payable as an accrued expense.

Accrued expenses (also called accrued liabilities)

Accrued expenses (or accrued liabilities) generally consist of amounts for services received under a written or implied contract. Accrued means "not yet paid". Large amounts may be separately named on the balance sheet. For example:

- accrued compensation
- accrued rent
- accrued interest

Accounts payable and accrued expenses both represent amounts owed for services provided to the company. Accounts payable reports only the invoices the company receives in the mail.

Revenues and Expenses Change Retained Earnings

A transaction that changes a revenue or expense will also change an asset or liability account. The revenue or expense included in net income becomes part of retained earnings to balance the accounting equation.

Assets = Liabilities + Shareholders Equity (Stock and Capital + Retained Earnings)

↖ ↗ (Assets and Liabilities) Changes with Revenues & Expenses

↑ (Retained Earnings) Revenues – Expenses = Net Income

Example 1 illustrates how a company reports $2,000 services provided to a customer and the customer pays before, during, or after the customer receives the service.

Financial statements report the following when <u>cash</u> is received <u>before</u> the company provides services:

Balance Sheet		Income Statement
Asset:	Liability:	
Cash +2,000	***Unearned Revenue*** + 2,000	Nothing

- Unearned revenue indicates the company owes goods or services to customers.
- Unearned revenue moves from the balance sheet to the income statement in a future period when the services are provided to the customer.

Financial statements report the following when the company receives <u>cash</u> in the <u>same period</u> the company provides services.

Balance Sheet		Income Statement
Asset:	Liability:	
Cash +2,000	Nothing	***Revenues*** + 2,000

- The company reports revenue in the period it provides services to customers.
- Cash received is not the reason the company reports revenue on the income statement.

Example 1 continued:

Financial statements will report the following when the company receives cash after it provides services:

Balance Sheet		Income Statement
Asset:	Liability:	
Accounts Receivable + 2,000	Nothing	***Revenues*** + 2,000

- The income statement reports revenue in the period the company provides the service.
- Accounts receivable reports the company expects the customer to pay the company in a future period.
- The company does not report revenue again when the customer pays cash.

Expense Example 2: illustrates how a company reports $2,000 advertising services received and the company pays before, during, or after the company receives the service.

Financial statements report the following when the company pays cash before the company receives the service.

Balance Sheet		Income Statement
Asset:	Liability:	
Cash – 2,000 ***Prepaid Expense*** + 2,000	Nothing	Nothing

- Prepaid expense reports the company paid before receiving a service.
- Prepaid expense will move from the balance sheet to the income statement when the company receives the service.

Financial statements will report the following when the company pays cash in the same period the company receives the service.

Balance Sheet		Income Statement
Asset:	Liability:	
Cash -2,000	Nothing	***Expense*** + 2,000

- The company reports the expense in the period the company receives the service.
- Cash paid is not the reason the company reports the expense on the income statement.

Financial statements will report the following when the company pays cash after the company receives the service.

Balance Sheet		Income Statement
Asset:	Liability:	
Nothing	***Accrued Liabilities*** +2,000	***Expense*** + 2,000

- The company reports the expense in the period the company receives the service.
- Accrued liabilities (or a payable) reports the amount the company owes for the services
- The company does not report the expense again when the company pays the liability.

An expense occurs when a company <u>uses an asset</u> to provide goods or services to customers.

Companies purchase assets to use to provide goods and services to customers.

(All assets will either be directly exchanged for cash or used to generate cash.)

Asset	→	**Expense**

1) A company receives the service as time passes. The prepaid expense is used up and is no longer prepaid.

Prepaid Rent Expense	→	***Rent Expense***
Prepaid Insurance Expense	→	***Insurance Expense***
Prepaid Advertising Expense	→	***Advertising Expense***

2) The company uses and no longer has the supplies.

Supplies	→	***Supplies Expense***

3) The company provided goods to customer and no longer owns the inventory.

Inventory	→	***Cost of Goods Sold***

4) The cost of a long-term asset is spread over the total time the company uses the asset to produce revenue.

Property, Plant, and Equipment	→	***Depreciation Expense***
Intangible Assets	→	***Amortization Expense***

5) Accounts receivable the company no longer expects customers to pay.

Accounts Receivable	→	***Bad Debt Expense***

Four different line items on the financial statements change when the company provides goods to customers:

1) Report sales (revenue) when the company provides goods to the customer.

2) The customer pays the company now (cash) or agrees to pay the company in a future period (accounts receivable).
    - Cash received in the current period increases cash
    - Cash received in a future period increases accounts receivable.

3) The company provides inventory to the customer (less inventory.)

4) Report the cost of the inventory provided to the customer (used) as an expense called cost of goods sold.

Example 3 illustrates how the financial statements report goods provided to customers.
Tick Tock, Inc. sold clocks that cost Tick Tock, Inc. a total of $50,000 for a total sales price of $72,000, on account. Customers agree to pay Tick Tock, Inc. in approximately 30 days. The balance sheet and the income statement will report the following:

Balance Sheet:

Assets:	
Accounts Receivable	$72,000 more
Inventory	($50,000) less

Income Statement:

Sales	$72,000 more
- Cost of Goods Sold	($50,000) more
= Gross Profit	$22,000

Total assets will increase $22,000.
Retained earnings (shareholders' equity) increases by $22,000

Gift Cards

Gift cards allow one customer to pay for another customer to purchase goods in the future.

A company receives cash when they sell the gift card; however, revenue is not recorded until the company provides goods or services to a customer (or when the gift card expires).

Example 4 illustrates how a company reports the sale and use of a $50 gift card to purchase goods that cost the company $30.

The initial sale of a $50 gift card is reported on the balance sheet (only) as follows:

Assets:		Liability:	
Cash	$50	Unearned Revenue	$50

The income statement reports revenue when the company provides goods to the customer (gift card holder).

Balance Sheet:

Assets:

Cash no change

Inventory ($30)

Liability:

Unearned Revenue ($50)

Income Statement:

Sales Revenue	$50
- Cost of goods sold	($30)
= Gross Profit	$20

Unearned revenues will decrease by $50 and move to the income statement as revenue.

The use of inventory creates an expense of $30 on the income statement.

Cash does not change when a gift card is used.

The balance sheet below shows how a company will report common accounts sorted by assets, liabilities, and Shareholders' equity in the order of liquidity. Accounts in italics indicate payment or receipt of cash is not in the current period.

Assets:

Cash
Accounts Receivable
Inventory
Supplies
Prepaid Expenses
"________" *Receivables*
Notes or Financing Receivable
Short-term Investments
Total Current Assets

Long-term Investments
L/T Notes or Financing Receivable

Property/Plant/Equipment (P/P/E):
Land
Building
Furniture and Fixtures
Equipment
Vehicles
Less Accumulated Depreciation
Net P/P/E

Intangible Assets
Goodwill
Patents, net
Copyrights, net
Trademarks, net
Total Intangible Assets

Other Long-term Assets

Liabilities:

Accounts Payable
Accrued Expenses or Accrued Liabilities
ST Unearned or Deferred Revenues
"______" *Payable (various payables)*
Income Tax Payable
Short-term Notes Payable
Current Maturities of Long-term Debt
Total Current Liabilities

LT Unearned or Deferred Revenue
Long-term Debt
Bonds Payable

Total Liabilities

Shareholders' Equity:

Common Stock
Additional Paid in Capital
Retained Earnings
- Treasury Stock
Other Comprehensive Income
Total Shareholder's Equity

Total Assets = **Total Liabilities & Shareholder's Equity**

Identify how a transaction changes the balance sheet and the income statement:

Accountants must record **every** transaction and report a summary of all transactions on the balance sheet and the income statement.

The answer to the following five questions helps the accountant determine how each transaction changes the financial statements.

	If yes:
1) Did the company provide goods or services to customers? If yes, was cash received now or later?	report revenue
2) Did the company receive a service? If yes, was cash paid now or later?	report expense
3) Did the company use an asset other than cash?	report expense
4) Does the company have more or less?	change an asset
5) Does the company owe more or less?	change a liability

Example 5 gives several transactions and illustrates the use of the five questions to determine accounts and amounts reported on the balance sheet and income statement. The transactions below occurred at Pillow Soft, Inc. (PS) during **February,** the second month of business.

1. Employees worked and earned $15,000. PS pays employees on the 2nd day of the following month.

1) Did the company provide goods and services to customers? **No**
2) Did the company receive a service? **Yes, salaries expense; $15,000**
   No cash was paid, see 5) below
3) Did the company use an asset other than ash? **No**
4) Does the company have more or less? **No, cash was not paid**
5) Does the company owe more or less? **Yes, salaries payable; $15,000**

2. PS paid an advertising firm $2,400 for sending marketing brochures to potential customers in the current month.

1) Did the company provide goods and services to customers? **No**
2) Did the company receive a service? **Yes, advertising expense; $2,400**
   Cash was paid, see 4) below
3) Did the company use an asset other than cash? **No**
4) Does the company have more or less? **Less, cash was paid; $2,400**
5) Does the company owe more or less? **No**

3. PS paid $6,000 for three months' rent for the use of a warehouse and office facilities at the end of January. PS used the facilities during February.

$6,000 / 3 months = $2,000 expense for one month

1) Did the company provide goods and services to customers? **No**
2) Did the company receive a service? **Yes, rent expense; $2,000**
   Cash was paid in January
3) Did the company use an asset other than cash? **Yes, prepaid rent; $2,000**
4) Does the company have more or less? **Yes, less prepaid rent; $2,000 (same as 3)**
5) Does the company owe more or less? **No**

4. PS paid $12,000 for six months coverage beginning February 1st.

($12,000 / 6 months = $2,000 each month)

1) Did the company provide goods and services to customers? **No**
2) Did the company receive a service? **Yes, insurance expense; $2,000**
   Cash was paid in January
3) Did the company use asset other than cash? **Yes, prepaid insurance; $2,000**
4) Does the company have more or less? **Yes, less prepaid; $2,000 (same as 3.)**
5) Does the company owe more or less? **No**

5. PS provided pillows with a cost of $28,000 to customers for a price of $62,000. PS expects customers to pay in 30 days.

1) Did the company provide goods and services to customers? **Yes, Sales; $62,000**
2) Did the company receive a service? **No**
   Cash was not received, see 4) below
3) Did the company use an asset other than cash? **Yes, Cost of Goods Sold; $28,000**
4) Does the company have more or less? **Less Inventory; $28,000**
   More Accounts Receivable; $62,000
5) Does the company owe more or less? **No**

6. PS received a $275 utility bill for February (not paid.)

1) Did the company provide goods and services to customers? **No**
2) Did the company receive a service? **Yes, utilities expense; $275**
   Cash was not paid, company owes, see 5)
3) Did the company use an asset other than cash? **No**
4) Does the company have more or less? **No**
5) Does the company owe more or less? **Yes, accounts payable; $275**

7. PS used property, plant, and equipment during February.

The balance sheet reports a cost of:	/	estimated useful life	= cost per month
Warehouse equipment	$50,000 /	7 years = 84 months	$ 595
Office Furniture	$15,000 /	10 years = 120 months	$ 125
Computer Equipment	$18,000 /	3 years = 36 months	$ 500
			$ 1,220

1) Did the company provide goods and services to customers? **No**
2) Did the company receive a service? **No**
3) Did the company use an asset other than cash? **Yes, Depreciation Expense; $1,220**
4) Does the company have more or less? **Less time to use the assets**
   Reported as negative accumulated depreciation; $1,220
5) Does the company owe more or less? **No**

8. PS used office supplies that cost $110 during February.

1) Did the company provide goods and services to customers? **No**
2) Did the company receive a service? **No**
3) Did the company use an asset other than cash? **Yes, Office Supplies expense; $110**
4) Does the company have more or less? **Less office supplies; $110**
5) Does the company owe more or less? **No**

The accountant must record and summarize all PS's transactions during the period and prepare the balance sheet and the income statement. The spreadsheet on the next page is used to record and summarize transactions that occurred during February.

Balance sheet accounts are cumulative and do not start over each period. The beginning balance for balance sheet accounts is the ending balance from the previous period ended January 31st.

Income statement accounts report the current period activity only and start over at zero the beginning of each period. Prior month income statement amounts became part of retained earnings at the end of the previous month.

	Cash	Prepaid Insurance	Accounts Receivable	Inventory	Prepaid Rent	Office Supplies
Begin	$136,620	$12,000		$60,000	$6,000	$300
2)	($ 2,400)					
3)					($2,000)	
4)		($2,000)				
5)			$62,000	($28,000)		
8)						($110)
TOTAL	**$134,220**	**$10,000**	**$62,000**	**$32,000**	**$4,000**	**$190**

	Warehouse Equipment	Office Furniture	Computer Equipment	Accumulated Depreciation	Retained Earnings
Begin	$50,000	$15,000	$18,000		12,620
7)				($1,220)	+ profit 10,995
TOTAL	**$50,000**	**$15,000**	**$18,000**	**($1,220)**	**23,615**

	Accounts Payable	Salary Payable	Notes Payable	Common Stock	Office Supplies Expense	Rent Expense
Begin	$60,300		$25,000	$200,000		
1)		$15,000				
4)						($2,000)
6)	$ 275					
8)					($110)	
TOTAL	**$60,575**	**$15,000**	**$25,000**	**$200,000**	**($110)**	**($2,000)**

	Salary Expense	Advertising Expense	Depreciation Expense	Insurance Expense	Sales	Cost of Goods Sold	Utility Expense
1)	($15,000)						
2)		($2,400)					
3)				($2,000)			
5)					$62,000	($28,000)	
6)							($275)
7)			($1,220)				
TOTAL	**($15,000)**	**($2,400)**	**($1,220)**	**($2,000)**	**$62,000**	**($28,000)**	**($275)**

Pillow Soft, Inc. uses a **multi-step** income statement because it sells goods. The income statement for the month ended February 28th follows:

Sales	$62,000	
- Cost of Goods Sold	($28,000)	
= Gross Profit	$34,000	
Operating Expenses:		
-Advertising Expense	($ 2,400)	
- Salary Expense	($15,000)	
- Rent Expense	($ 2,000)	
- Insurance Expense	($ 2,000)	
- Depreciation Expense	($ 1,220)	
- Utilities Expense	($ 275)	
- Office Supplies Expense	($ 110)	
= Net Earnings	$ 10,995	(assume no income tax expense)

Sales (revenue) is the price of goods or services PS provided to the customer. The value is the price to the customer.

Cost of goods sold is the cost of the inventory PS provided to customers.

Advertising, **salary**, and **utilities expenses** report services the company received and either paid for or will pay in the future. **Rent, insurance** and **office supplies expense** report the cost of assets the company used to operate the business. **Depreciation expense** reports the cost of using physical long-term assets. All activity reported on the above income statement occurred during February.

Retained earnings on the balance sheet now includes net earnings of $10,995.

The **balance sheet as of February 28th** reports the following:

Assets:		Liabilities:	
Cash	$134,220	Accounts Payable	$60,575
Accounts Receivable	62,000	Salaries Payable	15,000
Inventory	32,000	Total Current Liabilities	75,575
Office Supplies	190	Notes Payable	25,000
Prepaid Expenses	14,000	Total Liabilities	100,575
Total Current Assets	242,410		
		Shareholders' Equity:	
Warehouse Equipment	50,000	Common Stock	200,000
Office Furniture	15,000	Retained Earnings	23,615
Computer Equipment	18,000	Total Shareholders' Equity	223,615
- Accumulated Depreciation	(1,220)		
Net Prop, Plant, Equip.	81,780		
Total Assets	$324,190	Total Liabilities and Shareholders' Equity	$324,190

8. Reporting Long-term Assets

Asset or Expense?

Accountants must decide whether to report the cost as an asset on the balance sheet and expense the cost over time or report the cost as an expense on the current period income statement.

- Probable future economic benefit (PFEB) must exist to report an asset
- Assets that lose PFEB become an expense during the period of the loss
- Costs that provide no PFEB are expensed in the period incurred.

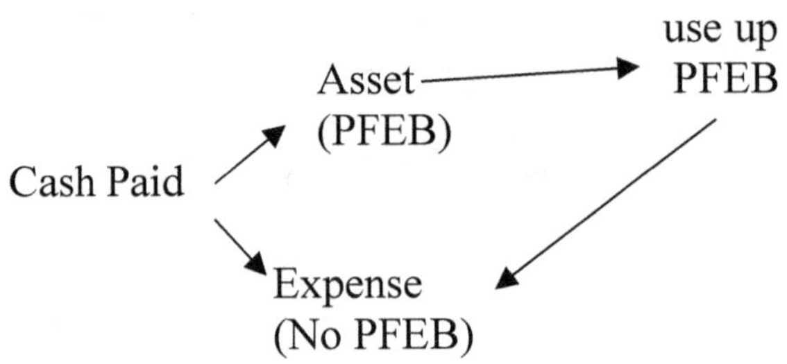

Costs paid more than once during the period do not provide probable future economic benefit. Future benefit typically refers to more than one period.

Property, Plant, and Equipment

Property, plant, and equipment (also called fixed assets, or plant assets) reports physical items a company uses for more than one year to operate the business, including:

Type of Asset	Typical Useful Life
Land	indefinite life; not replaced
Buildings	30 to 50 years
Furniture and Fixtures	5 to 10 years
Office Equipment	3 to 5 years
Computer Hardware	3 to 5 years
Computer Software	2 to 5 years
Leasehold Improvements	term of the lease
Machinery and Equipment	5 to 20 years
Autos	3 to 7 years

Companies must report property, plant, and equipment on the balance sheet at historical cost, net of accumulated depreciation (unless probable future economic benefit is lower than cost).

Historical cost includes the purchase price and all amounts paid to get the asset ready to use to produce revenues:

Related to Land:

sales tax, title search and transfer cost, attorney fees, real estate commission, removal of old buildings from the land, bulldozing, survey fees, and past due property taxes

Related to Buildings:

sales tax, title search and transfer costs, real estate commission, attorney fees, remodel before use, architect fees, and past due property taxes

Related to Equipment:

sales tax, delivery costs, installation costs, and training costs before use

Intangible Assets

Intangible assets report the cost of an exclusive right to something. The useful life of an intangible asset is the time the company intends to exercise the right to use the asset to generate revenue.

Intangible Assets	Typical Useful Life
Patents	17-20 years
Trademarks	10+ renewable; or indefinite life
Copyrights	70 years past the author's life
Franchises	Negotiated between franchisee and franchisor
Customer Lists	3-5 years, varies by industry
Goodwill	Indefinite life

Companies report intangible assets on the balance sheet at the amount **paid to outside parties** when the cost is incurred (consulting fees, attorney fees, filing fees, and all costs to obtain and successfully defend the right to use the asset).

Companies must expense **internal costs** related to obtaining or developing intangible assets as the cost is incurred. Internal costs primarily relate to employees who work for the company.

The reported value (cost) of an intangible asset is often minimal compared to the related potential future cash flows (fair market value.) For example, the fair market value of the trademark golden arches owned by McDonalds Corporation is millions of dollars and is reported on the balance sheet at a few thousand dollars. The balance sheet reports only payments to outsiders to obtain and protect the trademark.

The balance sheet reports the cost of acquiring intangible assets, net of accumulated amortization, to date

The income statement reports the cost of using intangible assets as amortization expense.

Goodwill

Goodwill is the amount a company paid to acquire 100% of another company over and above the fair market value of the net assets acquired. Goodwill represents the expected future cash flows related to a good management team, a good location, and name brand recognition. Companies pay for goodwill because the business is established and has the ability to generate more future cash flows than separate individual assets.

	The amount paid for the entire company
-	The fair market value of net assets acquired
=	Goodwill (prepaid future cash flows)

A company must carefully determine the value of purchased identifiable assets and liabilities.

- The value assigned to identifiable assets will be expensed each period.
- The value left is assigned to goodwill and is not expensed each period.

Goodwill has an indefinite life and therefore, is not moved (expensed) to the income statement systematically each period.

The balance sheet only **reports purchased goodwill.**

Internally generated goodwill is not reported on the balance sheet because no exchange occurs and a reliable value is difficult to determine.

Software Development Costs

Companies do not know the probable future economic benefit of software development costs until a significant portion of work has been completed.

Therefore, GAAP requires a company to report costs incurred:

- **before technological feasibility** as an expense on the income statement and report costs
- **after technological feasibility** on the balance sheet as an asset (often called software development costs).

Technological feasibility means the product works, a market exists, and the product is expected to be sold at a profit.

RESEARCH AND DEVELOPMENT

Research and Development: Internal

Research is the attempt to find new knowledge. Development is the translation of new knowledge into a product or service. Research and development costs follow the general rule that a cost must provide probable future economic benefit for a company to report an asset on the balance sheet.

The expectation of probable future economic benefit often varies from company to company and is difficult to substantiate. For consistency, GAAP requires companies to report research and development costs incurred

- prior to production as an expense (regardless of the probability of success) due to the uncertainty of the associated future economic benefit.
- to improve products currently in production and generating revenue as an asset because future economic benefit is probable.

Research and Development: Performed for Others

Companies report costs incurred to perform research and development for others as inventory until the project is completed and provided to a customer.

Revenue is reported, along with the cost of the research and development (inventory becomes a "cost of service" expense) when the research is completed.

Research and Development: Purchased from Another Company

A company may purchase another company primarily for its in-process research and development. Purchased research and development is reported as an asset and valued at fair market value at the time of purchase (cost).

Purchased research and development that has achieved technological feasibility is considered "developed" and is reported as an intangible asset and amortized over the expected useful life.

Purchased research and development that has not achieved technological feasibility is considered to be "in process research and development", and is reported as an intangible asset with indefinite life and tested periodically for impairment.

Subsequent Expenditures

Companies also capitalize (include in the cost of the asset) subsequent expenditures incurred after it begins using the asset to produce revenues. Subsequent expenditures consist of costs incurred to:

- **Extend the useful life**
- **Improve efficiencies**

Examples of subsequent expenditures include replacing a roof on a building, rebuilding the engine on a truck, replacing major parts of a machine.

Summary: General rules

Report as an asset (capitalize)

Property, plant, and equipment

- The purchase cost
- Costs incurred to get the asset ready to use to produce revenues
- Costs incurred to extend the useful life or improve efficiencies

Intangible Assets

- Costs paid outside the company; includes attorney fees, filing fees
- Costs to successfully defend the right to use intangible assets
- Purchased goodwill

Software Development Costs

- Costs incurred after "technological feasibility" (it works and a profitable market exists)

Research and Development Costs

- Costs incurred to improve or modify an existing product
- Long-term contract research and development performed for others before completion (reported as work-in-process long-term inventory)

Report as an expense:

- Routine maintenance and repairs (more than once a year)
- Internal development costs of intangible assets (salaries and facilities)
- Software development costs before "technological feasibility"
- Research and development before a marketable product
- Advertising expense (uncertain probable future benefit)

Report Assets at Historical Cost or Fair Market Value?

Accounting and finance professionals continuously debate whether long-term assets should be reported at historical cost or fair market value. Most professionals prefer assets reported at fair market value when fair market value is reliable. Reliable means one can verify the amount. Currently, accountants do not have a reliable method to determine the fair market value of long-term assets. Therefore, US GAAP requires companies to report long-term assets at historical cost (except publicly traded investments or when impairment occurs).

The fair market value of individual assets does not typically impact a financial decision unless the company intends to sell the asset in the near future or the fair market value is less than cost.
As such, accountants believe historical cost is more useful information than an unreliable fair market value (unless assets have permanently lost value).

The cost of the asset moves to the income statement over time as the company uses the asset. Accountants report historical cost to allow users to project future expenses.

9. Using Long-term Assets

Companies use long-term assets they must eventually replace. Therefore, a company must expense a portion of the cost of the asset on the income statement each period the asset is used to generate revenue.

Accountants do not know the actual cost of using long-term assets each period and must **estimate** and report an expense on the income statement.

Terms that relate to the estimate of the cost of using long-term assets each period include:

1) **Depreciable cost (base)** is the total net cost, the cost of the asset less the estimated residual value.

2) **Residual value (salvage value)** is the amount the company expects to receive when the company sells the asset at the end of use.

3) **Useful life** is the number of years the company expects to use the asset. Useful life is estimated based on past experience with similar assets and the company's intent to replace after certain times of use.

4) **Accumulated depreciation** is the total depreciation expense for all periods the asset has been used (all prior periods plus the current period).

5) **Book value** is the cost of the asset less accumulated depreciation. Book value represents the amount the company expects to expense in future periods. Book value is not equal to fair market value.

The balance sheet reports a long-term asset as:

Property, Plant, & Equipment	$ 100,000	Historical cost
- Accumulated Depreciation	($ 20,000)	Expense reported in prior periods
= Property, Plant & Equipment, net	$ 80,000	**Future expense**

Property, Plant & Equipment, net does NOT report the fair market value or the worth of the asset.

The net amount is also referred to as **book value or carrying value**.

According to GAAP, companies may use any depreciation method that systematically and rationally allocates the cost over the time the asset is used.

However, accountants typically use one of the following methods to estimate depreciation expense:

1) Straight-line
2) Double-declining balance
3) Units of production
4) Sum of years digits

Straight-line Method

The straight-line method results in an equal expense each year. The annual depreciation expense is computed as follows:

$$\frac{\text{Cost} - \text{Residual Value}}{\text{Useful Life in Years}} = \text{Annual Depreciation Expense}$$

More companies use the straight-line method because they have no reason to believe that revenues generated are directly impacted by the use of assets. Marketing strategies and customer demand typically have the most impact on revenue. A direct relationship between revenue and asset use is difficult to determine.

Double-declining Balance

The double-declining balance method results in a higher expense in the first year and a lower expense each subsequent year. The annual expense is computed as follows:

$$\frac{100\%}{\text{Useful life}} = \% \times 2 = \% \times \textbf{\textit{Book Value*}} = \text{Annual Depreciation Expense}$$

% (after × 2) ↑ Stays Same

*Book Value** ↑ Changes Each Year

Annual Depreciation Expense ↑ Lower Each Year

	Cost
-	Accumulated Depreciation
=	***Book Value****

Book value decreases over time as accumulated depreciation increases, which results in lower depreciation expense in each future year.

Companies with significant maintenance costs often use the double-declining balance method. Depreciation expense decreases and maintenance expense increases as the asset ages. The two expenses together give a somewhat constant annual expense to match consistent revenue generated from using the asset.

Units of Production

Companies that use the units of production method estimate depreciation expense based on an average cost to produce one unit.

The annual expense is computed as follows:

$$\frac{\text{Cost - Residual Value}}{\text{Total Estimated Units Produced}} = \text{Depreciation Expense per Unit}$$

and then,

Depreciation Expense per Unit
x Units Produced During the Period
= Depreciation Expense for the Period

Companies that manufacture using machines or mine natural resources use the units of production method when it is **relatively easy to reliably quantify the units of output**. The units of production method directly matches depreciation expense with the revenue generated during the period.

Sum-of-the-Years'-Digits (SYD)

The sum-of-the-years'-digits method results in depreciation expense that decreases systematically each year. The accountant multiplies the depreciable base by a declining fraction of remaining life each year. The denominator is always the sum of the estimated useful life (i.e. an estimated life of 10 years has a denominator of 55 (1 + 2 + 3 + 4 + 5 + 6 + 7 + 8 + 9 + 10). The numerator begins with the useful life and decreases by one each subsequent year.

For example, a useful life of 4 years will have a denominator of 10 (4 + 3 + 2 + 1) and the first year expense will be the fraction of the useful life divided by the denominator.

The first year's depreciation expense is: Cost – RV x 4 / 10

The second year's depreciation expense is: Cost – RV x 3 / 10

The third year's depreciation expense is: Cost – RV x 2 / 10

The fourth year's depreciation expense is: Cost – RV x 1 / 10

You are not required to know SYD and the following examples will not include the sum of the year's digits method because companies rarely use this method.

Example 1 illustrates the impact the different depreciation methods.

A company purchased a machine for \$260,000 at the beginning of the year. The company expects to use the new machine for 8 years and then sell it for \$25,000. The machine is expected to produce 300,000 total units and actually produced 55,000 units in year one, 42,000 units in year two, and 28,000 units in year three. The company would report depreciation expense on the income statement for the first three years as follows:

Straight-line (S-L)

$$\frac{\text{Cost} - \text{Residual Value}}{\text{Useful Life}} = \text{Depreciation Expense Each Year}$$

$$\frac{\$260{,}000 - \$25{,}000}{8 \text{ years}} = \mathbf{\$29{,}375 \text{ each year}}$$

Year 1:	\$29,375
Year 2:	\$29,375
Year 3:	\$29,375

The straight-line method reports the same amount of depreciation expense each year.

Double-declining Balance (DDB)

100% / Useful Life = % x 2 = % x Book Value

Year 1: 100% / 8 years = 12.5% x 2 = 25% x \$260,000* book value = **\$65,000**
* Cost of \$260,000 – \$0 prior year expense = \$260,000 book value

Year 2: 100% / 8 years = 12.5% x 2 = 25% x \$195,000** = **\$48,750**
** Cost of \$260,000 - \$65,000 prior year expense = \$195,000 book value (accumulated depreciation)

Year 3: 100% / 8 years = 12.5% x 2 = 25% x \$146,250*** = **\$36,563**
*** Cost of \$260,000 - \$65,000 - \$48,750 = \$146,250 book value (accumulated depreciation)

Year 1:	\$65,000
Year 2:	\$48,750
Year 3:	\$36,563

The double declining balance method reports a lower depreciation expense each year because book value is lower each year.

Example 1 (continued):

Units of Production (UP)

$$\frac{\text{Cost} - \text{Residual Value}}{\text{Total Estimated Units}} = \text{Cost per Unit} \times \text{Units Produced in the current period} = \text{Depreciation Expense}$$

$$\$260{,}000 - \$25{,}000 = \frac{\$235{,}000}{300{,}000 \text{ units}} = \$0.783 \text{ per unit}$$

$0.783 x Units produced in the current year = Expense for the Year

Year 1: $0.783 per unit x 55,000 units = **$43,065** depreciation expense

Year 2: $0.783 per unit x 42,000 units = **$32,886** depreciation expense

Year 3: $0.783 per unit x 28,000 units = **$21,924** depreciation expense

Depreciation expense for each method follows:

.

	Straight-line (S-L)	Double-declining Balance (DDB)	Units of Production (UP)
Year 1:	$29,375	$65,000	$43,065
Year 2:	$29,375	$48,750	$32,886
Year 3:	$29,375	$36,563	$21,924

Given sales total $500,000 and other operating expenses total $400,000, the income statement will report the following for year one and year three:

Year 1

	S-L	**DDB**	**UP**
Sales	$500,000	$500,000	$500,000
- Operating Expenses	($400,000)	($400,000)	($400,000)
- Depreciation Expense	($ 29,375)	($ 65,000)	($ 43,065)
= Operating Income	$ 70,625	$ 35,000	$ 56,935

Example 1 (continued):

Year 3

	S-L	**DDB**	**UP**
Sales	$500,000	$500,000	$500,000
- Operating Expenses	($400,000)	($400,000)	($400,000)
- Depreciation Expense	($ 29,375)	($ 36,563)	($ 21,924)
= Operating Income	$ 70,625	$ 63,437	$ 78,076

The method a company uses can significantly impact the earnings for a given time.
A higher depreciation expense results in lower operating income for the period. A company that reports higher depreciation expense in the first year will report lower depreciation expense in future years.

The depreciable cost of $260,000 historical cost less $25,000 residual value is $235,000. Each method gives a different depreciation expense each period; however, the total depreciation expense using all methods will be same $235,000 (cost – residual value) over the life of the asset.

A company typically does not actually use an asset for exactly the estimated useful life. Therefore, a company reports a gain or loss for the difference in the cash received from the sale of the asset and the book value when the asset is sold.

The estimated depreciation expense reported up to the date of the sale determines the amount of the gain or loss.

Example 2 uses the depreciation expense computed in ***Example 1*** to illustrate how a gain or loss at the time of sale depends on the cumulative prior year depreciation expense.

The accumulated depreciation and book value after three years under the three most commonly used methods would be:

	Straight-line (S-L)	**Double-declining Balance (DDB)**	**Units of Production (UP)**
Year 1:	$29,375	$65,000	$43,065
Year 2:	$29,375	$48,750	$32,886
Year 3:	$29,375	$36,563	$21,924
Accumulated Depreciation	$88,125	$150,313	$97,875

Cost	$ 260,000	$260,000	$ 260,000
- Accumulated Depreciation	($ 88,125)	($150,313)	($ 97,875)
= Book Value	$ 171,875	$109,687	$ 162,125

Book value is the cost the company has not yet reported as an expense on the income statement.

Example 2 (continued):

The gain or loss on the sale is the difference in the cash received and the cost the company has not expensed:

	Straight-line (S-L)	Double-declining Balance (DDB)	Units of Production (UP)
Cash Received	$150,000	$150,000	$150,000
- Book Value (not yet exp)	($171,875)	($109,687)	($162,125)
= Gain or (Loss) from the sale	($ 21,875)	$ 40,313	($ 12,125)
Accumulated Deprec Expense	($ 88,125)	($ 150,313)	($ 97,875)
Total Expense +- Gain or Loss	($110,000)	($110,000)	($110,000)

$260,000 cost less $150,000 cash = $110,000 Total on the Income Statement

A company will report a gain (or loss) when the company has previously reported more (or less) total depreciation than the actual net cost of the asset (initial cost less the cash received).

A company may use an asset longer than the estimated life. No depreciation expense is reported for years after the estimated useful life.

The name of the expense indicates the type of asset the company used.

The balance sheet reports the cost the company has not yet reported as an expense on the income statement (net cost). The income statement reports the expense for **one time period** (month, quarter, or year.)

Balance Sheet	Income Statement
Property, Plant, and Equipment - Accumulated Depreciation = Property, Plant and Equipment, Net	Depreciation Expense
Intangible Assets - Accumulated Amortization = Intangible Assets, Net	Amortization Expense
Natural Resources (Reduce the asset directly)	Cost of Goods Sold or Depletion Expense

Partial-year Depreciation Expense

A company that acquires long-term assets during the year only reports an expense for the portion of the year the company used the asset.

Example 3 illustrates how to determine and report partial-year depreciation expense.
A company purchases an automobile on September 1st for a cost of $24,000. The company expects to use the automobile for six years and then sell it for $4,000. Annual depreciation expense using the straight-line method is:

$$\frac{\$24{,}000 - \$4{,}000}{6 \text{ years}} = \$3{,}333 \text{ depreciation expense each year}$$

The company must report depreciation expense for the four months they used the automobile (September 1st through December 31st) in the first year.

$3,333 per year x 4 months out of 12 months (4/12) = $1,111

Depreciation expense and accumulated depreciation both increase by $1,111.

- Depreciation expense will be $3,333 in each of the next 5 years.
- Eight months of depreciation expense will be recorded in the last year ($2,222.)
- Total accumulated depreciation will equal $20,000 after 6 years from the purchase date (the depreciable base of $24,000 less $4,000 residual value).

A company that uses **double declining balance** will report depreciation expense of:

1st year: 4 months

$$\frac{100\%}{6 \text{ years}} = 16.7\% \times 2 = 33\% \times \text{BV of } \$24{,}000 = \$7{,}920 \times 4/12 = \mathbf{\$2{,}640}$$

($24,000 - $0) — **$2,640** Depreciation Expense

2nd year:

$$\frac{100\%}{6 \text{ years}} = 16.7\% \times 2 = 33\% \times \text{BV of } \$21{,}360 = \mathbf{\$7{,}049} \text{ depreciation expense}$$

($24,000 - **$2,640** = $21,360)

3rd year:

$$\frac{100\%}{6 \text{ years}} = 16.7\% \times 2 = 33\% \times \text{BV of } \$14{,}311 = \mathbf{\$4{,}723} \text{ Depreciation Expense}$$

($24,000 - $2,640 - **$7,049** = $14,311)

Depreciation expense for all years the asset is used (accumulated depreciation) cannot exceed the depreciable base of $20,000.

10. The Cash Flow Statement

The balance sheet reports the assets a company uses to operate the business and the amounts owed for goods, services, and borrowings. The balance sheet does not report activity that happened to change each line item (account).

The income statement reports the value of goods and services the company provides to customers and the cost to do so. Cash is not always exchanged in the same period as the related revenue or expense. The income statement does not report changes in cash.

The cash flow statement reports the cash transactions in three separate types of business activities.

Operating Activities

Companies report cash flows related to providing to customers and operating the business in the operating activities section.

Cash from operations may be used to grow the company (investing activities), be returned to investors (financing activities), or used to repay debt (financing activities).

GAAP allows companies to report operating activities using the indirect method or the direct method.

Investing Activities

Companies report cash flows related to buying and selling long-term assets and investments in the investing activities section.

Companies invest in long-term assets to operate the business and to earn a return on excess cash (investments).

Financing Activities

Companies report cash flows related to long-term liabilities and shareholders in the financing activities section.

Cash flows include borrowing and repaying long-term debt, cash received from issuing shares of stock, and payments to shareholders (dividends and stock repurchases) .

The Direct Method (of reporting operating activities)

The direct method states the cash received and paid for specific items during the period.

Format:

Cash collected from customers	248,500
Cash collected related to investments	6,500
Cash paid for inventory	(62,600)
Cash paid for salaries	(39,100)
Cash paid for income taxes	(22,900)
Cash paid for interest	(8,300)
Cash paid for other expenses	(12,800)
Cash generated from operating activities	**109,300**

The direct method is much easier for businesspeople to understand. The FASB and the IASB currently favor the direct method; however, almost all companies in the United States report an indirect cash flow statement.

The Indirect Method (of reporting operating activities)

The indirect method cash flow statement begins with net income. Net income does not represent the net cash inflows and outflows during the period.

Therefore, income statement items with a different amount of cash exchanged in the current period are listed as reconciling items to report cash generated from operations.

The indirect cash flow statement format:

Net income	100,000	
Depreciation and amortization expense	15,000	On the income statement; however, no cash
Gain on sale of equipment	(5,000)	
Stock Compensation expense	2,400	
Change in current assets and liabilities		
Accounts receivable	(4,200)	Revenue and expense amounts are different than cash received or paid
Interest receivable	6,800	
Accounts payable	(8,200)	
Income tax payable	2,500	
Cash generated from operating activities	**109,300**	

Non Cash Items

Non cash items are reported first after net income. Non-cash items will never be paid or collected. Depreciation and amortization expense, gains and losses on sale, and stock compensation expense are the most common non cash items.

Depreciation and amortization expense report the estimated cost of using long-term assets during the period. The company never pays depreciation and amortization expense. The company pays for the asset when the asset is purchased (reported in the investing activities section) and pays nothing when the asset is used.

Depreciation expense is added back to net income on the indirect cash flow statement because the expense reduced net income and cash did not decrease.

	Income Statement	Cash
Sales	$100,000	$100,000
Depreciation	($ 12,000)	$ 0
Income	$ 88,000	$100,000

Cash is $12,000 greater than Income; Therefore $12,000 is added to net income to get to cash generated from operations.

Stock compensation expense is a promised payment to employees in shares of stock. The expense decreases net income; however, is not paid in cash. Therefore, cash is greater than net income. The positive reconciling amount to net income results in greater cash from operations than net income.

Stock compensation expense works the same way as depreciation expense and is added to net income.

A gain (loss) on sale of equipment increases net income. A gain (loss) is the difference in the cash received and the net cost of the asset. The gain is subtracted (loss is added) on the indirect cash flow statement because a gain increases net income (loss decreases net income) and the company received no cash for the gain (and doesn't pay for the loss). The cash received from the sale of the asset is reported in the investing activities section. The cash received is not the gain.

	Income Statement	Cash	
Sales	$100,000	$100,000	
Gain	$ 5,000	$ 0	less cash than income; subtract
Loss	($ 10,000)	$ 0	more cash than income; add
Income	$ 95,000	$100,000	

Positive reconciling amounts: cash (received or paid) is greater than the amount included in net income (revenue or expense)

Negative reconciling amounts: cash (received or paid) is less than the amount included in net income (revenue or expense)

Example 1 illustrates how the cash flow statement reports cash related to gains and losses on long-term asset sales

In year 1, a company paid $120,000 for a machine expected to have a useful life of 10 years and be sold for $20,000. The estimated expense each year the machine is used is $10,000 (straight-line depreciation).

The machine was used for 8 years, accumulated depreciation was $80,000, and the machine was sold for $45,000 at the beginning of year 9.

$120,000	cost
($80,000)	accumulated depreciation ($10,000 x 8 years)
$ 40,000	book value
$ 45,000	**cash received**; reported in the **investing activity section**
$ 5,000	**gain;** cash received is greater than book value

	Income Statement	Cash	
Sales	$100,000	$100,000	
Gain	$ 5,000	$ 0	less cash than income; **subtract**
Income	$105,000	$100,000	

The indirect cash flow statement reconciles net income to cash generated from operations:

Income Statement	
Revenue	$100,000
- Depreciation expense	($15,000)
- Stock option expense	($ 2,400)
+ Gain on sale of assets	$ 5,000
= Net Income	$ 87,600

Cash from Operations:	
Net Income	$87,600
Depreciation Expense	$15,000
Stock Option Expense	$ 2,400
Gain on Sale of Assets	($5,000)
Cash from Operations:	$100,000

The indirect cash flow statement **lists only the differences in cash and net income.** Expenses the company does not pay results in more cash than net income (add the difference). Gains the company does not receive in cash results in less cash than net income (subtract the difference).

Changes in Current Assets and Current Liabilities

The income statement reports activity that occurs in the current period regardless of when the cash is exchanged. Current assets and current liabilities report the difference in the reported revenue or expense during the period and the cash exchanged during the period on the balance sheet.

The indirect cash flow statement reports the difference in revenues and expenses included in net income and the cash received or paid in the current period. The difference is reported on the cash flow statement as a positive or negative number depending on whether the balance increases or decreases.

	Increase	**Decrease**
Current Asset	negative number	positive number
Current Liability	positive number	negative number

A positive **number** means the company has more cash compared to net income

- did not pay all expenses incurred
- received more cash than revenue earned

A **negative number** means the company generated less cash compared to net income

- paid more expenses than incurred during the period
- customers did not pay the revenues.

Example 2 A company began the year with accounts receivable of $20,000 and provided services valued at $100,000. Customers paid the company $95,800 during the year.

Accounts Receivable

Debit	Credit
Beginning $ 20,000	
Sales $100,000	$95,800 Collect
Ending $ 24,200	

Sales is included on the income Statement:	$100,000
Collected is the cash received:	$ 95,800
Difference	$ 4,200 **less cash; negative** on CF Statement

Note: The difference in sales and cash is also equal to the difference in the beginning and ending accounts receivable balance.

- An increase in accounts receivable is a negative amount
  - less cash was received than revenues in the current period.
- A decrease in accounts receivable is a positive amount
  - the company received more cash during the period than current period revenues.

Example 2 continued:

A same company began the year with accounts payable of $20,000 and received services (expense) valued at $60,000 and paid $51,800 for services during the year.

Accounts Payable	
Paid Cash $51,800	$20,000 Beginning $60,000 Expense
	$28,200 Ending

Expense included on the income Statement: $60,000
Paid in the current period: $51,800
Difference $ 8,200 **more cash; positive** on CF Statement

Note: The difference in sales and cash is also equal to the difference in the beginning and ending accounts receivable balance.

- A decrease in accounts payable (or any current liability) is reported as a negative amount
  - more cash was paid than expenses (also paid some of last periods expenses)
  - the company has less cash than net income.

- An increase in accounts payable (or any current liability) is reported as a positive amount
  - part of the expense was not paid
  - the company has more cash than net income.

The same company began the year with prepaid expenses of $6,000 and received services valued at $5,000. The company also prepaid $7,500 during the year.

Prepaid Expenses	
Beginning $ 6,000 Prepaid $ 7,500	$5,000 Service Received
Ending $ 8,500	

Expense included on the income Statement: $ 5,000
Cash Paid: $ 7,500
Difference $ 2,500 **paid more = less cash; negative**

Note: The difference in expense and cash paid is also equal to the difference in the beginning and ending prepaid expense balance.

The indirect cash flow statement will report all differences as follows:

Net income	$35,000	($100,000 - $60,000 - $5,000)
Change in current assets and current liabilities:		
Accounts receivable	($4,200)	less cash than Revenue in NI
Accounts payable	$8,200_	more cash than Expense in NI
Prepaid expense	($2,500)	less cash than Expense in NI
Cash generated by operations	$36,500	

Cash Received from Sales	$ 95,800	
Cash Paid for Services	($51,800)	
Cash Prepaid	($ 7,500)	
Cash	$ 36,500	Change in cash is Cash Generated from Operations

Total cash from operating activities will be the same under both the direct and the indirect methods.

The direct and the indirect cash flow statement report the same investing and financing sections of the cash flow statement.

Investing Activities

The investing activity section reports the cash exchanges related to the purchase or sale of long-term assets and all investments.

The balance sheet reports the beginning (prior year) and ending (current year) balances of long-term assets. However, the balance sheet does not report the individual transactions that changed the balances from one period to the next.

Amounts reported on the cash flow statement present the cash portion of the portion of the change in the balance sheet amounts paid or received in cash.

Example 3 illustrates how the change in balance sheet amounts relate to the cash flow statement.

	Balance Sheet Equipment Account	Investing Section Cash ONLY
Prior Year Balance	$300,000	
+Purchased Equipment:		
with Debt	$ 60,000	
paid Cash	$ 36,000	($36,000)
- Sold Equipment:		
cost of Equipment	($200,000)	
cash Received		$150,000
Current Year Balance:	$196,000	

The investing activity section will present cash amounts only:

Proceeds from selling equipment	150,0000
Purchases of equipment	(36,000)
Cash generated from investing activities	114,000

The cash flow statement does not report the purchase and sale netted in one line (except for short-term investments the company intends to purchase and sell many times during the year.)

Companies often report cash paid for property, plant, and equipment on a line named **capital expenditures**.

Financing Activities

The financing activity section reports cash exchanges related to borrowing or repaying long-term debt and transactions with owners.

The balance sheet reports the beginning (prior year) and ending (current year) balances of long-term liabilities and shareholders' equity accounts.

The balance sheet does not report the individual cash transactions that changed the balance from one period to the next.

Example 4 illustrates how the cash flow statement reports only the cash portion of the change in balance sheet amounts.

	Balance Sheet L/T Notes Payable Account	Financing Section Cash ONLY
Prior Year Balance	$500,000	
Cash Borrowings	$ 15,000	$ 15,000
Cash Repayments	($25,000)	($25,000)
Purchased land	$100,000	
Current Year Balance	$590,000	

	Balance Sheet Common Stock Account	Financing Section Cash ONLY
Beginning Balance	$700,000	
Issued Stock for cash	$ 50,000	$ 50,000
Ending Balance	$750,000	

Financing Section	Retained Earnings Account	Cash ONLY
Beginning Balance	$150,000	
Dividends Declared	($ 25,000) not yet paid	
Paid $20,000 prior year dividend		($ 20,000)
Repurchased and retired common stock	($120,000)	($120,000)
Net Income	$130,000	
Ending Balance	$135,000	

The financing activity section will report:

Proceeds from borrowing long-term debt	15,000
Repayment of long-term debt	(25,000)
Proceeds from issuing common stock	50,000
Dividend payments	(20,000)
Repurchased Common Stock	(120,000)
Cash generated from/(used for) financing activities	**(100,000)**

The financing section reports only cash amounts received or paid.

Example 5 provides a complete cash flow statement followed by important things to note about the Company's strategy when reading the cash flow statement.

Net income	100,000
Depreciation expense	15,000
Gain on sale of equipment	(5,000)
Stock Compensation expense	2,400
Change in current assets and liabilities	
Accounts receivable	(4,200)
Inventory	6,800
Accounts payable	(8,200)
Income tax payable	2,500
Cash generated from operating activities	109,300
Proceeds from selling equipment	150,000
Purchases of equipment	(36,000)
Cash generated from investing activities	114,000
Proceeds from borrowing from banks	15,000
Repayment of loans to banks	(25,000)
Proceeds from issuing common stock	50,000
Dividends paid	(20,000)
Repurchase common stock	(120,000)
Cash generated from financing activities	(100,000)
Total change in cash	123,300

1) The company has positive cash flow from operations which gives them financial flexibility to invest to grow, repay liabilities, or return cash to investors.

2) Small changes in current assets and current liabilities compared to net income are normal and indicate customers generally pay the company and the company generally pays expenses timely. Large changes without a comparable change in revenues and expenses indicate otherwise.

3) The cost of using assets (depreciation expense) is $18,000 and the company paid $36,000 for new equipment. The company is purchasing more long-term assets than they currently used. Therefore, the company is attempting to grow internally.
Note: It is important to consider that the assets used were purchased at a lower cost than the current period purchases due to inflation.

4) The company appears to be using proceeds from selling equipment to repurchase common stock. Investors and creditors will wonder why the company sold such a significant amount of assets.

5) The company issued common stock to raise funds. The company may have used the funds to repay loans. Less debt generally strengthens the future financial position.

6) The company strategy is to reward investors. The company paid a large portion of net income to investors (dividends) and used a large amount of cash to repurchase common stock. Both transactions increase shareholder value.

A cash flow statement provides valuable insight into a company's strategy that the other three financial statements do not reveal. General strategies to look for include:

- Use excess cash to invest in stock or bonds.
- Grow the company through the purchase of other companies.
- Reinvest cash generated from operations into long-term assets
- Finance growth by borrowing from banks or investors.
- Finance growth through the issuance of stock to investors.
- Consistently pay investors a cash return on their investment (dividends and repurchase stock)
- Debt reduction

11. Recording Business Transactions

Double entry bookkeeping requires accountants to record business transactions one at a time. Venetian merchants first documented and used double entry bookkeeping in Italy in 1492.

The accountant makes **journal entries** to record the change to accounts for each transaction. A transaction is an exchanged.

- An account name is assigned for each item that changes.

- Journal entries have only positive numbers.

The words **debit** and **credit** have no specific meaning except to describe the format of a journal entry.

- A debit is the account name written on top.

- A credit is the account name written on bottom and indented to the right.

Account Name	$XXX	
Account Name		$XXX

Each journal entry may have more than one debit or credit.

Total debit amounts (top) must equal total credit amounts (bottom).

Each account name also has its own "T" account.
Draw a "T" first, write the account name across the top and write amounts on the left or right.

Write debit amounts on the left and write credit amounts on the right.

Account Name	
Debit	**Credit**
Amounts	Amounts

The type of account (asset, liability, shareholders' equity, revenue, expense) and the direction of the change (increase or decrease) determine whether an amount is a debit or a credit.

Asset and expense accounts increase with a debit, decrease with a credit, and always have a total balance (net amount) on the debit side (the up side).

Asset or Expense	
Debit	**Credit**
Amounts ↑	Amounts ↓
Net	

Shareholders' equity, liability and revenue accounts increase with a credit, decrease with a debit, and always have a total balance (net amount) on the credit side (the up side).

Shareholders' Equity, Liability or Revenue	
Debit	**Credit**
Amounts ↓	Amounts ↑
	Net

Record journal entries:

1) Determine the **account names** that change with the transaction.

2) Determine the **type of account name** that is changing
   (asset, liability, Shareholders' equity, revenue, expense.)

3) Determine if the change to each account name is an **increase or a decrease.**

4) Determine if the change is recorded as a **debit or credit** for each account name.
   (See above "T" account guide.)

5) Write all **debit account names on top.**
   Write all **credit account names on bottom, indented to the right.**

A transaction is an exchange: the debit is the item the company receives (now or later) and the credit is the item the company gives up (now or later).

Write the journal entry as:

Debit Account name **(Receive)**	$$$	
Credit Account name **(Give up)**		$$$

Receive (Get):

Receive an asset (asset ↑ now or later)

Receive a service (expense↑)

Owe less (liability↓)

Give up:

An asset (↓)

Make a payment (cash↓)

Issue common stock for ownership (equity ↑)

Provide goods or services (revenue↑)

After recording the journal entry – the next step is to post and summarize all amounts in each "T" account:

1) Draw a "T" and write the account name on the top of the T.
   Do this for each account name used.

2) Put all amounts in the journal entries in the "T" account of the name of the account used.

   Write all debit amounts (top) on the left side of the appropriate T account.
   Write all credit amounts (bottom) on the right side of the appropriate T account.

3) Total the debits amounts on the left side and the credits amounts on the right side.
   Write the subtotal amount for each side.

4) Subtract the smallest amount from the largest amount and net the increases and decreases.

Example 1 illustrates how an accountant will record three common transactions:

1) Borrowed $50,000 cash from the bank. The company will repay the debt in five years.

Account	Debit	Credit
Cash	*$50,000*	
L/T notes payable		*$50,000*

2) Purchased equipment for $32,000 cash.

Account	Debit	Credit
Equipment	*$32,000*	
Cash		*32,000*

3) Paid $12,000 cash for inventory.

Account	Debit	Credit
Inventory	*$12,000*	
Cash		*$12,000*

The Cash T account will show:

	Cash (Debit)	Cash (Credit)
(1)	50,000	32,000 (2)
		12,000 (3)
Subtotals:	50,000	44,000
Balance:	6,000	

Remember to **use the following questions** to determine which accounts change with each transaction:

Question:	Reported as a change to:
• Did the company provide goods or services to customers? o If yes, receive cash now or later?	Revenue
• Did the company receive a service? o If yes, pay cash now or later?	Expense
• Did the company use an asset during the period?	Expense
• Does the company have (own/control) more or less?	Asset
• Does the company owe more or less?	Liability
• Did the company exchange anything with owners?	Owners' Equity

Examples 2 and 3 illustrate how to think through each transaction and record the journal entries for each transaction. The amounts are then posted to the related T accounts to determine the ending balance for each account.

Example 2: BGJ, Inc. had three transactions during the first month of operations that change the balance sheet only.

1) The company received $20,000 cash from owners in exchange for shares of ownership.

a) Which account names change?	**Cash**	**Common stock**
b) What type of account is changing?	Asset	Shareholders' equity
c) Is the change to the account an increase or a decrease?	Increase	Increase
d) Is the change to the account a debit or credit?	Debit (get)	Credit (give up)

Account	Debit	Credit
Cash	20,000	
Common Stock		20,000

2) The company signed a note at the bank and received cash of $8,000. The company must repay the total amount in 18 months.

a) Which account names change?	**Cash**	**Long-term Notes payable**
b) What type of account is changing?	Asset	Liability
c) Is the change to the account an increase or a decrease?	Increase	Increase
d) Is the change to the account a debit or credit?	Debit (get)	Credit (give up)

Account	Debit	Credit
Cash	8,000	
Long-term notes payable		8,000

3) The company paid $2,000 cash for office furniture at the end of January.

a) Which account names change?	**Office furniture**	**Cash**
b) What type of account is changing?	Asset	Asset
c) Is the change to each account an increase or a decrease?	Increase	Decrease
d) Is the change to each account a debit or credit?	Debit (get)	Credit (give up)

Account	Debit	Credit
Office Furniture	2,000	
Cash		2,000

Example 2 continued:

Write the amounts recorded in each journal entry in the T account with the account name on the top. Write debit amounts on the left side and credit amounts on the right side.

Subtotal each side and subtract the smallest amount from the largest amount. Write the balance on the increase side.

Cash

Debit	Credit
20,000	
8,000	2,000
28,000	2,000
26,000	

Office Furniture

Debit	Credit
2,000	
2,000	

Common Stock

Debit	Credit
	20,000
	20,000

Long-term Notes Payable

Debit	Credit
	8,000
	8,000

The balance sheet will report the account names and final balances:

Assets		**Liabilities**	
Cash	$26,000	Long-term Notes Payable	$ 8,000
		Shareholders' Equity	
Office Furniture	$ 2,000	Common Stock	$ 20,000
Total Assets	$28,000	Total Liabilities and Shareholders' Equity	$28,000

Example 3: BGJ, Inc. had the following transactions during January, the first month of operations. Follow the thought process to record transactions and balance accounts.

1) The company purchased inventory for $18,000, on account.

	Inventory	**Accounts Payable**
a) Which account names change?		
b) What type of account is changing?	Asset	Liability
c) Is the change to each account an increase or a decrease?	Increase	Increase
d) Is the change to each account a debit or credit?	Debit (get)	Credit (give up)

Inventory	$18,000	
Accounts Payable		$18,000

2) The company sold inventory that cost $10,000 to customers for a price of $17,500, on account.

	Inventory	**Cost of Goods Sold**
a) Which account names change?		
b) What type of account is changing?	Asset	Expense
c) Is the change to each account an increase or a decrease?	Decrease	Increase
d) Is the change to each account a debit or credit?	Credit (give up)	Debit

	Accounts Receivable	**Sales**
a) Which account names change?		
b) What type of account is changing?	Asset	Revenue
c) Is the change to each account an increase or a decrease?	Increase	Increase
d) Is the change to each account a debit or credit?	Debit (get)	Credit (give up)

Cost of Goods Sold	$10,000	
Inventory		$10,000
Accounts Receivable	$17,500	
Sales		$17,500

3) Employees worked in January and the company paid the employees $1,100.

	Salary Expense	**Cash**
a) Which account names change?		
b) What type of account is changing?	Expense	Asset
c) Is the change to each account an increase or a decrease?	Increase	Decrease
d) Is the change to each account a debit or credit?	Debit (get)	Credit (give up)

Salary Expense	$1,100	
Cash		$1,100

Example 3 (continued):

4) The company received a utility bill for $200 for services received during January.

	Utilities Expense	**Accounts Payable**
a) Which account names change?		
b) What type of account is changing?	Expense	Liability
c) Is the change to each account an increase or a decrease?	Increase	Increase
d) Is the change to each account a debit or credit?	Debit (get)	Credit (give up)

Utilities Expense $200
    Accounts Payable $200

5) The company paid for insurance for three months (beginning with January), at a total cost of $3,000.

	Cash	**Prepaid Insurance**	**Insurance Expense**
a) Which account names change?			
b) What type of account is changing?	Asset	Asset	Expense
c) Is the change to each account an increase or a decrease?	Decrease	Increase	Increase
d) Is the change to each account a debit or credit?	Credit (give up)	Debit (get)	Debit (get)

Prepaid Insurance $2,000 (February and March)
Insurance Expense $1,000 (January)
    Cash $3,000

6) Customers paid the company $8,000 for amounts owed on account.

	Cash	**Accounts Receivable**
a) Which account names change?		
b) What type of account is changing?	Asset	Asset
c) Is the change to each account an increase or a decrease?	Increase	Decrease
d) Is the change to each account a debit or credit?	Debit (get)	Credit (give up)

Cash $8,000
    Accounts Receivable $8,000

7) The company paid $500 for advertising services received during January.

	Cash	**Advertising Expense**
a) Which account names change?		
b) What type of account is changing?	Asset	Expense
c) Is the change to each account an increase or a decrease?	Decrease	Increase
d) Is the change to each account a debit or credit?	Credit (give up)	Debit (get)

Advertising Expense $500
    Cash $500

Example 3 (continued):

8) The company invested $5,000 cash in short-term investments.

	Cash	**S/T Investments**
a) Which account names change?	**Cash**	**S/T Investments**
b) What type of account is changing?	Asset	Asset
c) Is the change to each account an increase or a decrease?	Decrease	Increase
d) Is the change to each account a debit or credit?	Credit (give up)	Debit (get)

Account	Debit	Credit
S/T Investments	$5,000	
Cash		$5,000

Post all journal entries made in examples in T accounts and balance the accounts.

Cash

Ref	Debit	Credit	Ref
2	20,000		
2	8,000	2,000	2
		1,100	(3)
		3,000	(5)
(6)	8,000		
		500	(7)
		5,000	(8)
	36,000	11,600	
	24,400		

Office Furniture

Ref	Debit	Credit
2	2,000	
	2,000	

Common Stock

Debit	Credit	Ref
	20,000	2
	20,000	

Example 3 (continued):

Inventory

	Debit	Credit	
(1)	18,000	10,000	(2)
	8,000		

Accounts Payable

	Debit	Credit	
		18,000	(1)
		200	(4)
		18,200	

Long-term Notes Payable

	Debit	Credit	
		8,000	17-2
		8,000	

Cost of Goods Sold

	Debit	Credit	
(2)	10,000		
	10,000		

Accounts Receivable

	Debit	Credit	
(2)	17,500	8,000	(6)
	9,500		

Sales

	Debit	Credit	
		17,500	(2)
		17,500	

Utility Expense

	Debit	Credit
(4)	200	
	200	

Salary Expense

	Debit	Credit
(3)	1,100	
	1,100	

Short-term Investments

	Debit	Credit
(8)	5,000	
	5,000	

Advertising Expense

	Debit	Credit
(7)	500	
	500	

Prepaid Insurance

	Debit	Credit
(5)	2,000	
	2,000	

Insurance Expense

	Debit	Credit
(5)	1,000	
	1,000	

Example 3 (continued):

Summarize all the accounts and balances in an unadjusted trial balance:

Accounts	Debit	Credit
Cash	24,400	
Accounts Receivable	9,500	
Inventory	8,000	
Prepaid Insurance	2,000	
Short-term Investments	5,000	
Office Furniture	2,000	
Accounts Payable		18,200
Long-term notes payable		8,000
Common Stock		20,000
Sales		17,500
Cost of Goods Sold	10,000	
Utilities Expense	200	
Salaries Expense	1,100	
Advertising Expense	500	
Insurance Expense	1,000	
Total	63,700	63,700

The total debits must equal the total credits because the total debits equals the total credits in each journal entry.

Place all accounts and amounts on the trial balance on the appropriate financial statement.

The income statement reports:

	Sales	17,500	
-	Cost of Goods Sold	(10,000)	
=	Gross Profit	7,500	
-	Operating Expenses		
	Utilities	(200)	
	Salaries	(1,100)	
	Advertising	(500)	
	Insurance	(1,000)	
=	Income Before Taxes	4,700	
	Income Tax Expense	0	
=	Net Income	4,700	included in retained earnings

Example 3 continued:

Include earnings for January in retained earnings as of January 31st.

Beginning Retained Earnings	$ 0	First month of operations
+ Current period earnings	$ 4,700	
- Dividends	$ 0	
Ending Retained Earnings	$ 4,700	

The balance sheet reports:

Assets		Liabilities	
Cash	24,400	Accounts Payable	18,200
Accounts Receivable	9,500		
Inventory	8,000	Total Current Liabilities	18,200
Prepaid Insurance	2,000		
Short-term Investments	5,000	Long-term Notes Payable	8,000
Total Current Assets	48,900	Total Liabilities	26,200
Office Furniture	2,000	Shareholders' Equity	
		Common Stock	20,000
		Retained Earnings	4,700
		Total Shareholders' Equity	24,700
Total Assets	50,900	Total Liabilities and Shareholders' Equity	50,900

Contra asset accounts reduce another asset account. As such, increases and decreases are opposite of an asset account.

Contra Asset Account

Debit Amounts ↓	Credit Amounts ↑
	Net

Example 4 provides the two journal entries for two transactions that change a contra asset account.

1) The company used equipment during the period; $5,000

Depreciation Expense	$5,000	
Accumulated Depreciation		$5,000

Accumulated depreciation is a contra asset that decreases property, plant and equipment.

The company does not expect to collect $3,000 that customers owe the company

Bad Debt Expense	$3,000	
Allowance for Uncollectible Accounts		$3,000

Allowance for uncollectible accounts is a contra asset That decreases accounts receivable.

Accountants use journal entries and T accounts to record and summarize transactions. The financial statements report the accounts and final balances. Prior to the use of computers, accountants manually wrote, posted, and summarized all accounts. Today, accountants enter journal entries into the computer and the accounting software automatically enters amounts into the T account and totals each account.

The computer system (software) generates a detail general ledger that reports all increases and decreases to each account and the final balance. A summary general ledger states only the final balance for all accounts in a format similar to a trial balance.

12. Adjusting Entries

Employees make entries into the computer system as the company purchases goods and services and provides goods and services to customers. The computer system automatically records journal entries as operations occur.

A company follows the process below to provide goods and services. The accounting system automatically records a journal entry as employees enter information into the system.

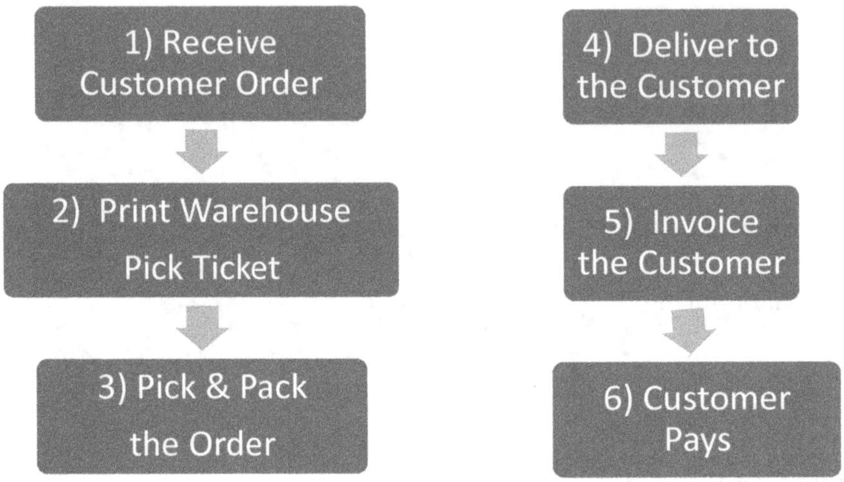

1) A customer service representative enters the order in to the computer system (the system) or the customer directly enters the order online.

2) The warehouse receives the order and prints a "pick ticket" stating the customer information and the items to be shipped to the customer.

3) Warehouse personnel take the items off the shelf and pack the items in a box to be shipped.

4) The company ships the package to the customer and warehouse employees enter a **"ship confirm"** into the computer system. The system has a record of the price to the customer and the cost of inventory sold and automatically records the sale and use of inventory upon "ship confirm" in the system as:

Account	Debit	Credit
Accounts Receivable	$$$	
Sales		$$$

Account	Debit	Credit
Cost of Goods Sold	$$$	
Inventory		$$$

5) The system generates a customer invoice with the order. The invoice may be included in the box to the customer or sent separately. The computer system automatically adds the name and amount to the list of amounts each customer owes.

6) The accountant enters the details of the customer's payment and the system records the following entry when the customer pays.

Account	Debit	Credit
Cash	$$$	
Accounts Receivable		$$$

A company also receives goods and services daily. Typical operating procedures related to receiving and paying for goods and services follow:

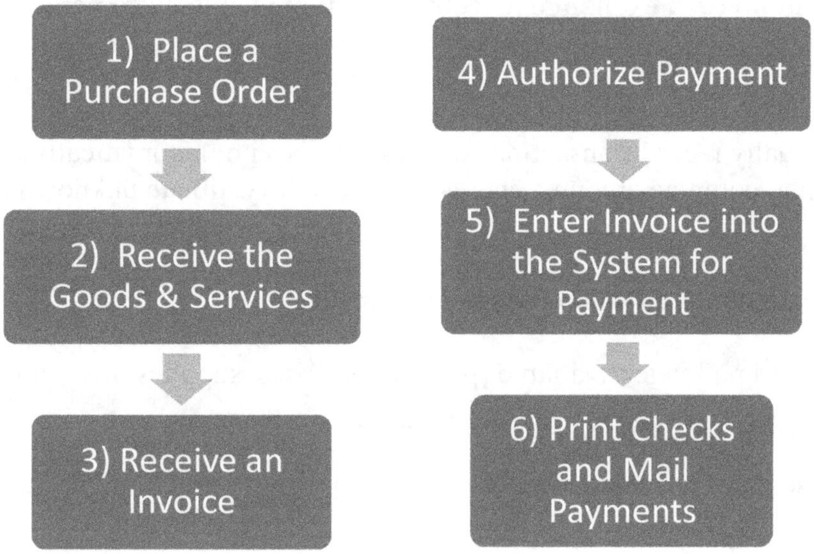

1) A functional manager identifies a necessary good or service and places an order with an approved supplier.

2) The company receives the goods or services ordered.

3) The accounting department receives an invoice.

4) The accounts payable clerk who works in the accounting department sends the invoice to the functional manager who verifies the company received the goods or services and authorizes the invoice for payment.

5) The functional manager returns the approved invoice to the accounting department. The accounts payable clerk enters the invoice into the computer system for payment. The name of the supplier, the invoice number, the due date, the amount and the **asset or expense account name** that changes is entered into the computer system. The computer system automatically records the following journal entry:

Account Name *	$$$	
Accounts Payable		$$$

6) Once a week, the accounting department prints and mails checks to suppliers for all invoices entered in the system with a due date in the next week. The computer system automatically makes the following journal entry when checks are printed:

Accounts Payable	$$$	
Cash		$$$

Therefore, a common question business people ask is "Why does a company need educated accountants if the accounting system does it all?"

The answer is: **The computer system does not automatically record transactions that are not repetitive and with <u>no cash exchange</u>** (except goods provided to customers) or occur as **<u>time passes.</u>**

Accountants must manually record transactions the system does not automatically record using additional information to compute amounts and use judgment to estimate unknown amounts.

Adjusting entries the accounting system does not automatically record, include:

1) assets used and no longer available (prepaid expenses, supplies, inventory)
2) the cost of using long-term assets (PPE and Intangibles)
3) goods and services provided to customers who paid in a previous period
4) revenue the company earns as time passes with no related cash receipt. (interest revenue, rent revenue)
5) the company received services; however, no invoice has been received
6) other expenses and losses the accountant must report in the same period as the related sale. The accountant does not know and must estimate the amount. (bad debt expense, warranty expense, bonus expense)

Accountants make adjusting journal entries at the end of the period (month, quarter, year) before they prepare financial statements.

Accounts that change with adjusting entries:

1) Assets used during the period and the related expense account:

Supplies	and	Supplies Expense
Inventory	and	Cost of Goods Sold
Accumulated Depreciation	and	Depreciation Expense
Accumulated Amortization	and	Amortization Expense

2) Services received; however, no invoice was received before the end of the period.

Salaries expense	and	Salaries payable
Interest expense	and	Interest payable
Tax expense	and	Tax payable
_________ expense	and	Accrued Liabilities

Accounts that change with adjusting entries (continued):

3) The company provided goods or services and did not invoice the customer. Therefore, no documentation is provided to the accounting department or the system did not automatically record the revenue (warehouse employees did not "ship confirm").

Sales (goods)	and	Accounts receivable
Cost of Goods Sold	and	Inventory
Service revenue	and	Accounts receivable

4) The customer paid the company cash in a prior period and the company provided the goods or services in the current period. The accountant originally recorded the cash received as unearned revenue.

Revenue	and	Unearned revenue

5) Revenue is earned, or expense is incurred, as time passed. The company did not receive or pay cash in the current period.

Interest expense	and	Interest payable
Interest revenue	and	Interest receivable
Rent revenue	and	Rent receivable
Dividend revenue	and	Dividend receivable
Insurance expense	and	Prepaid insurance *
Rent expense	and	Prepaid rent *

* A service received and a prepaid asset used as time passed.

Accountants follow a specific process to identify accounts with balances that need to be adjusted:

First: Prepare an unadjusted trial balance and:

- identify the current assets the company uses during the period and determine the remaining value.
- review expense account balances for missing expenses related to transactions that occur each month and estimate unknown amounts (consider typical monthly expenses consistently invoiced).
- review sales for reasonableness (with help from sales managers).
- consider unusual services received and identify services received with late invoices. estimate the cost of using long-term assets during the period (depreciation).
- Review account balances for reasonableness (missing transactions).

Second: Determine the correct amount for each asset and liability account.

Third: Adjust each account for the difference in the unadjusted account balance and the correct balance at the end of period.

Example 1 demonstrates the process the accountant follows to identify necessary adjusting journal entries. The accountant begins with an unadjusted trial balance as of the end of the period. The unadjusted trial balance includes all transactions the system automatically records as employees throughout the company enter data. The amounts come from the T account balance. Questions the accountant answers to identify and record adjusting entries follow the unadjusted trial balance.

Unadjusted Trial Balance as of December 31st

Accounts	Debit	Credit
Cash	26,830	
Accounts Receivable	16,000	
Allowance for Uncollectible Acct.		400
Inventory	13,000	
Office Supplies	1,450	
Prepaid Insurance	7,200	
Prepaid Rent	12,000	
Short-term Investments	45,000	
Long-term Notes Receivable	60,000	
Equipment	100,000	
Accumulated Depreciation		12,000
Accounts Payable		580
Unearned Revenue		6,000
Long-term Notes Payable		250,000
Common Stock		21,000
Sales		62,000
Service Revenue		4,000
Cost of Goods Sold	32,000	
Depreciation Expense	12,000	
Bad Debt Expense	0	
Operating Expenses	11,400	
Rent Expense	17,600	
Wage Expense	1,500	
Total	355,980	355,980

1) Does the company still expect customers to not pay $400 of the accounts receivable? If not, an adjustment is made to report the estimated amount customers may not pay. The adjusting entry will increase the allowance for uncollectible accounts and bad debt expense.

2) Does the company have inventory in the warehouse that cost $13,000? If not, an adjustment is made to report the cost of inventory actually in the warehouse.

3) Does the company have office supplies on hand that cost $1,450? If not, the office supplies account is adjusted to equal the amount of office supplies the company actually has.

Example 1 (continued):

4) Has some of the prepaid insurance coverage and prepaid rent expired during the period as time passed? If so, each prepaid account balance must be reduced to report the benefit received.

5) Did the accounting system record revenue related to investments and notes receivable? If the company did not receive cash, the accountant must calculate and record interest/dividend revenue and interest/dividend receivable.

6) Did the company use long-term assets during the period? If so, the accountant must estimate and record any unrecorded depreciation and amortization expense.

7) Did the company pay and record the interest expense associated with the long-term notes payable and long-term debt? If not, the accountant must compute/estimate and record interest expense and interest payable.

8) Does the company now owe $6,000 to customers who paid in a prior period (unearned revenue)? The accountant must adjust the unearned revenue account to equal the amount owed to customers.

9) Does the total sales amount reflect sales managers sales reports? If not, make adjustments for unrecorded/not yet invoiced sales that occurred during the period.

10) Do the expense accounts report all services that the accountant knows the company consistently receives each month. If not, search for late invoices or estimate the amount of the unrecorded service received based on past history.

11) Do revenue accounts reflect all services the company provided during the period? If not, the accountant must record the revenue and the receivable (rent, interest).

The accountant gathered the information needed to answer the above questions and identified and recorded the following necessary adjustments:

1. The accountant reviewed the list of customers who owe the company and determined customers may not pay the company $1,200.

a) Which account names change?	**Allow for Uncoll Accts**	**Bad Debt Expense**
b) What type of account is changing?	Asset	Expense
c) Is the change to each account an increase or a decrease?	Increase	Increase
d) Is the change to each account a debit or credit?	Credit	Debit

What is the current balance in the allowance for uncollectible accounts account? $400
What should the balance be as of December 31st? $1,200

Example 1 (continued):

Make the adjusting entry to record the use of the asset (loss of future benefit).

Bad Debt Expense	$800	
Allowance for Uncollectible Accts		$800

Allow for U. A.	
	400
	800
	1,200

Bad Debt Expense	
0	
800	
1,200	

2. Warehouse employees counted inventory valued at $11,800.

	Inventory	Cost of Goods Sold
a) Which account names change?	**Inventory**	**Cost of Goods Sold**
b) What type of account is changing?	Asset	Expense
c) Is the change to each account an increase or a decrease?	Decrease	Increase
d) Is the change to each account a debit or credit?	Credit	Debit

What is the current balance in the inventory account? $13,000

What should the balance be as of December 31st? $11,800, *the value the company actually counted at the end of the period.*

Make the adjusting entry to record the use of the asset.

Cost of Goods Sold	$1,200	
Inventory		$1,200

Inventory	
13,000	
	1,200
11,800	

Cost of Goods Sold	
32,000	
1,200	
33,200	

Example 1 (continued):

3. The company counted $920 in office supplies available to use at the end of the year.

	Office Supplies	**Supplies Expense**
a) Which account names change?	**Office Supplies**	**Supplies Expense**
b) What type of account is changing?	Asset	Expense
c) Is the change to each account an increase or a decrease?	Decrease	Increase
d) Is the change to each account a debit or credit?	Credit	Debit

What is the current balance in the office supplies account? $1,450

What should the balance be on December 31st? $920, the amount the company has

Office Supplies:

Unadjusted balance	1,450	
Balance should be	**920**	
Adjustment needed	530	reduce office supplies

Office Supplies

Debit	Credit
1,450	
	530 adjust
920 have	

Make the adjusting entry to record the expense of using the office supplies.

	Debit	Credit
Office supplies expense	$530	
Office supplies		$530

4. The company signed a six-month lease to rent office space on September 1st. The company paid for the entire six months at a cost of $12,000 on September 1st and recorded the entire payment to prepaid rent.

	Prepaid Rent	**Rent Expense**
a) Which account names change?	**Prepaid Rent**	**Rent Expense**
b) What type of account is changing?	Asset	Expense
c) Is the change to each account an increase or a decrease?	Decrease	Increase
d) Is the change to each account a debit or credit?	Credit	Debit

What is the current balance in the prepaid rent account? $12,000

What should the balance be in the prepaid rent account on December 31st? $4,000

Paid $12,000 for six months = $2,000 per month.

Two months are left and four months have been used up on December 31st.

Cost per month	$ 2,000	$2,000
x Number of months passed	4	2
= Adjustment to be made	$ 8,000	$4,000
	used up = expense	future benefit = asset

Example 1 (continued):

Make the adjusting entry to record the expense of using the space as time passed:

	Debit	Credit
Rent Expense	$8,000	
Prepaid Rent		$8,000

Rent Expense

Debit	Credit
17,600	
8,000	
25,600	

Prepaid Rent

Debit	Credit
12,000	
	8,000
4,000	

2 months left

4. On April 1st, of the current year, the company paid $7,200 for 24 months of insurance coverage. The accountant recorded the payment to prepaid insurance.

	Prepaid Insurance	**Insurance Expense**
a) Which account names change?	**Prepaid Insurance**	**Insurance Expense**
b) What type of account is changing?	Asset	Expense
c) Is the change to each account an increase or a decrease?	Decrease	Increase
d) Is the change to each account a debit or credit?	Credit	Debit

What is the current balance in the prepaid insurance account? $7,200
What should the balance be on December 31st? $4,500 (15 months left)

Cost of $7,200 / 24 months = $300 per month April 1st to December 31st is nine months used.

Using up an asset is an expense: 9 months x $300 = $2,700 is the expense.

Cost per month	$ 300	$ 300
x Number of months passed	9	15
= Adjustment to be made	$2,700	$4,500
	used up = expense	Future benefit = asset

Make the adjusting entry to record the asset used up.

	Debit	Credit
Insurance Expense	$2,700	
Prepaid Insurance		$2,700

Insurance Expense

Debit	Credit
0	
2,700	
2,700	

used up

Prepaid Insurance

Debit	Credit
7,200	
	2,700
4,500	

future benefit

Example 1 (continued):

5. On January 1st the company put $45,000 into a one-year government bond that earns 1%.

a) Which account names change?	**Interest Receivable**	**Interest Revenue**
b) What type of account is changing?	Asset	Revenue
c) Is the change to each account an increase or a decrease?	Increase	Increase
d) Is the change to each account a debit or credit?	Debit	Credit

What is the current balance in the interest revenue account? $0

What should the balance be as of December 31st? $450

Interest = principle x rate x time: $45,000 x 0.01 x 12/12 months = $450

Make the adjusting entry to record the revenue earned as time passed.

Account	Debit	Credit
Interest Receivable	$450	
Interest Revenue		$450

5. On June 1st the company loaned $60,000 to another company in need of cash. The other company agreed to repay the full amount in two years and pay interest of eight percent annually each May 31st. Record the adjustment for the interest earned.

a) Which account names change?	**Interest Receivable**	**Interest Revenue**
b) What type of account is changing?	Asset	Revenue
c) Is the change to each account an increase or a decrease?	Increase	Increase
d) Is the change to each account a debit or credit?	Debit	Credit

What is the current balance in the interest revenue account? $0

What should the balance be as of December 31st? $2,800

Interest = principle x rate x time: $60,000 x .08 x 7 /12 months = $2,800
June 1 to December 31st is seven months earned this year.

Make the adjusting entry to record the revenue earned as time passed.

Account	Debit	Credit
Interest Receivable	$2,800	
Interest Revenue		$2,800

Example 1 (continued):

6. On January 1st of <u>last year</u>, the company purchased a tractor for \$100,000. The company expects to use the tractor for seven years. The company used the tractor during the current year.

	Depreciation Expense	**Accumulated Depreciation**
a) Which account names change?	**Depreciation Expense**	**Accumulated Depreciation**
b) What type of account is changing?	Expense	Contra Asset
c) Is the change to each account an increase or a decrease?	Increase	Increase
d) Is the change to each account a debit or credit?	Debit	Credit

What is the current balance in the depreciation expense account? \$12,000

What should be the total expense for the period ended December 31st?

Cost \$100,000 / 7-year life = \$14,286 each year

Make the adjusting entry to record the expense of using the long-term asset.

Account	Debit	Credit
Depreciation Expense	\$2,286	
Accumulated Depreciation		\$2,286

Depreciation Expense (Debit)	Depreciation Expense (Credit)
12,000	
2,286	
14,286	

Accumulated Depreciation (Debit)	Accumulated Depreciation (Credit)
	12,000
	2,286
	14,286

7. On March 1st, the company borrowed \$250,000 from the bank they must repay in three years. The bank charges interest at a 6% annual rate and the company must pay interest each year on February 28th.

	Interest Expense	**Interest Payable**
a) Which account names change?	**Interest Expense**	**Interest Payable**
b) What type of account is changing?	Expense	Liability
c) Is the change to each account an increase or a decrease?	Increase	Increase
d) Is the change to each account a debit or credit?	Debit	Credit

What is the current balance in the interest expense account? \$0

What should the balance be as of December 31st? \$12,500

Interest = principle x rate x time: \$250,000 x .06 x 10 /12 months = \$12,500
March 1st to December 31st is ten months incurred this year.

Make the adjusting entry to record the expense incurred as time passed.

Account	Debit	Credit
Interest Expense	\$12,500	
Interest Payable		\$12,500

Example 1 (continued):

8. On August 1st the company received cash from a customer in the amount of $6,000 for services to be provided equally over the next six months. The service was provided monthly beginning on August 1st. The receipt of cash was recorded as unearned revenue.

a) Which account names change?	**Unearned Revenue**	**Service Revenue**
b) What type of account is changing?	Liability	Revenue
c) Is the change to each account an increase or a decrease?	Decrease	Increase
d) Is the change to each account a debit or credit?	Debit	Credit

What is the current balance in the unearned revenue account? $6,000

What should the balance be as of December 31st? $1,000, the amount owed on 12/31

$6,000 / 6 month = $1,000 per month

August 1st to December 31st is five months earned.
5 months x $1,000 per month = $5,000 earned
1 month x $1,000 remains unearned

Make the adjusting entry to record the revenue earned.

	Debit	Credit
Unearned Revenue	$5,000	
Service Revenue		$5,000

Service Revenue	
	4,000
	5,000
	9,000 earned this period

Unearned Revenue	
	6,000
5,000	
	1,000 still owed

Example 1 (continued):

9. During the month of December, the company provided $7,000 in services to a customer. The accounting department did not know about the service and did not send an invoice.

	Accounts Receivable	Service Revenue
a) Which account names change?	**Accounts Receivable**	**Service Revenue**
b) What type of account is changing?	Asset	Revenue
c) Is the change to each account an increase or a decrease?	Increase	Increase
d) Is the change to each account a debit or credit?	Debit	Credit

What is the current balance in the sales account? $62,000

What should the balance be as of December 31st? $7,000 more

What should be recorded? Services provided in the amount of $7,000.
The customer owes $7,000.

Make the adjusting entry to record the revenue earned.

Account	Debit	Credit
Accounts Receivable	$7,000	
Service Revenue		$7,000

10. The company received $900 of invoices in early January of the next year for a variety of services the company received during December of the current year.

What should be recorded? Services received totaled $900.
The company owes $900 more.

Account	Debit	Credit
Operating Expenses	$900	
Accounts Payable		$900

The accountant prepares the following adjusted trial balance after recording and posting amounts into T accounts.

Accounts	Unadjusted Trial Balance Debit	Unadjusted Trial Balance Credit	Adjustment	Unadjusted Trial Balance Debit	Unadjusted Trial Balance Credit
Cash	26,830			26,830	
Accounts Receivable	16,000		7,000	23,000	
Allowance for Uncollectible Acct.		400	800		1,200
Inventory	13,000		(1,200)	11,800	
Office Supplies	1,450		(530)	920	
Prepaid Insurance	7,200		(2,700)	4,500	
Prepaid Rent	12,000		(8,000)	4,000	
Interest Receivable	-		3,250	3,250	
Short-term Investments	45,000			45,000	
Long-term Notes Receivable	60,000			60,000	
Equipment	100,000			100,000	
Accumulated Depreciation		12,000	2,286		14,286
Accounts Payable		580	900		1,480
Unearned Revenue		6,000	(5,000)		1,000
Interest Payable			12,500		12,500
Long-term Notes Payable		250,000			250,000
Common Stock		21,000			21,000
Sales		62,000			62,000
Service Revenue		4,000	12,000		16,000
Interest Revenue		-	3,250		3,250
Cost of Goods Sold	32,000		1,200	33,200	
Depreciation Expense	12,000		2,286	14,286	
Operating Expenses	11,400		900	12,300	
Bad Debt Expense	-		800	800	
Rent Expense	17,600		8,000	25,600	
Insurance Expense	-		2,700	2,700	
Office Supplies Expense	-		530	530	
Interest Expense	-		12,500	12,500	
Wage Expense	1,500			1,500	
Total	355,980	355,980		382,716	382,716

General rules to follow to record adjusting entries:

- When an expense increases, an asset will also decrease or a liability will also increase.
- When revenue increases, an asset will also increase or unearned revenue will decrease.
- Do not use the cash account in adjusting entries (with the exception of the bank reconciliation adjusting entry not yet discussed).
- Reduce estimated revenues or expenses when the actual amount is lower than the amount estimated and recorded.

13. The Accounting Cycle

Accountants refer to the process of preparing financial statements at the end of each month (or quarter or year) as "closing the books". The previous chapters discussed recording entries and adjusting accounts. The accountant must also close out temporary accounts to prepare the balance sheet and income statement.

The Entire Process:

1) The accounting system automatically records transactions related to customer sales, cash receipts, and cash payments when employees enter data into the accounting system.
The system then posts amounts in "T" accounts and balances the "T" accounts.

2) The system provides an **unadjusted trial balance,** a listing of all accounts and **preliminary balances** before adjustments. The purpose of the unadjusted trial balance is to help the accountant identify accounts and amounts to adjust. An unadjusted trial balance is formatted as (random example):

Account Name	Debit	Credit
Cash	50,000	
Accounts Receivable	30,000	
Inventory	20,000	
Equipment	78,000	
Accumulated Depreciation		15,000
Accounts Payable		10,000
Long-term Notes Payable		100,000
Common Stock		5,000
Retained Earnings (beginning)		28,000
Dividends	5,000	
Sales Revenue		65,000
Salary Expense	40,000	
	223,000	223,000

Accountants call the trial balance the **general ledger.**

3) Accountants make a**djusting entries** to record transactions that did not change cash and do not require a physical exchange (not yet recorded).

4) The system posts the amounts in all adjusting journal entries to each "T" account and determines a **final balance** for each account.

5) The system provides an **adjusted trial balance** (general ledger). The adjusted trial balance lists all accounts and **final balances** in the same format as the unadjusted trial balance.

6) The accountant prepares the **income statement** that reports all revenue, expense, gain, and loss accounts and associated amounts stated on the adjusted trial balance.

7) The accountant records **closing entries** to move all income statement accounts (revenues, expenses, gains, and losses) and dividends to retained earnings. Income statement accounts are **temporary (or nominal) accounts** because they must start at zero at the beginning of each period to report the current period's activity only. **Balance sheet accounts are permanent (or real) accounts** that do not start over at $0 at the beginning of the next period.

The accountant records closing entries in three steps:

1) Adjust all expense and loss accounts to zero and transfer the amounts to retained earnings.

1st: credit the total balance for all expense and loss accounts
2nd: debit retained earnings for the total of all credits

Retained earnings	*$XXXXX*	
_____expense		*$XXX*
_____ expense		*$XXX*
_____ expense		*$XXX*
_____ expense		*$XXX*
Cost of goods sold		*$XXX*
Loss on sale		*$XXX*

All expense and loss accounts have a debit balance. A credit to the account for the total account balance will change the account balance to zero.

2) Adjust all revenue and gain accounts to zero and transfer the amounts to retained earnings.

1st: debit the total balance for all revenue and gain accounts
2nd: credit retained earnings for the total of all credits

Sales	*$XXX*	
Interest income	*$ XX*	
Dividend income	*$ XX*	
Service revenue	*$XXX*	
Gain on sale	*$ XX*	
Retained earnings		*$XXXX*

All revenue and gain accounts have a credit balance. A debit to the account for the total account balance will change the account balance to zero.

3) Adjust the dividend account to zero and transfer the amount to retained earnings.

1st: Credit the dividend account to adjust the dividend account balance to zero.
2nd: Debit retained earnings for the same amount to move dividends to retained earnings.

Retained earnings	*\$XXX*	
Dividend		*\$XXX*

Example 1 illustrates how to record closing entries. The closing entry amount to make the account balance equal zero is in the box. All revenue, expense, gain, and loss accounts are transferred to retained earnings.

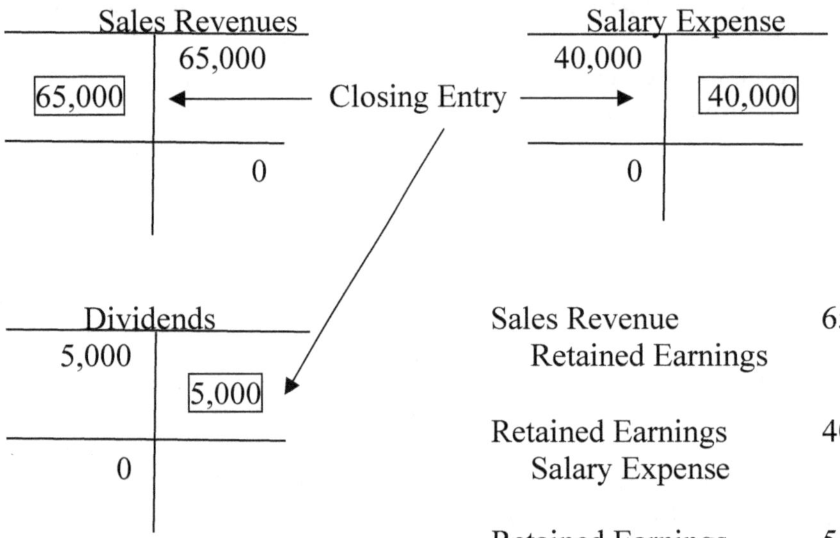

Sales Revenue	65,000	
Retained Earnings		65,000
Retained Earnings	40,000	
Salary Expense		40,000
Retained Earnings	5,000	
Dividends		5,000

Closing entries transfer all items on the income statement and dividends to retained earnings. The final ending balance of retained earnings is reported on the balance sheet.

Retained Earnings	
	Beginning Balance \$28,000
Expenses \$40,000	Revenues \$65,000
Losses \$0	Gains \$0
Dividends \$5,000	
	Ending Balance \$48,000

Retained Earnings consists of cumulative profits and losses the company keeps to reinvest in the business since the first day of operations.

Purpose of Closing entries:

- move income statement account balances to retained earnings.
- adjust income statement account balances to zero so that accounts start over and include only the next period's activity.

8) After closing entries, the accountant prepares the **Statement of Shareholders' Equity.** The statement presents equity account names across the top and a description of each transaction is reported on the left side. The column of the account that changes contains the amount. The ending balances for all accounts on the statement of shareholders' equity equal the equity account amounts reported on the balance sheet.

9) The accountant prepares the **balance sheet.** The balance sheet reports all asset, liability, and equity account names and related total amounts on the adjusted trial balance. The balance sheet reports retained earnings <u>at the end of the period</u> (which includes current period earnings and dividends).

10) The accountant prepares the **Statement of Cash Flows.**

11) The accountant writes the **footnotes** presented with the financial statements.

12) The accountant provides the financial statements and the footnotes to internal management and external stakeholders.

The accounting department performs steps three through twelve at the end of the period (month, quarter, and year) to prepare financial statements. The time required to close the books and provide financial statements is dependent on the size of the company and the accounting system's capabilities (normally three days to three weeks).

- Accountants must have strong controls in place to ensure all automated transactions are properly recorded.

- Accountants use most of their time to identify, value, and make adjusting entries.

Example 2 illustrates all steps in the accounting cycle from recording transactions, adjusting entries, closing entries and summarizing transactions to prepare financial statements.

XYZ Company had the following transactions during the month of January, the first month of operations:

1. Received \$150,000 cash from investors for ownership in the company.
2. Purchased \$45,000 inventory; on account.
3. Paid \$7,200 for liability insurance for the entire year on January 2nd.
4. Sold inventory that cost \$32,000 to customers for \$62,000, on account.
5. Purchased manufacturing equipment that cost \$39,000 (7-year life). Paid \$7,000 cash and agreed to pay the balance plus interest in 6 months, 8% annual interest.
6. The company paid \$1,500 to employees who worked during the month.
7. Paid for the inventory purchased in (2.) above
8. Purchased office supplies for \$250. (\$100 remained at the end of January)
9. Paid \$1,300 for a trademark XYZ expects to be use for 10 years beginning in March.
10. Invested \$50,000 in a short-term certificate of deposit earning a 6% annual rate. Interest will be received on February 1st of next year.
11. XYZ paid \$3,000 dividends to shareholders at the end of the month.

Record the Initial Transaction

1. Received \$150,000 cash from investors for ownership in the company.

Received – Cash
Gave up – Ownership – Common Stock

Cash is an asset, increased: debit
Common Stock is shareholders' equity, increased: credit

		Debit	Credit
Cash		**\$150,000**	
	Common stock		**\$150,000**

2. Purchased \$45,000 inventory; on account.

Received – Inventory
Gave up – Pay later: liability, accounts payable: "On account" means pay later

Inventory is an asset, increased: debit
Accounts payable is a liability, increased: credit

		Debit	Credit
Inventory		**\$45,000**	
	Accounts Payable		**\$45,000**

Example 2 continued:

3. *Paid $7,200 for liability insurance for the entire year on January 2nd.*

Received – Insurance coverage in the future; Prepaid Insurance
Gave up – Cash

Prepaid insurance is an asset, increased: debit
Cash is an asset, decreased: credit

	Debit	Credit
Prepaid Insurance	**$7,200**	
Cash		**$7,200**

4. *Sold inventory that cost $32,000 to customers for $62,000, on account.*

Received – Cash later; Accounts receivable is an asset, increased: debit
Gave up -- Provided Goods – Sales Revenue, increased: credit

Gave up – Provided goods to customer, inventory decreased: credit
Used the asset inventory, is an increase to an expense (CGS): debit

	Debit	Credit
Accounts Receivable	**$62,000**	
Sales Revenue		**$62,000**
Cost of Goods Sold	**$32,000**	
Inventory		**$32,000**

5. *Purchased manufacturing equipment that cost $39,000 (7-year life). Paid $7,000 cash and agreed to pay the balance plus interest in 6 months, 8% annual interest.*

Received – Equipment $39,000
Gave up – Cash $7,000
Gave up – Pay later, short-term notes payable

Equipment is an asset, increased: debit
Cash is an asset, decreased: credit
Short-term notes payable is a liability, increased: credit

	Debit	Credit
Equipment	**$39,000**	
Cash		**$ 7,000**
S/T Notes Payable		**$32,000**

Example 2 continued:

6. *The company paid $1,500 to employees who worked during the month.*

Received – A service, employees worked: wage expense
Gave up – Cash

Wages expense is an expense, increased: debit
Cash is an asset, decreased: credit

	Debit	Credit
Wages Expense	**$1,500**	
Cash		**$1,500**

7. *Paid for the inventory purchased in 2 above.*

Received – Owe less, decreases accounts payable
Gave up – Cash

Accounts payable is a liability, decreased: debit
Cash is an asset, decreased: credit

	Debit	Credit
Accounts Payable	**$45,000**	
Cash		**$45,000**

8. *Purchased office supplies for $250 ($100 remained at the end of January.)*

Received – Office Supplies
Gave up – Cash

Office supplies is an asset, increased: debit
Cash is an asset, decreased: credit

	Debit	Credit
Office Supplies	**$250**	
Cash		**$250**

9. *Paid $1,300 for a trademark XYZ expects to use for 10 years beginning in March.*

Received – Trademark
Gave up – Cash

Trademark is an asset, increased: debit
Cash is an asset, decreased: credit

	Debit	Credit
Trademark	**$1,300**	
Cash		**$1,300**

Example 2 continued:

10. *Invested $50,000 in a short-term certificate of deposit earning a 6% annual rate. Interest will be received on February 1st next year.*

    Received – Short-term Investment
    Gave up - Cash

    S/T Investment is an asset, increased: debit
    Cash is an asset, decreased: credit

Short-term Investment	**$50,000**	
Cash		**$50,000**

11. *XYZ paid $3,000 dividends to shareholders.*

Dividends	**$3,000**	
Cash		**$3,000**

T Accounts for Journal Entries: Steps 2, 4, and 5

Make a "T" account for each account in each journal entries, record all journal entry amounts in the T accounts on the proper debit or credit side, and balance each account. The "A" out to the side of the amount indicates it is an adjusting entry made at the end of the period.

Cash

	Debit	Credit	
(1)	150,000	7,200	(2)
		7,000	(5)
		1,500	(6)
		45,000	(7)
		250	(8)
		1,300	(9)
		50,000	(10)
		3,000	(11)
	150,000	115,250	
	34,750		

Common Stock

	Debit	Credit	
		150,000	(1)
		150,000	

Inventory

	Debit	Credit	
(2)	45,000	32,000	(4)
	13,000		

Accounts Payable

	Debit	Credit	
(7)	45,000	45,000	(2)
		0	

Prepaid Insurance

	Debit	Credit	
(3)	7,200		
		600	A
	6,600		

Accounts Receivable

	Debit	Credit
(4)	62,000	
	62,000	

Sales

	Debit	Credit	
		62,000	(4)
		62,000	

Cost of Goods Sold

	Debit	Credit
(4)	32,000	
	32,000	

Equipment

	Debit	Credit
(5)	39,000	
	39,000	

Short-term Notes Payable

	Debit	Credit	
		32,000	(5)
		32,000	

Wage Expense

	Debit	Credit
(6)	1,500	
	1,500	

Office Supplies

	Debit	Credit
(8)	250	
		150
	100	

Trademark

	Debit	Credit
(9)	1,300	
	1,300	

Short-term Investments

	Debit	Credit
(10)	50,000	
	50,000	

Insurance Expense

	Debit	Credit
A	600	
	600	

	Depreciation Expense	
A	464	
	464	

Accumulated Depreciation		
	464	A
	464	

	Interest Expense	
A	213	
	213	

Interest Payable		
	213	A
	213	

	Office Supplies Expense	
A	150	
	150	

	Interest Receivable	
A	250	
	250	

Interest Revenue		
	250	A
	250	

	Retained Earnings		
		0 Beginning	
C	3,000	62,250	C
C	34,927		
		24,323	

Dividends		
0 Beginning		
3,000		
	3,000	C
0		

"C" is for closing entries

Example 2 continued:

Prepare an Unadjusted Trial Balance before Adjusting Journal Entries

Unadjusted Trial Balance

Accounts	Debit	Credit
Cash	34,750	
Accounts Receivable	62,000	
Inventory	13,000	
Office Supplies	250	
Prepaid Insurance	7,200	
Short-term Investments	50,000	
Equipment	39,000	
Trademarks	1,300	
Accounts Payable		0
Short-term Notes Payable		32,000
Dividends	3,000	
Common Stock		150,000
Sales		62,000
Cost of Goods Sold	32,000	
Wage Expense	1,500	
Total	244,000	244,000

Prepare Adjusting Journal Entries for the Month of January: The transaction number on the right refers to the original transaction that relates to the adjustment.

Record assets used during the month of January:

	Debit	Credit	
3. Insurance Expense	600		\$7,200 / 12 months = \$600 each month
Prepaid Insurance		600	
5. Depreciation Expense	464		\$39,000 / 7 years = \$5,571 each year
Accumulated Depreciation		464	\$5,571 / 12 months = \$464 each month
8. Office Supplies Expense	150		\$250 purchased - \$100 ending = \$150 used
Office Supplies		150	

9. The trademark is not used in January. Therefore, no amortization expense is recorded.

Record one month of services received (5. to the company and 10. to another entity) during January with no cash received or paid in January.

	Debit	Credit	
5. Interest Expense	213		\$32,000 x 8% x 1/12 = \$213 each month
Interest Payable		213	
10. Interest Receivable	250		\$50,000 x 6% x 1/12 = \$250 each month
Interest Revenue		250	

Example 2 continued:

Record the adjusting journal entry amounts in the T accounts and balance the T accounts
See the previous T accounts. The "A" beside the amount indicates an adjusting entry.

Prepare an Adjusted Trial Balance with FINAL Accounts and Amounts
The adjusted trial balance lists every account name and the related final balance in the T account in the correct column.

Accounts	Debit	Credit
Cash	34,750	
Accounts Receivable	62,000	
Inventory	13,000	
Office Supplies	100	
Prepaid Insurance	6,600	
Interest Receivable	250	
Short-term Investments	50,000	
Equipment	39,000	
Accumulated Depreciation		464
Trademarks	1,300	
Accounts Payable		0
Interest Payable		213
Short-term Notes Payable		32,000
Common Stock		150,000
Dividends	3,000	
Sales		62,000
Cost of Goods Sold	32,000	
Wage Expense	1,500	
Insurance Expense	600	
Depreciation Expense	464	
Office Supplies Expense	150	
Interest Expense	213	
Interest Revenue		250
Total	244,927	244,927

Prepare the Income Statement for the Month of January.
Report all revenues and expenses listed on the adjusted trial balance on the income statement.

Sales	62,000	
- Cost of Goods Sold	32,000	
= Gross Profit	30,000	
- Operating Expenses:		
Wage Expense	1,500	
Insurance Expense	600	
Depreciation Expense	464	
Office Supplies Expense	150	
= Income from Operations	27,286	
Interest Expense	(213)	
Interest Revenue	250	This example has no
= Net Income	27,323	income tax expense.

Example 2 continued:

Prepare Closing Journal Entries

Transfer all revenue, expense, gain, loss, and dividend accounts to retained earnings.

Account	Debit	Credit	Note
Sales	62,000		All revenues and gains
Interest Revenue	250		
Gain on Sale of Assets	0		
Retained Earnings		62,250 (total of all debits)	

Account	Debit	Credit	Note
Retained Earnings	34,927 (total of all credits)		
Cost of Goods Sold		32,000	All expenses and losses
Wage Expense		1,500	
Insurance Expense		600	
Depreciation Expense		464	
Office Supplies Expense		150	
Interest Expense		213	
Loss on Sale of Assets		0	

Account	Debit	Credit	Note
Retained Earnings	3,000		
Dividends		3,000	Dividends reduce retained earnings

Retained Earnings	
	0
34,927	62,250
3,000	
	24,323

Prepare a Statement of Shareholders' Equity for the Month of January

	Common Stock	Retained Earnings
January 1, 20XX	$ 0	$ 0
Issued Common Stock	$150,000	$ 0
Declared Dividends		$ 3,000
Net Income		$ 27,323
January 31, 20XX	$150,000	$ 24,323

Example 2 continued:

Prepare a Balance Sheet as of January 31st

List all assets, liabilities and shareholders' equity accounts and the final balances on the adjusted trial balance in proper format.

Assets		**Liabilities**	
Cash	34,750	Interest Payable	213
Accounts Receivable	62,000	Short-term Notes Payable	32,000
Inventory	13,000		
Office Supplies	100		
Prepaid Insurance	6,600	Total Current Liabilities	32,213
Interest Receivable	250		
Short-term Investment	50,000		
Total Current Assets	166,700	Total Liabilities	32,213
		Owner's Equity	
P/P/E: Equipment	39,000	Common Stock	150,000
- Accumulated Depreciation	(464)	Retained Earnings	24,323
Net P/P/E:	38,536	Total Owner's Equity	177,323
Intangible Assets:			
Trademark	1,300		
Total Assets	206,536	Total Liabilities and Owner's Equity	206,536

Prepare a Statement of Cash Flows (Direct Method)

Cash collected from customers	$ 0
Cash paid for supplies	(250)
Cash paid for inventory	(45,000)
Cash paid to employees	(1,500)
Cash paid for insurance	(7,200)
Cash used for operating activities	(53,950)
Equipment purchased	(7,000)
Trademark purchased	(1,300)
Short-term investments purchased	(50,000)
Cash used for investing activities	(58,300)
Paid dividends to shareholders	(3,000)
Common stock issued	150,000
Cash from financing activities	147,000
Total Change in Cash	$ 34,750
Beginning Cash	0
Ending Cash	$ 34,750

14. Revenue Recognition

Revenue is the exchange of goods and services for an asset (simple way to think about it).

ASC Definition of "Revenue": Inflows or other enhancements of assets of an entity (a seller) or settlements of a liability (or combination of both) from delivering or producing goods, rendering services, or other activities that constitute the entity's (seller's) ongoing major or central operations.

The Issues:

- **When** to recognize revenue
- **How much** revenue to recognize each period

Accounting for Revenue (ASC 606):

Step 1: Identify the contract with the customer (legal rights of the seller and customer)

Step 2: Identify the performance obligations in the contract: single or multiple

Step 3: Determine the transaction price
- ***ASC:*** The amount the seller expects to be entitled to receive in exchange for transferring goods or services to the customer, not including amounts collected on behalf of third parties)

Step 4: Allocate the transaction price to each performance obligation (bundled price)

Step 5: Recognize revenue when each performance obligation is satisfied

Revenue is recognized at:

- **One point in time**
  - When goods or services transfer to the customer
  - When the customer obtains control
- **Over more than one period of time**
  - The customer consumes the benefit of the sellers' work as it is performed over time (service contracts)
  - The customer controls the asset as it is created (construction)
  - An asset that has no alternative use to the seller and the seller has legal right to receive progress payments (construction)
- **At each point in time a performance obligation is satisfied**
  - Multiple performance obligations in one contract

Issue 1: Does a contract exist?

ASC Definition of a "Contract":
An agreement between two or more parties that creates legally enforceable rights and obligations.

A valid contract has:

- Commercial substance
- Approved – committed to perform the obligations
- Identified rights and obligations – goods and services to be transferred
- Identified payment terms
- Payment is probable (customer has intent and ability to pay)

Contracts can be *implicit* based on the typical business practices of a company
Examples: Retail store that provides goods   Universities that provide classes

If Yes: Recognize Revenue

If No: Do Not Recognize Revenue IF

- Neither the seller nor the buyer has performed an obligation under the contract
- Either the seller or the buyer can terminate at any time without penalty or payments

Contract modifications:

- Adding a distinct good or service is accounted for as a new separate contract
- The total price is reallocated to all obligations in the contract when an added performance obligation does not have a stand-alone price.
- Update the assessment of progress if performance occurs over time

Issue 2: How many performance obligations?

ASC Definition of a "Performance Obligation": A promise in a contract with a customer to transfer to the customer: (a) a good or service (or a bundle of goods/services) that is distinct or (b) a series of distinct goods or services that are substantially the same and that have the same pattern of transfer to the customer.

ASC Definition of a "Customer": A party that has contracted with an entity (seller) to obtain goods and services that are an output of the entity's (seller's) **ordinary activities** in exchange for consideration.

A good or service is a **distinct** (separate) performance obligation if:

1) The customer can benefit from the good or service on its own or combined with other goods or services

Ways a customer may benefit:

- Use it
- Consume it
- Sell it for greater than scrap value
- Hold it to generate future cash flows

Evidence a customer can benefit:

- Customers regularly pay for the good or service

2) The obligation is separately stated/identified in the contract

3) The obligation is NOT highly interrelated with other goods or services in the contract (can be provided separately).

Highly interrelated:

- One promise is required to fulfill another promise.
- One promise modifies another promise
- One promise is dependent on another promise

Practical approach to identifying a distinct performance obligation:

- Could the customer benefit from the goods or services separately?
- Could the customer obtain different promises from different suppliers?
- Does the seller provide the goods or services at/over different time periods?
- What does the seller have to do to be entitled to payment?

Issue 3: Allocating One Price for Multiple Performance Obligations

Allocate the total transaction price to each performance obligation using a percent of the total sales price for the goods or services if sold separately.

Example: ABC, Inc. sells software with a one-year maintenance contract for a total price of $1,000. ABC, Inc. also sells each one separately for the stand-alone price below.

	Stand-alone price	% of Total	Allocated Revenue
Software:	$ 600	40%	$ 400
Services	$ 900	60%	$ 600
Total	$1,500	100%	$ 1,000

Recognize $400 of revenue for the software upon delivery (control passes)

Recognize $600 of revenue for services over the year as time passes

	Debit	Credit	
Cash	**$1,000**		
Sales Revenue		**$400**	when delivered
Deferred Revenue		**$600**	becomes revenue each mo.
Deferred Revenue	**$50**		
Service Revenue		**$50**	monthly revenue

Companies must estimate a stand-alone price when the company does not normally sell the goods and services separately:

Common approaches to **estimate** a stand-alone price (the price a seller would sell a promised good or service separately to a customer):

1) **Adjusted market assessment approach**: estimate based on competitor prices

2) **Expected cost-plus margin approach**: estimate the cost to provide and add a reasonable profit margin

3) **Residual approach:** subtract the total of the other known stand-alone selling prices from the total selling price of all obligations

Issue 4: Option to Receive Additional Goods or Services

Software upgrades, loyalty points for free goods, airline miles

Separate performance obligation if a material right is provided to the customer they would not receive otherwise.

The seller must allocate a portion of the transaction price to the option granted to the customer.

- Estimate a stand-alone selling price for the option and record that portion of the price to deferred revenue
- Recognize revenue when the customer exercises the deferred option, or it expires.

Issue 5: Recognize Revenue When ...

Recognize revenue at <u>one point in time</u> when goods or services are transferred to the customer and <u>control has passed</u>:

Control is likely to have passed to the customer if the customer has:

- An obligation to pay seller
- Legal title to the asset
- Physical possession of the asset
- Assumed the risk and rewards of ownership
- Accepted the goods or received the service

Recognize revenue: <u>Over time</u> if one of the following:

- The customer receives the benefit of the service as the service is performed over time
- The customer controls the asset as the seller creates the goods, or

  The seller creates the asset exclusively for the buyer and has legal right to receive progress payments for progress (long-term manufacturing or construction contracts)

Revenue is estimated based on progress towards completion

Total Revenue
<u>x % Complete to Date</u>
= Total Revenue to report to date

Accounting for Revenue

1st Determine when the performance obligation is met:

Credit "Revenue" in the period the performance obligation is met.

2nd Determine when the payment was (will be) received:

If payment is received in the period the performance obligation is met:

Account	Debit	Credit
Cash	$xxx	
Revenue		$xxx

If payment is received in a period after the performance obligation is met:

In the period the performance obligation is met:

Account	Debit	Credit
Accounts Receivable	$xxx	
Revenue		$xxx

When payment is received:

Account	Debit	Credit
Cash	$xxx	
Receivable		$xxx

If payment was received in a period prior to meeting the performance obligation:

When payment is received:

Account	Debit	Credit
Cash	$xxx	
Unearned Revenue		$xxx

Then – In the period the performance obligation is met:

Account	Debit	Credit
Unearned Revenue	$xxx	
Revenue		$xxx

15. Revenue: Other Issues

Warranties

Quality Assurance (not sold separately) -- NOT a separate performance obligation.

- Estimate the expense based on past history (percentage of sales)
- Report the expense and the liability in the same period as the sale

Period of Sale	**Claim Occurs**
Warranty Expense	Warranty Liability
Warranty Liability	Inventory or Cash

Extended Warranty (sold separately) -- separate performance obligation that covers more than just the quality of the product on the delivery date.

- recognize revenue over the period covered by the extended warranty
- estimate the warranty expense and liability each period

When the customer purchases:

Cash
    Deferred Warranty Revenue

As time passes (each month): Total amount / # months

Deferred Warranty Revenue
    Warranty Revenue

Estimate the cost (each month): Total amount / # months

Warranty Expense	Warranty Liability
Warranty Liability	Inventory or Cash

Contingent Revenue ("Variable Consideration"):

Price depends on the outcome of future events

(Incentives, price concessions, rebates, refunds, discounts)

Estimate the most likely amount the seller will receive using either:

- **Expected Value:** The weighted average expected value using the percentage probability of occurrence of various amounts.
- **Most Likely:** The most probable amount (all or none)

The seller must revise the estimate each period based on the most likely circumstances.

Contingent Revenue Example:

A theatre shows a movie for three months for $60,000 and a bonus of $60,000 is earned if 10,000 people view the movie. The company estimated the probability of the movie being viewed by 10,000 people at 60%. The theatre manager believes 12,000 viewers is reasonable.

The theatre company will record the estimated value of revenue equally over the 3-month period they show the movies, using one of the following methods to estimate total revenue.

Alternative 1: Expected Value (Probable)

$60,000 + $60,000	= $120,000 x 60%	=	$72,000
$60,000 + $0	= $ 60,000 x 40%	=	$24,000
	Total		$96,000 Estimated total amount
			$32,000 revenue recorded each month

Alternative 2: Most likely (probable) amount 60% is more likely than not (most probable)

$60,000 + $60,000 = $120,000 estimated total amount

$40,000 revenue recorded each month

For both methods – the company will adjust the estimated total revenue recorded to the actual revenue earned in the last month.

If the theatre company **did not earn a bonus, the accounting will be:**

Alternative 1: Expected Value			**Alternative 2: Most likely (60%, all)**		
Record for each of the 3 months:					
Accounts Receivable	$32,000		Accounts Receivable	$40,000	
Revenue		$32,000	Revenue		$40,000
(Total revenue of $96,000)			(Total revenue of $120,000)		
Record at the end of 3 months:					
Revenue	$36,000		Revenue	$60,000	
Accounts Receivable		$36,000	Accounts Receivable		$60,000

Total Revenue is now $60,000 in both alternatives

Contingent Revenue Example continued:

If the theatre company **DOES earn a bonus, the accounting will be:**

Alternative 1: Expected Value			**Alternative 2: Most likely (60%, all)**		
Record for each of the 3 months:					
Accounts Receivable	$32,000		Accounts Receivable	$40,000	
Revenue		$32,000	Revenue		$40,000
(Total revenue of $96,000)			(Total revenue of $120,000)		
Record at the end of 3 months:					
Accounts Receivable	$24,000		No adjustment: $120,000 revenue has been previously recorded		
Accounts Receivable		$24,000			

Total Revenue recorded is $120,000 in both alternatives

License Fees to <u>use</u> Intellectual Property (software, music, movies)

Types of licenses that allow the use of intellectual property:

Transfer a right of unlimited use:	Recognize revenue at the point the right is transferred
Provide a right of access:	Recognize revenue over the time of access
Embedded in a good or service:	Recognize revenue for the use when the revenue for the good or service is recognized

Bill and Hold Arrangements

The buyer requests the seller to ship the products at a date after control transfers.
Revenue is recognized on the billing/invoice date and before the seller has delivered the goods to the buyer **only when all** the following has occurred:

- The customer controls the product.
- There is good reason for the seller to hold the goods.
- The product is specifically identified as belonging to the customer and is ready for shipment.

Point of Sale: Principal or Agent

Principal

- Controls the goods or service prior to the customer obtaining control
- Is primarily responsible for delivering the goods or services to the customer
- Assumes the risk of inventory loss and payment (bad debt expense).
- Establishes the price

A principal records revenue at the point of sale (control passes to the customer) as follows:

Accounts Receivable (or cash)	$Price		(increase)
Sales Revenue		$Price	(increase)
Cost of Goods Sold	$Cost		(increase)
Inventory		$Cost	(decrease)

Agent

- Facilitates the sale
- Is not responsible for providing the goods or services to the customer
- Does not set the selling price
- Earns a commission for matching buyers and sellers.

An agent reports revenue for the net commission received from facilitating the sale.

An agent does not report cost of goods sold or cost of services or gross profit.

The agent's entry to record revenue for the amount they are entitled to receive:

Accounts Receivable (or cash)	$	
Fee Revenue		$

AGENT: Income statement:	**PRINCIPAL:** Income statement
Fee Revenue	Sales
- Operating Expenses	- Cost of Goods Sold
	= Gross Profit

16. Sales and Accounts Receivable

A company reports accounts receivable on the balance sheet when the company provides goods or services to a customer who agrees to pay in the future based on previously agreed to terms (*on account*). The most common payment term is *n 30* and customers generally pay within 30 to 45 days.

Most business to business transactions occur on account because it is not practical for business customers to pay when they receive the goods or services. Companies do not charge customers interest on accounts paid according to terms.

Common accounts receivable transactions:

1) **Sales** on credit with payment terms.
2) **Cash received** from customers for a credit sale on account.
3) **Write-off a** specific customer account and amount.
4) **Estimate** uncollectible amounts (bad debt expense).

Accounting systems typically record **sales and cash received** from customers as employees enter data into the system. Accountants review amounts customers owe and determine when the company no longer expects payment.

A **write off** is recorded when the accountant identifies **specific invoices** a customer will not pay.

Accountants estimate and record **bad debt expense** at the end of the month before preparing financial statements.

The four transactions change the balance sheet and the income statement:

Balance Sheet:	**Income Statement:**
Cash (2)	Sales (1)
	- Cost of Sales
Accounts Receivable (1, 2, 3)	=Gross Profit
- Allowance for uncollectible (3, 4)	Operating Expense:
= Accounts Receivable, net	- Bad Debt Expense (4)

Uncollectible Accounts and Write-offs

Companies know from experience that customers will not pay all accounts owed because of:

- disputes over the receipt of goods and services (most common)
- pricing disputes.
- customer cash shortages or bankruptcy.

Large companies have a collections department with employees who "encourage" customers to pay past due accounts receivable. Smaller companies use collection agencies to ask the customer to pay. However, it eventually becomes obvious that some customers will not pay and the company removes the invoices (write-off) from the detail list of customers who owe the company.

Bad Debt Expense

Bad debt expense reports the **current period change** in the amount the company **estimates** customers will not pay (no future economic benefit). As such, the company must decrease accounts receivable and report the decrease as an expense. Bad debt expense is an operating expense related to selling goods and services to customers on credit.

The amount reported on the income statement for **bad debt expense is always an estimate**. Companies do not know which customer will not pay for several months to a year or two from the date of the sale. However, given history, it is probable that customers will not pay a certain amount of accounts receivable. A company must report all expected write-offs in the period of the related sales to properly report earnings for the period.

Example 1: Assume customers owe the company $2,000 that the company estimates (based on past experience) that customers will not pay.

The company could wait to report the expense until they know the exact customer and amount. However, the company would report the sale in a different period than the related expense.

		Year 1	Year 2
	Sales	100,000	0
-	Bad Debt Expense	0	(2,000) (write-off occurs)
=	Operating Income	100,000	(2,000)

Example 1 (continued):

GAAP requires companies to report all expenses incurred to generate revenue in the same period as the revenue.

		Year 1
	Sales	100,000
-	Bad Debt Expense	(2,000)
=	Operating Income	98,000

Therefore, a company **must estimate bad debt expense** using past history and customer specific information to properly report earning for a period of time.

Accountants believe it is better to estimate an amount and revise the estimate as data becomes available than to report sales and the related bad debt expense in different periods.

Allowance for Uncollectible Accounts

Allowance for uncollectible accounts reports the **total** amount the company estimates customers will not pay (using past history). The balance sheet reports the expected probable future economic benefit as the Accounts Receivable, "net" amount.

On the Balance Sheet		Reports
Accounts receivable	→	Total customers owe
- Allowance for uncollectible accounts	→	- Total customers may not pay (estimated)
= Accounts receivable, net	→	= Total company expects to receive

Accounts receivable, net should be a reasonable estimate that will not mislead a user about the amount a company expects to receive in the future.

Example 2: A company with sales of $100,000 normally writes-off (does not receive) approximately 2% of sales. Customers paid $75,000 and owe $25,000 at the end of year 1. The financial statements will report:

Income Statement

Sales	100,000	
Operating Expenses:		
- Bad Debt Expense	(2,000)	Estimated

Balance Sheet:

Accounts Receivable:	$25,000	*Customers owe*
-Uncollectible accounts:	($2,000)	*Unknown customers who may not pay*
Accounts receivable, Net	$23,000	*Amount the company expects to receive*

The company will write-off "accounts receivable" and decrease "uncollectible accounts" when the company identifies the specific customer who will not pay.

The company will also remove the invoice from the accounts receivable aging report (list of customers who owe).

The company does not report an expense at the time of a write-off because the company previously estimated and reported the expense in the period of the sale.

A write-off does not change the value reported for "accounts receivable, net" because both accounts change by the same amount.

Example 3 illustrates how a write-off changes the accounts and amounts reported on the balance sheet. Customers owe the company $100. The company estimated customers will not pay $5 of the $100 owed. During the period, the company identified a specific customer that will not pay $2 and removed the account (write-off) from the detail list of customers that owe the company.

	Before the Write-off	**Write-off Occurs**	After the Write-off
Accounts Receivable	$100	**($2)**	$98
Allowance for Uncollectible Accounts	($ 5)	**$2**	($ 3)
Accounts Receivable, Net	**$ 95**	**$0**	**$95**

The write-off decreases both the accounts receivable and allowance for uncollectible accounts for the same amount and does not change accounts receivable, net.

Example 3 (continued):

The allowance for uncollectible accounts changes as follows:

	Allowance for Uncollectible Accounts	
Beginning Balance	$0	First year of business
Estimate of Uncollectible Amounts	**$5**	Current period estimate
Write-offs	**($2)**	During the current period
Ending Balance	$3	

Accountants must use judgment to estimate total uncollectible accounts and the bad debt expense for the current period. The current period estimate will also include a revision to prior period estimates.

Companies do NOT go back and restate (change) prior period financial statements when the estimated amount is different than actual write-offs.

- Companies that previously underestimated bad debt expense must report additional bad debt expense in the current period to make up the difference.
- Companies that previously overestimated bad debt expense will report lower bad debt expense in the current period.

Beginning Allowance for Uncollectible Accounts

\- Write-offs during the period

= Unadjusted balance at the end of the period

\+ Estimate bad debt expense for current period sales*

+- Adjustment of prior period estimates (when using % of accounts receivable)*

= Ending Allowance for Uncollectible Accounts
(the current estimate of the amount customers may not pay)

Accountants estimate bad debt expense based on current period sales (% of sales method) or current period accounts receivable balances (% of accounts receivable aging method). See next chapter.

Days to Collect

An important aspect of managing cash is collecting accounts receivable as quickly as possible. The longer it takes a customer to pay, the higher the risk of collection. Companies closely monitor the average number of days from the sale until the customer pays.

$$\frac{\text{Current Period Credit Sales}}{\text{Average Accounts Receivable*}} = \text{Accounts Receivable Turnover}$$

$$\frac{\text{365 days}}{\text{Accounts Receivable Turnover}} = \text{Average days to collect}$$

* Average accounts receivable = prior year plus current year divided by two.

Example 4 illustrates how analysts determine the average days to collect. A company had the following sales and accounts receivable for the first three years of operations:

	Sales	Accounts Receivable
Year 1	$400,000	$ 55,000
Year 2	$500,000	$ 60,000
Year 3	$570,000	$ 100,000

Days to collect accounts receivable is computed as follows:

Year 2

$$\frac{\$500{,}000}{((\$55{,}000 + \$60{,}000) / 2)} = 8.7 \text{ x}$$

$$\frac{365}{8.7} = 42 \text{ days}$$

Year 3

$$\frac{\$570{,}000}{((\$60{,}000 + \$100{,}000) / 2)} = 7.1 \text{ x}$$

$$\frac{365}{7.1} = 51 \text{ days}$$

The increase in average days to collect from 42 to 51 indicates customers are paying slower on average or some customers owe significantly past due amounts. Both situations increase the risk of collection. The average days to collect should be compared to the payment terms offered to customers (most common is 30 days). It is common for customers pay 5 to 10 days after the due date.

Bad debt expense and the allowance for uncollectible accounts typically increase as the average days to collect increases.

Minimizing the Risk of Collection

Companies attempt to minimize the risk of non-payment in a variety of ways. Unfortunately, strategies employed to collect receivables have a cost. Managers should do a careful analysis to determine if the benefit is greater than the cost before implementing the following strategies:

- Establish pre-determined credit limits for customers according to the strength of their financial position.
    - Lower (or higher) credit limits generally lead to lower (or higher) sales.
    - Management should determine if profits from additional sales will be higher than the expected bad debt expense related to additional sales.
- Ensure invoices for goods and services provide sufficient detail necessary for approval of payment by the customer in a timely manner.
    - Detail invoices often require customized software.
- Send out second invoices just after the due date as a reminder that payment is past due. Label the invoice as late or past due.
    - Additional invoices require more labor, postage, and supplies.
- Hire a collections manager and implement a more aggressive collections policy. Call or fax customers who have past due invoices and ask for immediate payment.
    - Requires additional employees, space, and computer equipment.
- Use a collection agency to call past due customers
    - Companies pay a percentage of the amount customers pay to the collection agency
- Encourage payment with a credit card.
    - Compare credit card fees to the historical bad debt expense

Credit Card Sales

Most businesses offer credit card payment of goods and services to facilitate quick payment and convenience. The seller has a receivable from the bank who finances the credit card the customer uses to pay. The process is:

- The company sends the details of the credit card transactions to the credit card bank (electronically) and requests payment from the credit card bank.
- The credit card bank pays the company and assumes the risk of non-payment from the customer.
- The bank charges the company a fee.
  The fee varies by bank and sales volume (typically 1 to 4%).
- Credit card banks generally pay the company within three to five days of notification of the amount due.
- The risk of collection transfers from the seller to the credit card bank.

Seller

Account	Debit	Credit
Credit Card Receivable	$100	
Sales		$100
Cash	$98	
Credit Card Expense (fee)	$ 2	
Credit Card Receivable		$100

Bank

Account	Debit	Credit
Credit Card Receivable	$100	
Cash		$98
Credit Card Income		$ 2

Notes Receivable

Companies may convert an accounts receivable that becomes significantly past due to a note receivable if the customer intends to pay. The customer will agree to pay monthly payments and interest on the amount owed until the total amount owed is paid over time.

The company earns interest on the note receivable as time passes and the income statement reports <u>interest income.</u>

Account	Debit	Credit
Notes Receivable	$12,000	
Accounts Receivable		$12,000

Account	Debit	Credit
Cash	$1,000	
Interest Income		$ 80
Notes Receivable		$920

17. Accounting for Accounts Receivable

A company reports sales and accounts receivable when the company provides goods or services to customers who agree to pay on account. All customers will not pay all amounts owed due to pricing and quantity disputes, or an occasional bankruptcy. Companies report uncollectible accounts as bad debt expense because the asset accounts receivable has lost probable future economic value.

Three transactions occur during the period that impact accounts receivable:

1) **Sale on credit** increase accounts receivable.

2) **Customer pays** and accounts receivable decrease.

3) **Write-off** accounts receivable when the company identifies a specific customer will not pay

The last transaction is an adjustment recorded at the end of the period:

4) **Estimate bad debt expense** for the current period.
    - Increase or decrease the allowance account

Account names that report sales and accounts receivable transactions:

Income Statement:

Sales reports the value of goods or services the company provided to customers.

Bad debt expense reports the **current** period estimate of the change in the amount the company does not expect customers to pay.

Balance Sheet:

Accounts receivable reports the total amount customers owe.

Allowance for uncollectible accounts reports the total estimated amount the company expects customers will NOT pay based on past-history.

Accountants record four journal entries for sales and accounts receivable transactions.

1) Sales on credit (during the period)

Accounts receivable ↑
Sales ↑

2) Receive cash from customers

Cash ↑
Accounts receivable ↓

3) Write-off accounts receivable

Allowance for uncollectible accounts ↓
Accounts Receivable ↓

The accountant (or the accounting system) makes entries 1, 2, & 3 during the period when the transaction occurs.

4) Estimate bad debt expense at the end of the period

Bad debt expense
Allowance for Uncollectible Accounts

An increase in amounts customers are NOT expected to pay

or

Allowance for Uncollectible Accounts
Bad Debt Expense

A decrease in amounts customers are NOT expected to pay

A decrease in the amount the company does not expect the customer to pay occurs only when the company overestimated the uncollectible amount in prior periods.

Accounts receivable increases with a debit and decreases with a credit:

1) Increases when a sale is made on account (credit).
2) Decreases when the customer pays the company cash (debit).
3) Decreases when the company writes-off an account and no longer expects the customer to pay (credit).

Accounts Receivable	
Beginning Balance	
Credit Sales	Customer Collections
	Write-offs
Ending Balance	

The **allowance for uncollectible accounts** is a contra-account that increases with a credit and decreases with a debit:

1) Decreases when an account is written-off.
2) Increases or decreases when the accountant estimates bad debt expense. (The change depends on the method used.)

Allowance for Uncollectible Accounts	
	Beginning Balance
Write-offs	
	Unadjusted Balance
	Estimate Bad Debt Expense*
	Ending Balance

* Bad debt expense is a credit to the allowance account when uncollectible accounts increase and a debit to the allowance account when the company has overestimated bad debt expense in the prior periods and must reduce the estimate in the current period.

Sales increase with a credit and decrease with a debit:

1) Increase when a sale is made on account (credit).

Sales

	Begins with 0
	Provide to Customers
	Ending Balance

Bad Debt Expense increases with a debit and decreases with a credit:

1) Increases when the company's total estimated uncollectible amounts increases.
2) Decreases when the company's total estimated uncollectible amounts decreases.

Bad Debt Expense

Begins with 0	
Increase in Uncollectible Amounts	Decrease in Uncollectible Amounts
Ending Balance	

Methods Accountants Use to Estimate Bad Debt Expense

An accountant must estimate bad debt expense at the end of each month and record the adjusting entry before they prepare financial statements.

- The company provides monthly financial statement to internal managers to use to make operating decisions.
- External stakeholders receive quarterly and annual financial statements to use to allocate capital (invest and make loans).

% of Sales Method:

- ***Used monthly to provide financial statements to internal managers***

The accountant uses the **percent of sales** approach each month to report only the bad debt expense related to **current period sales** on the income statement.

  Current period credit **sales**
x **% of sales** the customer historically does not pay
= **Bad debt expense** for the current period (reported on the income statement)

The additional amount the company does not expect customers to pay is reported as bad debt expense and added to the current balance in the allowance for uncollectible accounts (reduces accounts receivable, net).

	Debit	Credit
Bad Debt Expense	$XXX	
Allowance for Uncollectible Accounts		$XXX

The **goal of the percent of sales method** is to quickly estimate and report bad debt expense related only to the current month's sales and provide management with a monthly income statement.

Sales
- Cost of Sales
= Gross Profit
- Operating Expense
  Bad Debt Expense
  Other Expenses
= Operating Income

The accountant who uses only the percent of sales method does not consider if the current balance in the allowance account is a good estimate of the total estimated uncollectible.

The % Sales approach is only appropriate when financial statements are only used internally.

The Balance Sheet must be adjusted before financial statements are provided outside the company.

% of Accounts Receivable Method:

- ***Used quarterly or annually to provide financial statements to external stakeholders***

External stakeholders heavily consider a company's financial position (balance sheet) when making decisions to allocate capital. The company's ability to use assets to repay debt levels impacts an external stakeholder's decision to invest or loan funds.

Investors and creditors evaluate whether the company will have enough cash on hand to pay amounts the company owes. Accounts receivable, net reports the cash the company expects to collect within 30 to 45 days.

Accounts Receivable	→	Total customers owe
- Allowance or Uncollectible Accounts	→	Expect customers will not pay
= Accounts Receivable, Net	→	Company expects customers to pay

Therefore, the accountant must ensure that accounts receivable, net reflects the company's reasonable estimate of the amount customers may not pay.

The **percent of accounts receivable** method considers all amounts owed from customers

Total accounts receivable (cumulative)
x % of accounts receivable customers historically do not pay
= The ending balance of the allowance for uncollectible accounts
(total amount the company does not expect customers to pay)

The accountant will record an adjustment to the estimated prior period total uncollectible amount:

Bad Debt Expense	*To increase the uncollectible*
Allowance for Uncollectible Accounts	*amounts*

or

Allowance for Uncollectible Accounts	*To decrease the uncollectible*
Bad Debt Expense	*amounts*

The change to the allowance account also adjusts prior period bad debt expense estimates the accountant made using the percent of sales method.

After the adjusting entry, the allowance account balance will equal the amount the company currently estimates customers will not pay.

Percent of Accounts Receivable Method (continued)

The **bad debt expense** the company reports on the income statement is the **change in the estimate** after considering current period sales, prior estimates, and current write-offs.

Prior period estimate: customers won't pay	→	Beginning Allowance Balance
Current period write-offs	→	- Know customers will not pay
Uncollectible amounts related to prior periods	→	= Allowance before Adjustment
+ Additional estimated bad debt for current sales and prior estimated adj.	→	+ Current Period Bad Debt Expense
= The current amount the company does not expect customers to pay	→	= Ending Allowance Balance

Allowance for Uncollectible

Debit	Credit
	Beginning Balance
Current Write-offs	
	Allowance before Adjustment
	Bad Debt Expense Adjustment
	Ending Balance

Example 1 illustrates how an accountant estimates and records bad debt expense using the ***% of Sales Method.***

XYX Company began 20Y1 with $3,000 in the allowance for uncollectible accounts. The company estimates customers will not pay 4 percent of the $50,000 current year sales. During 20Y1, the company identified a customer that will not pay $400 and removed the account from the list of customers who owe the company. Customers owe the company $22,000 at the end of 20Y1.

The accountant's entry to write-off the uncollectible account during the 20Y1 is:

Account	Debit	Credit
Allowance for U.A.	$400	
Accounts Receivable		$400

Example 1 (continued):

Sales	$50,000
x Historical % Sales	4%
= Bad Debt Expense	$ 2,000

The accountant's entry to record the estimated bad debt expense for 20Y1 is:

Bad Debt Expense	$2,000	
Allowance for U.A.		$2,000

The balance sheet will report the allowance for uncollectible accounts amount:

Beginning allowance balance:	$3,000	
+ **Bad debt expense**	**$2,000**	increases the allowance
- Write-offs	($ 400)	decreases the allowance
= **Ending allowance balance**	**$4,600**	

The balance sheet and income statement will report:

Balance Sheet		Income Statement	
Accounts Receivable	$ 22,000	Sales	$50,000
- Allowance for Uncollectible Accts	($ 4,600)	Other Expense	($43,000)
= Accounts Receivable, Net	$ 17,400	**Bad Debt Expense**	**($2,000)**
Total Assets	$200,000	Net Income	$ 5,000

The allowance account is not significant to total assets on a percentage basis (2.3%).
Bad debt expense is significant to net income on a percentage basis (40%).

Investors and creditors generally consider a balance sheet item that is greater than 5% of total assets or an income statement item that exceeds 3% of net income to be large enough to make a difference in a decision (significant).

Example 2 illustrates how an accountant estimates bad debt expense using ***the % of accounts receivable method.***

XYZ Company began 20Y1 with $3,400 in the allowance for uncollectible accounts. Sales during 20Y1 totaled $320,000. During 20Y1, the company identified customers who will not pay $2,600. Customers owe the company a total of $100,000 at the end of 20Y1. XYZ estimates that 2.5% of total accounts receivable will not be collected.

The entry to write-off uncollectible accounts for Y1:

Allowance for U.A.	$2,600	
Accounts Receivable		$2,600

At the end of 20Y1, the accountant estimates the total amount of accounts receivable XYZ does not expect customers to pay:

Accounts receivable, at year end	$100,000
x % of accounts receivable historically not collected	2.5%
= The total amount XYZ does not expect to receive (the ending balance in the allowance account)	$ 2,500

Allowance for Uncollectible

	$3,400
$2,600	
	$ 800
	$ 1,700 Bad Debt Expense
	$2,500 Calculated Amount

Bad Debt Expense	$1,700	
Allowance for Uncollectible Accounts		$1,700

The balance sheet and income statement will report:

Balance Sheet

Accounts Receivable	$100,000
- Allowance for uncollectible accts.	($ 2,500)
= Accounts Receivable, Net	$ 97,500
...	
Total Assets	$600,000

Income Statement

Sales	$320,000
Other Expense	($303,300)
Bad Debt Expense	($ 1,700)
...	
Net Income	$ 15,000

The Percent of Accounts Receivable Aging Approach

All companies have an aging report that shows amounts owed for each customer and the number of days each invoice is past due. Amounts customers owe the company for longer periods of time have lower probability of collection. Therefore, accountants use an aging report to consider the age of invoices and each customer's payment history when they estimate bad debt expense.

The format of a **summary aging report**:

	Total	Current	30 days Past Due	60 Days Past Due	90 Days Past Due
Customer 1	$ 51,125	41,125	2,975	7,025	0
Customer 2	$ 8,000	7,000	0	400	600
Customer 3	$ 17,462	15,102	0	0	2,360
Customer 4	$ 37,512	25,400	12,112	0	0
Total	$114,099	88,627	15,087	7,425	2,960

A **detail aging report** lists every invoice due and gives a total for each past due category by individual customer.

The accountant who estimates bad debt expense using the percent of accounts receivable aging method follows the same procedures as the percent of accounts receivable method. However, the accountant **estimates the probability of collection for each category on the aging report** instead of the total accounts receivable.

Example 3 illustrates how an accountant uses the ***% of Accounts Receivable Aging Method*** to estimate bad debt expense.

XYZ Company had an allowance for uncollectible accounts of $90,000 at the beginning of 20Y1. During 20Y1, the company wrote-off $30,000 of identified specific customer accounts. The accounts receivable aging report at the end of 20Y1, along with the accountant's estimate of uncollectible accounts for each category, follows:

Age	Total Accounts Receivable	Estimated % Uncollectible	Estimated Amount Uncollectible
Current	$1,000,000	1%	$10,000
0-30 days	$ 600,000	2%	$12,000
31-60 days	$ 250,000	5%	$12,500
61- 90 days	$ 200,000	8%	$16,000
90 days +	$ 150,000	15%	$22,500
Total	$2,200,000		$73,000
	Ending A/R Balance		**Ending Allowance Balance**

Example 3 (continued)

The balance sheet will report an allowance for uncollectible accounts of $73,000; the total the company does not expect customers to pay.

The income statement will report bad debt expense for the current period and adjustments to prior period estimates.

Beginning balance	$90,000	
- Write-offs	($30,000)	
= Unadjusted balance	$60,000	left from prior period estimates
- Estimated amount uncollectible	**($73,000)**	need more in the allowance account
= Bad debt expense	**($13,000)**	

The accountant records an entry to write-off the uncollectible accounts during the 20Y1:

Allowance for U.A.	$30,000	
Accounts Receivable		$30,000

The accountant records an entry to adjust bad debt expense at the end of 20Y1:

Bad Debt Expense	$13,000	
Allowance for U.A.		$13,000

The income statement will report **bad debt expense** of **$13,000; the difference** in the $60,000 remaining from prior period estimates and the current $73,000 end of year estimate.

The balance sheet will report the following:

Accounts Receivable	$2,200,000
- Allowance for Uncollectible Accounts	($ 73,000)
= Accounts Receivable, Net	$2,127,000

Customer Payments on an Account Previously Written Off

A company may write off an account that the customer unexpectantly pays at a later date (rare occurrence.) In this situation, the accountant must reverse the journal entry previously recorded for the write-off and record the payment in the period the company receives cash.

The accountant previously wrote-off $500 and removed the invoices from the list of customers (and invoices) who owe the company:

Account	Debit	Credit
Allowance for Uncollectible Accounts	$500	
Accounts Receivable		$500

The accountant must now reverse the prior entry to write-off the account:

Account	Debit	Credit
Accounts Receivable	$500	
Allowance for Uncollectible Accounts		$500

And records the receipt of cash for payment on the account:

Account	Debit	Credit
Cash	$500	
Accounts Receivable		$500

Accounts receivable, net will increase because the allowance for uncollectible accounts decreases.

Summary of Different Approaches to Estimate Bad Debt Expense

Percent of Sales Approach

- Use to prepare **internal monthly financial statements**; quick and easy
- Reports the expected bad debt expense for **current period sales only**.
- Does not evaluate accounts receivable, net for reasonableness; however, only internal management use monthly financial statements.
    - Companies will must use the percent of accounts receivable approach before providing financial statements to investors and creditors.

Percent of Accounts Receivable Aging Approach

- Use before providing financial statements to investors and creditors (quarterly or annually)
- Accounts receivable, net is reported at estimated probable future economic benefit
- Bad debt expense is the difference in the prior period estimate and the current period estimate of uncollectible amounts.
- Gives the best estimate of uncollectible amounts because the accountant considers how long accounts have been outstanding.

18. Factoring Accounts Receivable

Accounts receivable, like any other asset, can be sold or used as collateral for a loan. Accounting for the sale of accounts receivable is similar to accounting for the sale of other assets and a gain or loss is reported on the income statement. Selling accounts receivable is referred to as **factoring.**

A company that factors accounts receivables sells to or takes a loan against the receivable with a financial institution or a company formed for the specific purpose of factoring accounts receivables.

- The buyer of the accounts receivables collects the receivables and charges a fee.
- The seller receives less than 100% of the face amount of the receivable
- The seller gives up the right to the collection of the accounts receivable
- A portion of the cash paid for accounts receivable may be withheld from the seller to cover bad debt expense.

Companies that factor receivables must account for the transaction as

1) a sale

or

2) a secured borrowing – use the accounts receivable as collateral.

Factoring accounts receivable is **accounted for as a sale** when **control** of the asset is **surrendered** and **each** of the following occurs:

1. The asset is isolated beyond the reach of the company that transferred the receivable to the buyer.

2. Buyer has the right to pledge or factor the assets it receives.

3. Seller does not maintain effective control over the transferred assets; the assets are not going to return to the seller.

When all 3 of the above does not occur, the accounts receivable continues to be reported on the balance sheet of the seller and the transaction is **accounted for as a secured borrowing** (a loan with the accounts receivable as collateral).

Accounts receivable sales are commonly done under the following arrangements:

- Factor with Recourse
- Factor without Recourse

Secured Borrowing (Accounts receivable is collateral for a loan)
The accounts receivable remains on the balance sheet

Record in separate transactions:

- Borrow and repay the note
- Record accounts receivable transactions

Step 1: Record the net cash received and the fee

Cash	$Net cash received	
Finance Expense	$Fee	
Notes Payable		$Loan amount

Step 2: Repay the note

Notes Payable	$Loan amount	
Interest Expense	$computed	
Cash		$Principle + Interest

Step 3: Record collection of accounts receivable – typical journal entry
Step 4: Record write-offs and bad debt expense – typical journal entries

Sell Accounts Receivable <u>with recourse</u>:

- The seller retains all the risk of bad debt expense and guarantees the buyer (factor) will be paid if the customer does not pay the buyer.
- An estimate of uncollectible amounts is recorded as a liability on the seller's balance sheet (called a recourse liability.)

Record the sale of the accounts receivable with recourse:
The accounts receivable moves from the seller's to the buyer's balance sheet.

Seller:

Cash	$net cash received	
Receivable from factor	$buyer keeps to cover sales adjustments	
Loss on sale of receivables	$fee + estimated bad debt expense	
Recourse liability		$estimated bad debt expense (liab)
Accounts receivable		$total gross accounts sold

Buyer:

Accounts receivable	$total gross accounts purchased	
Payable to seller		$potential sales adjustments
Financing revenue		$interest
Cash		$net cash paid

Sell Accounts Receivable <u>without recourse</u>:

The accounts receivable moves from the seller's to the buyer's balance sheet.

- The company that buys the accounts receivable is responsible for bad debt expense
- The fee is higher to cover the potential bad debt expense

Record the sale of the accounts receivable with without recourse:

Seller:

Account	Debit	Credit
Cash	$net cash received	
Receivable from factor	$buyer keeps to cover sales adjustments	
Loss on sale of receivables	$fee	
Accounts receivable		$total gross accounts sold

Buyer:

Account	Debit	Credit
Accounts receivable	$total gross accounts purchased	
Payable to seller		$potential sales adjustments
Financing revenue		$fee
Cash		$net cash paid

Account	Debit	Credit
Bad debt expense		
Allowance for Doubtful Accounts		

Summary: Borrow Against or Sell (Factor) Accounts Receivable

1) Borrow Against: Use the A/R as collateral

Leave the Accounts Receivable on the balance sheet

- Account for the collections and write-offs as normal

Get cash and report a Notes Payable

- Repay with Interest Expense
- The lender can take the accounts receivable and collect it if the loan is not repaid

2) Sell Accounts Receivable with Recourse (seller must pay for amounts not collected)

Seller:

Remove the A/R from the balance sheet
Get less cash than the A/R and record a loss on sale of A/R
Report a liability for potential bad debt expense

Buyer:

Reports the A/R on their balance sheet
Pay less cash than the gross A/R
Report Fee Income for the difference

3) Sell Accounts Receivable with NO Recourse (Seller does not for uncollectible amounts)

Seller:

Remove the A/R from the balance sheet
Get less cash than the A/R and record a loss on sale of A/R for the fee and sales adjustments

Buyer:

Reports the A/R on their balance sheet
Pay less cash than the gross A/R
Report Fee Income for the difference

19. Accounts Receivable: Sales Discounts and Sales Returns

Accounts receivable is recorded when goods or services are provided to a customer and cash is expected to be received in the future. Most business-to-business transactions occur *on account*. The term *on account* means the customer will pay the company in the future based upon previously agreed to terms. The most common payment term is n 30 and customers generally pay within 30 to 45 days. A company does not charge interest on accounts receivable (some charge interest after it becomes past due).

Companies may offer a **trade discount** to customers. A trade discount occurs when goods are sold to a customer at a price lower than the list price. Trade discounts are also referred to as volume discounts. A trade discount is not recognized separately when accounting for sales or receivables. The sale is recorded at the price net of the trade discount.

Sales discounts are early payment discounts offered to customers. Sales discounts should only be offered to customers when a company is in immediate need of cash and is not able to borrow money at a lower interest rate. The cost of a two percent offered to a customer who purchases once or twice a month can cost as much as twenty percent annually.

Examples of customer payment terms:

1) **2/10, n 30** means a 2% discount is given if paid in 10 days, or the full amount is due in 30 days

2) **1/15, n 60** means a 1% discount is given if paid in 15 days, or the full amount is due in 60 days

3) **n 30** means no discount is offered and the full amount is due in 30 days

Gross and Net Methods:

The **gross method** is used when a company does not normally offer a discount or when customers generally do not take discounts offered. Sales discounts are reported on the income statement as a reduction to sales when the **gross method** is used.

Sales
- Sales Discount
= Net Sales

- The account called sales discounts is a contra revenue account.

- Accounts receivable is always recorded (debit and credit) at the gross amount.

Example 1: Gross Method: A sale for $100 with terms of 2/10, net 30:

Sale	Payment after 10 days: Discount is NOT taken	Payment on or before day 10: Discount is taken
Acct. Rec. $100	Cash $100	Cash $98
Sales $100	Acct. Rec. $100	Sales Discount $ 2
		Acct. Rec. $100

The **net method** is used when customers generally take the discount offered. The sale is recorded at the net price and no sales discount is recorded if the customer takes the discount.

If the customer does not take the discount, the additional amount received from the customer is recorded as interest revenue.

- The net price is considered to be the value of the goods provided.
- Additional cash received above the net price is considered additional sales revenue.
- Accounts receivable is always recorded (debit and credit) at the gross amount.

Report on the Income Statement:

	Net Sales
+	Sales Discounts Forfeited
=	Total Sales

Example 2: Net Method: A sale for $100 with terms of 2/10, net 30:

Sale	Payment on or before 10 days: Discount is taken	Payment after day 10: Discount is NOT taken
Acct. Rec. $98	Cash $98	Cash $100
Sales $98	Acct. Rec. $98	Sales Disc Forfeited $ 2
		Acct. Rec. $98

Sales Returns:

Sales must be adjusted for returns when

- the customer has the right of return, **and**
- the amount of returns can be reliably estimated.

The amount of estimated sales returns is generally determined using a historical percentage of sales.

	Normal Historical % of Returns
x	Current Period Sales
=	Total Estimated Current Period Returns

- The amount of returns must be estimated and reported in the same period as the related sales.

Account	Debit	Credit
Sales Returns	$XXX	
Allowance for Sales Returns		$XXX

- The value of inventory expected to be returned to inventory and resold must also be estimated and recorded in the same period as the related sales.

Account	Debit	Credit
Inventory – Estimated Returns	$XXX	
Cost of Goods Sold		$XXX

One of two accounts is credited depending on if the customer has paid for the goods:

- Allowance for returns: use when the customer pays on account
- Refund liability: use when the customer pays cash or uses a credit card

Example 3: Sales Returns

During 20Y1, Jewel Manufacturing sold inventory on account for $200,000. The inventory had a cost of $120,000 (60% of the selling price.) Jewel's past experience indicates that approximately 5% of sales will be returned. Customers actually returned $8,000 of goods in early 20Y2. Returned goods are typically restocked and sold to other customers.

Estimated returns at the end of 20Y1:

	Debit	Credit	
Sales Returns	$10,000		(5% x 200,000 sales)
Allowance for Returns (or refund liability)		$10,000	

	Debit	Credit	
Inventory – Est. returns ↑	$6,000		
Cost of Sales ↓		$6,000	(60% of estimated returns)

The change to net amounts on the financial statements occurs when the company estimates returns.

Actual returns in 20Y2:

	Debit	Credit	
Allowance for Returns	$8,000		
Accounts Receivable		$8,000	(no change to A/R, net)

or

	Debit	Credit
Refund Liability	$8,000	
Cash		$8,000

and

	Debit	Credit	
Inventory	$4,800		
Inventory – Est. Returns		$4,800	(60% of returns)

Note: The inventory entry is made only when returned items are placed in inventory to be resold to other customers.

Presentation of Sales on the Income Statement

Gross Sales to Customers
- Sales Discounts taken (gross method)
- Estimated Sales Returns

= Sales, Net

The income statement will say **"Sales, Net"** when gross sales is reduced by a material estimated amount.

Presentation of Accounts Receivable on the Balance Sheet

Gross Receivables from Customers
- Estimated Allowance for Uncollectible Accounts
- Estimated Allowance for Sales Returns

= Accounts Receivable, net

The balance sheet reports accounts receivable, net when gross accounts receivable is reduced by a material estimated amount.

20. Inventory Overview

Inventory consists of items held only to sell to customers. A company either purchases ready-to-sell inventory from a supplier or manufactures inventory themselves.

Accounting and reporting issues primarily relate to:

- Inventory in transit.
- The value of inventory reported on the balance sheet.
- The value of cost of goods sold reported on the income statement.

Inventory shipped to customers can take as long as a week or more to reach a customer. Inventory the seller has shipped and the customer has not yet received is **in transit.**

The shipping terms negotiated between the buyer and the seller determine the legal owner of inventory in transit. The legal owner of the goods in transit is responsible for any loss that occurs while in transit. The party that owns the goods in transit is generally compensated for assuming the risk and uses the cost savings (buyer) or higher price (seller) to insure the goods in transit. Freight on board (FOB) destination or FOB shipping describe the shipping terms.

FOB Destination means:

- the buyer owns the inventory when it gets to the destination (upon receipt).
- the seller owns and is responsible for the goods in transit.

FOB Shipping means:

- The buyer owns the inventory when the seller ships the goods.
- The buyer owns and is responsible for the goods in transit.

Warehouse employees count the quantity of each inventory item to value inventory. The count does not include items in transit that the company owns. Accountants must review the invoices of purchases and shipments a few days before and after the end of each period to determine if an adjustment to inventory is necessary for owned in-transit inventory the company owns.

The legal owner reports goods in transit as inventory on their balance sheet.

Goods on Consignment:

A company that stores another company's goods in their warehouse holds goods on consignment. The company that holds goods on consignment does not legally own the goods and does not report goods on consignment on its balance sheet. Goods on consignment is common when one company takes orders and ships goods to customers for another company.

Amazon.com warehouses and ships goods on consignment for other companies. A local resale clothing shop sells goods on consignment for others.

The legal owner with title to the goods will report the inventory on its balance sheet.

The Value of Inventory

The accountant must determine the total cost of all owned inventory items at the end of the period.

1) Warehouse workers count the quantity of each inventory.

2) The accountant determines the cost of each item paid to suppliers.

3) Quantity x cost for one quantity = the cost of each item.

4) The total cost of inventory is the total cost of all items.

For example, a company sells four different items. Warehouse workers counted and verified the quantity of each item on hand at the end of the period. The cost for one item of inventory includes all necessary costs to purchase (cost plus freight-in) or manufacture (material, labor, overhead) the inventory.

	Quantity	x	Cost for One	=	Total Cost	
Item A	100		$25		$2,500	
Item B	50		$10		$ 500	
Item C	200		$15		$3,000	
Item D	500		$ 5		$2,500	
Total Cost					$8,500	reported on the balance sheet

Companies report warehouse costs to purchase and store inventory as operating expenses.

Shrinkage

Generally accepted accounting principles require companies to count inventory at least once each year. Some companies count at the end of each month or each quarter. Other companies count certain items and adjust some inventory items each day according to a schedule that results in a count of all items at least once during the year (cycle counting.)

The quantity counted is then compared to the accountant's inventory report and the missing inventory is considered **"shrink."**

Companies report shrink on the income statement as part of cost of goods sold.

Employee theft, damage to inventory, or warehouse employees place a wrong item into a box for shipment (human error) causes shrink.

The actual quantity of inventory in the warehouse may also be higher than the accounting records indicate due to employee errors when recording the quantity of inventory items received or shipped.

- Inventory is adjusted higher in this situation.

Cost of Goods Sold

Companies begin the period with inventory and purchased goods to provide to customers.

The total value of goods available to sell to customers less the value of goods held at the end of the period is the cost of goods sold during the period.

The formula to determine cost of goods sold is:

If purchase goods ready for sale:

Beginning Inventory
\+ Purchases
\+ Freight-in
\- Purchase Returns
= Goods Available for Sale
\- Ending Inventory *
= Cost of Goods Sold

If manufacture goods to sell:

Beginning Inventory
\+ Direct Materials
\+ Direct Labor
\+ Manufacturing Overhead
= Total Cost of Goods for Sale
\- Ending Inventory*
= Cost of Goods Sold

* Ending inventory is valued at the quantity on hand x the cost for each unit determined using the FIFO, LIFO, or average cost method.

The total cost of all items available to sell during the period is reported on either the income statement or the balance sheet.

Total Cost of Items
Available to Sell

OR

Cost of Goods Sold	**Inventory**
The cost of items sold during the period	The cost of items remaining in the warehouse at the end of the period

21. Inventory Valuation: Methods

Generally accepted accounting principles (GAAP) allow a company to choose a method to use to value inventory. The most common methods include:

1) specific identification

2) first in first out (FIFO)

3) last in last out (LIFO)

4) average

Separately Identifiable Items

A company uses the **specific identification method** when each item looks different and the company can easily identify each individual item. The sum of the cost of each item on hand at the end of the period is the total value of inventory reported on the balance sheet. Likewise, the company reports the cost of each individual item sold when the sale occurs.

Companies that use the specific identification method include auto dealerships, jewelry stores, home builders, and sellers of other high dollar items.

Similar Items Purchased at Different Costs

Most companies purchase the same item at different costs. The cost will vary because suppliers change the price or the company purchases the same item from a different supplier.

For example, suppose a company purchased 120 phone cases for $24.50 each and a week later purchased 180 of the same phone case for $25.25 each. The company sold 200 phone cases and 100 remain in the warehouse. All phone cases remaining in the warehouse look the same and the company cannot determine if the cost of each phone case available to sell cost $24.50 or $25.25.

GAAP allows a company to a choose a method to use to estimate the value of ending inventory when the company cannot determine the cost of similar items purchased at different costs.

One method is not more accurate than another method.

- All methods estimate the cost of inventory because the actual cost of items sold is unknown.

Accountants use either "first in first out" (FIFO), "last in first out" (LIFO), or "average" to value inventory and cost of goods sold.

First In First Out (FIFO)

The FIFO method assumes the first items purchased are sold first. Items purchased last are assumed to remain in inventory.

Last In First Out (LIFO)

The LIFO method assumes the last items purchased are sold first. Items purchased first are assumed to remain in inventory.

Average

The average method values inventory at the average purchase cost.

$$\frac{\text{Total Available Cost}}{\text{Total Available Quantity}} = \text{Average cost}$$

then:

Average cost per item
x Quantity on hand
= Inventory $ reported on the balance sheet

Each of the three methods used to value inventory (LIFO, FIFO, Average) give a different <u>estimated</u> cost of goods sold (expense) and <u>estimated</u> value of inventory (asset.)

Inventory at the beginning of the period

\+ Purchases, net during the period

= Total cost of all items available to sell

- Estimated cost of items in the warehouse, end of the period (balance sheet)

= Estimated cost of goods sold during the period (income statement)

Periodic Method

Example 1 illustrates the difference in the three acceptable inventory methods. In this example, the company does not determine the cost of inventory sold until the end of the period (periodic_method).

The Company had the following transactions during the first quarter:

		Units	Cost-per-unit
January 1	Beginning Balance	900	$11
January 15	Purchased	500	$10
February 2	Sold	600	
February 5	Purchased	400	$12
February 18	Sold	700	
March 15	Purchased	600	$11

First, list all individual purchases in chronological order.
Second, total the cost of all items available for sale during the period.

	Quantity	x	Cost for 1	=	Total Cost
1/1	900	x	$11	=	$ 9,900
1/15	500	x	$10	=	$ 5,000
2/5	400	x	$12	=	$ 4,800
3/15	600	x	$11	=	$ 6,600
	2,400		Total Available		$ 26,300
	(1,300)		Total Sold		$????
	1,100		End of Period Inventory		$????

The company knows the quantity of items sold.

The company does not know the cost of each item sold and must use a method to estimate the cost.

FIFO (first in first out) assumes items **purchased first** are **sold first.** Start at the top with the first items purchased and move down until the total quantity sold is 1,300.

	Sold					
1/1	900	x	$11	=	$ 9,900	
1/15	400	x	$10	=	$ 4,000	
	1,300				$13,900	Cost of Goods Sold

Total Available	$26,300	
- Cost of Goods Sold	$13,900	reported on the income statement
= Inventory	$12,400	reported on the balance sheet

FIFO assumes the company sold the first items purchased first and the last items purchased remain in inventory.

Example 1 (continued):

LIFO (last in first out) assumes items **purchased last** are **sold first**. Start with the last items purchased and move up until the total quantity sold is 1,300.

	Sold				
3/15	600	x	$11	=	$ 6,600
2/5	400	x	$12	=	$ 4,800
1/15	300	x	$10	=	$ 3,000
	1,300				$14,400 Cost of Goods Sold

Total Available	$26,300	
- Cost of Goods Sold	$14,400	reported on the income statement
= Inventory	$11,900	reported on the balance sheet

LIFO assumes the company sold the last items purchased first and the first items purchased remain in inventory.

Average Cost: Inventory is valued at the average purchase cost.

$$\frac{\text{Total Available Cost}}{\text{Total Available Quantity}} = \frac{\$26{,}300}{2{,}400} = \$10.96 \text{ average cost per item}$$

$10.96 average cost per item x 1,300 units sold = $14,248 cost of goods sold

Total Available	$26,300	
- Cost of Goods Sold	$14,248	reported on the income statement
= Inventory	$12,052	reported on the balance sheet

Summary of the three methods (periodic method):

	LIFO	Average	FIFO
Total Goods Available for Sale	$26,300	$26,300	$26,300
Cost of Goods Sold (Income Statement)	$14,400	$14,248	$13,900
Inventory (Balance Sheet)	$11,900	$12,052	$12,400

Each method results in a different reported value of inventory and cost of goods sold on the financial statements. The reported amount is an estimate that varies based on the method used.

The actual cost of goods sold and items on hand at the end of the period is unknown.

- Items that look the same have different costs.
- It is impossible to know the actual cost of the one taken from the warehouse shelf and sold when they all look the same.

Selecting a Method to Value Inventory

A company must continue to value inventory using the method they select unless business changes justify a change to a different method. The most common reason to change the inventory method is the desire to use the same method to value all inventory after an acquisition.

A company may use a different method for direct materials and finished goods.

The *Internal Revenue Service's LIFO Conformity Rule* requires a company that uses LIFO for income taxes to also use LIFO for financial reporting.

The inventory method used determines:

- The amount of income reported for the period.
- The amount of income tax paid for the period.
- How close the value reported for inventory is to replacement cost
  (FIFO reports inventory closest to the cost of replacing the inventory)
- How close the value of cost of goods sold is to replacement cost.
  (LIFO reports cost of goods sold closest to the cost of replacing the goods.

Company's do not select a method to mirror the physical movement of inventory.

A method is used because the actual sequence of physical movement is unknown.

The most common reason a company initially selects a particular method is **the impact on income before taxes and income taxes paid.**

In times of inventory cost <u>inflation:</u>

FIFO:

- The items sold were purchased at a **lower cost** and cost of goods sold is lower.
- A lower cost of goods sold leads to **higher income** before taxes and higher taxes paid for the period.

LIFO is the opposite: higher cost of goods sold and lower income

In times of inventory cost <u>deflation:</u>

FIFO:

- The items sold were purchased at a **higher cost** and cost of goods sold is higher.
- A higher cost of goods sold leads to **lower income** before taxes and lower taxes paid for the period.

LIFO is the opposite: lower cost of goods sold and higher income

Most products, with the exception of technology, generally experience inflation over time.

Financial statements will report the following using LIFO and FIFO when **<u>consistent inflation</u>** occurs:

Reports:	**<u>LIFO</u>**	**<u>FIFO</u>**
Inventory at:	Old Cost	Replacement Cost
Cost of Goods Sold at:	Replacement Cost	Old Cost

- Note: the opposite occurs (switch the LIFO and FIFO results) in deflation

A company that reports cost of goods sold at the most recent replacement cost gives a closer reflection of economic earnings because sales are also reported at a current price.

The methods do not allow for companies to report both inventory and cost of goods sold at the most recent replacement cost.

Public companies and companies that obtain financing generally choose the method they expect will report a lower cost of goods sold and higher net income. Private companies that are more concerned about cash flows than reported net income generally choose the method they expect to give the highest cost of goods sold, the lowest income and the lowest taxes paid. Approximately half of the companies in the US use the FIFO method.

LIFO Reserve

It is difficult to compare the operating income of companies that use FIFO to companies that use LIFO because inventory and cost of goods sold is not valued the same. Therefore, FASB requires companies that use LIFO to report a ***LIFO Reserve*** for the difference in the value of inventory using LIFO and what inventory would be using FIFO.

The LIFO Reserve is the difference in inventory using FIFO and inventory using LIFO.

Example 2 illustrates the information a company that uses LIFO to value inventory provides in the footnotes to enable investors to compare companies that use different methods:

	Current Year	Prior Year
Total Inventories using FIFO	$80,000	$72,000
LIFO Reserve	(2,000)	(1,500)
Total Inventories Reported using LIFO	$78,000	$70,500

22. Inventory Accounting: Perpetual and Periodic Methods

Inventory is purchased from suppliers, returned to suppliers and sold to customers. Accountants will use one of the following methods to record inventory movement.

- **Perpetual method:** record an entry to the inventory account each time inventory moves
- **Periodic method:** record the total change in inventory at the end of each period

Perpetual Method

Companies that sell large quantities of many different items normally have sophisticated computer systems in place to track inventory movement and record the change to inventory each time inventory is purchased, returned or sold. Tracking of inventory is often accomplished by using bar codes and scanners.

Accounting for inventory using the **perpetual method**:

1) The inventory account is used to record the cost of inventory purchases, including freight-in.

2) The inventory account is used to record inventory returns at cost.

3) The inventory account decreases and cost of goods sold increases at the time each sale occurs. The computer system computes the cost of each item sold.

A perpetual inventory system can generate a report of the quantity and cost of inventory on hand at any given time during the period. The account balance may not equal the amount that is actually on hand at the end of the period due to human error, theft or damage to goods. Inventory is counted at the end of the period to determine the cost of all inventory items actually on hand.

The accountant must make a final adjustment to adjust the inventory account balance to the actual value of the quantities in the warehouse at the end of the period.

Inventory		
Beginning Purchases Freight-In	Sold	
Unadjusted Balance		
Adjustment	Adjustment	to agree to count balance can be either
Count Value		a debit or credit to inventory

Periodic Method

Smaller companies or companies with many small locations with low quantities of inventory do not have elaborate computer systems that track every movement of inventory. Therefore, nothing is recorded to change the inventory account during the period.

Inventory is counted and valued at the end of the period. The inventory account is adjusted to be equal to the actual value of inventory on hand at the end of the period. Inventory no longer in the warehouse is assumed to be sold and is reported as cost of goods sold.

Companies that use the **periodic method** record **changes to the inventory account ONLY at the end** of each period.

Inventory purchases, freight-in, and purchase returns are recorded as they occur to properly record amounts owed for inventory.

- The purchases account (an expense) is used to record purchases of inventory.
- The purchase returns account (contra expense) is used for inventory returns.
- The freight-in account (an expense) is used for the cost of acquiring inventory.

The total_change to inventory and the total cost of goods sold is recorded only at the end of the period.

The sale is recorded as it occurs; however, the cost of inventory for each sale is **not** recorded because it is not known at the time of the sale.

End of Period Adjustments:

1) The total balance in the purchases, freight-in, and purchase returns accounts are transferred to the cost of goods sold account.

    CGS
    Purchase Returns
        Freight-In
        Purchases

2) The difference in the beginning and ending inventory value is transferred to the cost of goods sold account.

    CGS
    Inventory — Debit inventory if inventory increases. Credit inventory if inventory decreases.

Journal Entries to Record Inventory Transactions

Periodic		Perpetual
The inventory account is not used until the end of the period.		The inventory account is used each time inventory moves.

Purchases
    Accounts Payable
	Purchases	Inventory
		    Accounts Payable

Freight-in
    Accounts Payable
	Freight-In	Inventory
		    Accounts Payable

Accounts Payable
    Purchase Returns
	Returns	Accounts Payable
		    Inventory

Accounts Receivable
    Sales
	Sales	Accounts Receivable (price to
		    Sales customer)

No entry to record Cost of Goods Sold		Cost of Goods Sold (cost to the Inventory company)
	Adjusting Entry	

Cost of Goods Sold*
Purchase Returns
    Freight-In
    Purchases
		Cost of Goods sold
		Inventory ***

Inventory (change) ** Cost of Goods Sold		

* Cost of goods sold is for the net amount of the other three accounts in the journal entry.

** The inventory account is a debit if inventory increased and a credit if inventory decreased. Cost of goods sold is the other account used.

*** The inventory account is a debit when the value of inventory counted is actually higher and a credit if inventory counted is actually lower than the accounting records indicate. Cost of goods sold is the other account used.

Example 1 provides a comparison of the periodic method and the perpetual method.
Both methods result in the same value of inventory and cost of goods sold reported on the financial statements.

A company purchased inventory at a cost of $64,000 plus freight-in of $1,000 on June 3. The company returned goods with a cost of $6,000 on June 12. Goods with a cost of $21,000 were sold to customers for $42,000 on June 14. Inventory counted in the warehouse at the end of June totaled $48,000. Purchases and sales were all on account. Beginning inventory was $12,000.

Gross Method:

Periodic Method		**Perpetual Method**
Purchases $64,000 Accounts Payable $64,000	**Purchases** June 3	Inventory $64,000 Accounts Payable $64,000
Freight-In $1,000 Accounts Payable $1,000		Inventory $1,000 Accounts Payable $1,000
Accounts Payable $6,000 Purchase Returns $6,000	**Returns** June 12	Accounts Payable $6,000 Inventory $6,000
Accounts Receivable $42,000 Sales $42,000	**Sales** June 14	Accounts Receivable $42,000 Sales $42,000
		Cost of Goods Sold $21,000 Inventory $21,000
	Adjusting Entries June 30	
Cost of Goods Sold $59,000 Purchase Returns $ 6,000 Purchases $64,000 Freight-in $ 1,000 (To transfer purchases, purchase returns and freight-in to cost of goods sold.)		Cost of Goods Sold $2,000** Inventory $2,000 (Adjust for shrink) ** See the inventory T account on the next page.
Inventory $36,000* Cost of Goods Sold $36,000 *Adjust inventory to the actual amount. (Beginning of $12,000 to ending of $48,000)		

Example 1 continued

The T accounts for inventory and cost of goods sold will reflect the following:

Periodic Method

Inventory	
12,000	
12,000	
36,000	Adjustment
48,000	

Cost of Goods Sold	
59,000	36,000 adjustment
23,000	

Perpetual Method

Inventory	
12,000 64,000 1,000	6,000 21,000
50,000	
	2,000 Adjustment
48,000	

Cost of Goods Sold	
21,000 2,000	adjustment
23,000	

Important to Note: Total inventory and total cost of goods sold is the same for both methods.

23. Inventory Value: Perpetual Method

Companies that use the perpetual method determine the cost of each unit sold at the time of each sale.

Under **LIFO perpetual**, the cost of each item sold is the last cost just before the sale (not the last cost at the end of the period.) The last cost will change with each new purchase.

Under the **perpetual moving average cost method**, a moving average is used to determine the cost of inventory **just before the sale**. The average cost changes with each new purchase.

Under **FIFO perpetual**, the cost of each item sold is the first cost purchased just before the sale. The first item purchased is always the same regardless of when the sale occurs. Periodic FIFO and perpetual FIFO result in the same value for inventory and cost of goods sold.

Example 1 illustrates the three different methods of accounting for inventory using the **perpetual method.** The Company had the following transactions during the first quarter:

		Units	Cost-per-unit
January 1	Beginning Balance	900	\$11
January 15	Purchased	500	\$10
February 2	Sold	(600)	
February 5	Purchased	400	\$12
February 18	Sold	(700)	
March 15	Purchased	600	\$11

Perpetual FIFO

1st Set up purchases and sales in date order. Only units on hand before the sale are included in units sold, starting with the first one purchased.

		Purchases		Sales		
		Units	Cost per-unit	Sold	Cost per unit	CGS
January 1	Beginning Balance	900	\$11			
January 15	Purchased	500	\$10			
February 2	Sold	(600)		600	\$11	\$6,600 from 1/1
February 5	Purchased	400	\$12			
February 18	Sold	(700)		300	\$11	\$3,300 from 1/1
				400	\$10	\$4,000 from 1/15
March 15	Purchased	600	\$11			
				Total CGS:		\$13,900

Ending Inventory consists of:

1/15	100 at \$10	= \$ 1,000 (500 purchased less 400 sold on 2/18)
2/5	400 at \$12	= \$ 4,800
3/15	600 at \$11	= \$ 6,600
Total 1,000		\$12,400

Perpetual LIFO

1st Set up purchases and sales in date order. Only units on hand before the sale are included in units sold. Start with the last one purchased just before the sale.

		Purchases		Sales			
		Units	Cost per-unit	Sold	Cost per unit	CGS	
January 1	Beginning Balance	900	$11				
January 15	Purchased	500	$10				
February 2	Sold	(600)		500	$10	$5,000	from 1/15
				100	$11	$1,100	from 1/1
February 5	Purchased	400	$12				
February 18	Sold	(700)		400	$12	$4,800	from 2/5
				300	$11	$3,300	from 1/1
March 15	Purchased	600	$11				
			Total CGS:			$14,200	

February 2nd sales: The last ones purchased before the sale are the 500 units from 1/15. Those units are sold first and then 100 from 1/1 are sold. The total sold equals 600 units. 800 units remain to be sold later from the beginning in inventory on 1/1.

February 18th sales: The last ones purchased before the sale are the 400 units from 2/5. Those units are sold first and then 300 units from beginning 1/1 inventory are sold. The January 15th purchase was sold on 2/2 and is not available to sell.

This leaves 500 units from the beginning in inventory on 1/1 (900 – 100 1st sale – 300 2nd sale) and the 600 purchased on March 15th on hand at the end of the period.

Ending Inventory:			
Beginning Inventory 1/1	500 x $11 =	$ 5,500
Last Purchase 3/15	600 x $11 =	$ 6,600
Total Ending Inventory	1,100	$12,100

All units purchased on 1/15 and 2/5 were sold.

Perpetual LIFO: The total available less cost of goods sold must equal ending inventory.

Total Available	$26,300	BI + all purchases
- Cost of Goods Sold	($14,200)	computed in the schedule
Ending Inventory	$12,100	

Perpetual Moving Average

List purchases and sales in date order. **A new moving average is computed after each purchase.** The cost of each sale is recorded at the last moving average cost per unit.
Sales do not change the moving average cost per unit.

		Purchases				Sales		
		Units	x Cost per-unit	= Total	Moving Average	Sold	x Cost per unit	= CGS
January 1	Beginning	900	$11	$9,900				
January 15	Purchased	500	$10	$5,000				
	Moving Average	1,400		$14,900	$10.64			
February 2	Sold	(600)		$(6,384)		600	$10.64	$6,384
	Ending Balance	800		$ 8,516				
February 5	Purchased	400	$12	$4,800				
	Moving Average	1,200		$13,316	$11.10			
February 18	Sold	(700)		$(7,770)		700	$11.10	$7,770
	Ending Balance	500		$5,546				
March 15	Purchased	600	$11	$6,600				
	Ending Inventory	**1,100**		**$12,146**	**$11.04**	Total CGS		**$14,154**

Total Available	$26,300
- Cost of Goods Sold	($14,154)
= Ending Inventory	$12,146

Perpetual Moving Average Process:

1) Compute a new moving average cost after each purchase.
   Total cost divided by total units = moving average cost per unit

2) CGS is computed as units sold x the **last** moving average.
   Sales will not change the moving average.

3) Compute an ending balance for units and inventory dollars after each sale.

24. Lower of Net Realizable Value (LCNRV) Lower of Cost or Market (LCM)

Companies **initially** value inventory at cost using either FIFO, LIFO, or the average method.

GAAP then requires a company to make sure that inventory is not reported on the balance sheet at an amount that is greater than probable future economic benefit (PFEB), the cash expected to be received from the sale of the inventory.

The net realizable value (PFEB) often decreases when the sale price decreases due to:

- New replacement products
- Competitor price changes
- Seasonal sales

Companies test the value using Lower of Net Realizable Value or Lower of Cost or Market.

- Inventory is reduced to the PFEB if the cost is greater than PFEB.
- Inventory is never reported at an amount higher than original cost.

Inventory write-downs are reported as part of cost of goods sold when write-downs are part of ordinary business or not material.

A **loss on impairment of inventory** is reported as part of operating expenses when an inventory write-down is significant and occurs because of an unusual business situation.

In future periods, a lower reported cost of inventory becomes a lower cost of goods sold.

<u>FIFO or Average Cost:</u> Lower of Cost or Net Realizable Value (LCNRV)

Companies who use the FIFO or average cost methods use the lower of cost or net realizable value method (LCNRV) to ensure inventory is not reported on the balance sheet at a value higher than PFEB.

Steps to implement LCNRV:

1) Value inventory at cost using FIFO or average cost.

2) Determine the Net Realizable Value (NRV) for each item.

   Sales Price
   <u>- Direct Costs to Sell (commission & shipping to customer)</u>
   = Net Realizable Value (NRV)

3) Report inventory on the balance sheet at the <u>lower</u> of cost or net realizable value.

   Cost of Inventory
   <u>- NRV (PFEB) of Inventory</u>
   = If positive: decrease inventory to NRV

4) Report the decrease to inventory on the income statement as cost of goods sold.

   Cost of Goods Sold
           Inventory

   Some companies will use other accounts to track amounts separate from CGS:

   Loss on Inventory Value (reported as CGS)
           Allowance to Reduce Inventory to Market

Example 1: <u>FIFO or Average Cost:</u> Lower of Cost or Net Realizable Value (LCNRV)

Information related to all the company's products is provided below.

Product	Selling Price	Cost to Sell	Cost
A	1,200	120	1,000
B	1,800	180	1,800
C	2,500	150	2,200
D	1,200	180	950

Determine the amount that inventory will be reported on the balance sheet using **Lower of Cost or Net Realizable Value** by individual product.

By Individual Product: Determine net realizable value for each individual product

Product	Selling Price	-	Cost to Sell	=	Net Realizable Value	Cost	Lower of Cost or Net Realizable Value
A	1,200		120		1,080	1,000	1,000
B	1,800		180		1,620	1,800	1,620
C	2,500		350		2,150	2,200	2,150
D	1,200		180		1,020	950	950
						5,950	5,720

Net realizable value (NRV) of $5,720 is lower than cost of $5,950 by $230.

- Inventory must be adjusted down to LCNRV.

Account	Debit	Credit
Cost of Goods Sold (Loss of inventory value)	$230	
Inventory (or Allowance to reduce to Mkt)		$230

Inventory will be reported on the balance sheet at $5,720

A company may also perform LCNRV by groups of inventory items, or for the total value of inventory.

Examples follow – however, you will not be asked to determine LCNRV by groups or in total on a quiz or exam. Be aware that companies have a choice in the method they use.

LCNRV by Group, A&B and C&D: Net realizable value for each group of products.

Product	Selling Price	Cost to Sell	Net Realizable Value	Cost	Lower of Cost or Net Realizable Value
A	1,200	120	1,080	1,000	
B	1,800	180	1,620	1,800	
			2,700	2,800	2,700
C	2,500	350	2,150	2,200	
D	1,200	180	1,020	950	
			3,170	3,150	3,150
				5,950	5,850

Net realizable value (NRV) is lower than cost by $100. Inventory must be adjusted down to NRV.

	Debit	Credit
CGS (Loss of inventory value)	$100	
Inventory (Allowance to reduce to Mkt)		$100

Inventory will be reported on the balance sheet at $5,850 under the group method of NRV.

LCNRV in Total: Determine net realizable value for total inventory

Product	Selling Price	Cost to Sell	Net Realizable Value	Cost	Lower of Cost or Net Realizable Value
A	1,200	120	1,080	1,000	
B	1,800	180	1,620	1,800	
C	2,500	350	2,150	2,200	
D	1,200	180	1,020	950	
			5,870	5,950	5,870

Net realizable value (NRV) is lower than cost by $80. Inventory must be adjusted down to NRV.

	Debit	Credit
CGS (Loss of inventory value)	$80	
Inventory (Allowance to reduce to Mkt)		$80

Inventory will be reported on the balance sheet at $5,870 under the total method of NRV.

LIFO: Lower of Cost or Market (LCM)

Companies who use LIFO must use the lower of cost or market method (LCM) to report inventory on the balance sheet at a value that is not higher than PFEB.

The LIFO method will value inventory at the first and oldest cost. Therefore, if the company has existed for years, it is possible that remaining inventory at cost will be very low. Very low inventory cost gives a higher gross profit than the true economic reality. The LCM method attempts to minimize this and report a reasonable gross profit.

GAAP defines **"market"** as the inventory's current replacement cost (purchase or manufacture); however, **"market" may not be:**

1) **higher** than net realizable value (NRV)

    Estimated selling price
    – Cost to sell
    = Net Realizable Value (NRV) (CEILING)

or

2) **lower** than the NRV less the normal profit margin (FLOOR)

The **ceiling** prevents a company from reporting a value for inventory higher than PFEB.

The **floor** prevents a company from reporting a value for inventory lower than a reasonable, normal cost.

Then: Report inventory on the balance sheet at the lower of cost or "market".

Cost of Inventory

\- "Market" value of Inventory (either replacement cost, ceiling, or floor)

= If positive: decrease inventory to market

Example 2: LIFO: Lower of Cost or Market (LCM)

Information related to the company's products is provided below. Normal gross profit on all products is 20% of cost.

Product	Replacement Cost	Net Realizable Value (NRV)	Cost
A	1,200	1,620	1,000
B	1,800	1,980	1,600
C	2,500	2,250	1,900
D	700	800	1,300

1st Set up a table and **compute the 3 "market" prices and define market value.** The middle value of the 3 will always be the "market" value.

- Replacement cost
- NRV
- NRV – normal GP

2nd Compare the original cost to "market" and put the lowest amount in the LCM column.

3rd Compare the total of original cost to the LCM total and determine the write-down.

- Reduce inventory for the difference **if LCM is lower than cost.**

LCM by Individual Product: Consider each product.

Product	Replacement Cost	(Ceiling) NRV	(Floor) NRV – Profit **	(1st) (Middle) Market	Cost	(2nd) LCM
A	1,200	1,620	1,420	1,420	1,000	1,000
B	1,800	1,980	1,660	1,800	1,600	1,600
C	2,500	2,250	1,870	2,250	1,900	1,900
D	700	800	540	700	1,300	700
			Total		**5,800**	**5,200**

** Profit = 20% of cost A = 200 B = 320 C = 380 D = 260

LCM is lower than cost by $600 so inventory must be adjusted down to LCM.

	Dr	Cr
CGS (Loss of inventory value)	$600	
Inventory (Allowance to reduce to Mkt)		$600

A company may also perform LCM by groups of inventory items, or for the total value of inventory. Examples follow – however, you will not be asked to determine LCM by groups or in total on a quiz or exam. Be aware that companies have a choice in the method they use.

LCM by Group, A& B, C&D: Determine market and LCM for each group of products. Use only the total column for each group.

Product	Replacement Cost	(Ceiling) NRV	(Floor) NRV – Profit **	Market	Cost	LCM
A	1,200	1,620	1,420		1,000	
B	1,800	1,980	1,660		1,600	
Group	**3,000**	**3,600**	**3,080**	**3,080**	**2,600**	**2,600**
C	2,500	2,250	1,870		1,900	
D	700	800	540		1,300	
Group	**3,200**	**3,050**	**2,410**	**3,050**	**3,200**	**3,050**
			Total of each group		**5,800**	**5,650**

LCM is lower than cost by $150 so inventory must be adjusted down to LCM.

	Debit	Credit
CGS (Loss of inventory value)	$150	
Inventory (Allowance to reduce to Mkt)		$150

LCM in Total: Determine market and LCM for total inventory only

Product	Replacement Cost	(Ceiling) NRV	(Floor) NRV – Profit **	Market	Cost	LCM
A	1,200	1,620	1,420		1,000	
B	1,800	1,980	1,660		1,600	
C	2,500	2,250	1,870		1,900	
D	700	800	540		1,300	
Total	6,200	6,650	5,490	**6,200**	**5,800**	**5,800**

LCM is higher than or equal to original cost. Inventory is reported at cost and **no adjustment is made.**

25. Accounting for Long-term Assets

Purchases and Sales

Example 1 provides several types of costs related to long-term assets. An (A) out to the side means the cost is reported as part of the cost of the asset on the balance sheet and expensed over the total time the asset is used to produce revenues. An (E) out to the side means the cost is expensed in the period the cost is incurred. The journal entry the accountant makes to record the costs incurred is presented below the list of costs.

<u>Building</u>

1. Purchase price of the building	$250,000 (A)
2. Property taxes on the building for previous years	$ 22,000 (A)
3. Real estate commission on the building	$ 18,000 (A)
4. Inspection fees related to the building	$ 2,900 (A)
5. Insurance for the building for the first month used	$ 800 (E)
6. Remodel of the building before use	$ 13,400 (A)

Costs 2, 3, 4, 6 must be paid to be able to use the asset.
Cost 5 is a monthly expense that must be paid each month; no future benefit.

Building	306,300	
Insurance expense	800	
Cash		307,100

<u>Land</u>

1. Purchase price of land	$125,000 (A)
2. Real estate commission on the land purchased	$ 10,000 (A)
3. Survey costs related to the land	$ 2,800 (A)
4. Bulldozing costs before using the land	$ 7,200 (A)
5. Removal of a building before using the land	$ 8,300 (A)
6. Property tax on the land after begin using the land	$ 4,400 (E)

Costs 2, 3, 4, 5 must be paid to be able to use the asset.
Cost 6 is an expense that must be paid each period; no future benefit.

Land	153,300	
Property tax expense	4,400	
Cash		157,700

Example 1 (continued)

Equipment

1. Purchase price of equipment	$ 65,000 (A)
2. Routine maintenance on the equipment	$ 8,000 (E)
3. Shipping expense for the equipment	$ 3,200 (A)
4. Monthly training on the equipment during use	$ 5,200 (E)
5. Installation of the equipment	$ 6,500 (A)
6. Engine upgrade on the equipment; extends life 5 years	$ 9,200 (A)
7. Training on the equipment prior to use	$ 1,200 (A)

Costs 3, 5 and 7 must be paid to be able to use the asset.
Cost 2 and 4 are expenses that must be paid each month; no future benefit.
Cost 6 gives additional future benefit; extends the life

Equipment	85,100	
Maintenance expense	8,000	
Training expense	5,200	
Cash		98,300

Trademark

1. Fees to file for a trademark with the Government	$ 12,000 (A)
2. Salaries of employees working on the trademark	$ 7,400 (E)

Legal fees are paid outside the company. Salaries are internal costs.

Trademark	12,000	
Salaries expense	7,400	
Cash		19,400

Lump Sum Purchase

A lump sum purchase is a group of assets purchased together for one total cost. The accountant assigns the cost of each type of asset based on the individual fair market value of each asset. Assets with different useful lives cannot be combined.

Example 2 illustrates how the cost of each asset in a lump sum purchase is determined. The company purchased assets with the following fair market values for a total cost of $1,000,000.

	Fair Market Value	% of Total	Allocated Cost
Building	$ 350,000	31.8%*	$ 318,000
Land	$ 700,000	63.6%	$ 636,000
Furniture	$ 50,000	4.6%	$ 46,000
Total	$1,100,000		$ 1,000,000

* $350,000 / $1,100,000 = 31.8% ** $1,000,000 x 31.8% = $318,000

The journal entry to record the lump sum purchase is:

	Debit	Credit
Building	$318,000	
Land	$636,000	
Furniture	$ 46,000	
Cash		$1,000,000

Recording Depreciation / Amortization Expense

A company must report property, plant, and equipment, net of accumulated depreciation expense on the balance sheet. **Depreciation expense** reported on the income statement is the current period cost of using a property, plant, and equipment

Accountants record the expense of using long-term assets as an adjusting entry at the end of each period before they prepare financial statements.

The journal entry to record the expense of using property, plant and equipment for the current period is:

	Debit	Credit
Depreciation Expense	**$xxx**	
Accumulated Depreciation		**$xxx**

The journal entry to record the expense of using intangible assets for the current period is:

	Debit	Credit
Amortization Expense	**$xxx**	
Asset (or Accumulated Amortization)		**$xxx**

Sale (Disposal) of a Long-term Asset

Example 3 illustrates how accountants record the sale of an asset. A company purchased an automobile for a salesman for $35,000 on January 2nd of the first year of operations. The company expects to use the automobile for 5 years and then sell it for $8,000. Depreciation expense was recorded using the straight-line method on December 31st of each year. On June 1st of the 4th year, the company sold the auto for $12,000.

The sale of the car is recorded as follows:

Account	Debit	Credit	Note
Realized Loss on Sale	**$ 4,550**		**(4)** Loss on Income Statement
Cash	**$12,000**		**(1)** Increase in an Asset
Accumulated Depreciation	**$18,450**		**(3)** Remove from Bal Sheet
Automobile		**$35,000**	**(2)** Remove from Bal Sheet

(1) Record the cash received from the sale; debit cash for $12,000

(2) Credit the automobile for the total historical cost of $35,000.

(3) Debit accumulated depreciation for the total recorded up to the date the asset is sold.

The automobile is sold in the middle of year four. The expense of using the car for the first five months of year four must be recorded. Depreciation expense each year is computed as follows:

$$\frac{\$35{,}000 - 8{,}000}{5 \text{ years}} = \$5{,}400 \text{ each year for three years}$$

Depreciation expense for the first five months of year four is computed as follows:
$5,400 per year x 5 months / 12 months in a year = $2,250

Total accumulated depreciation at the time of the sale is computed as follows:

First 3 years:	$5,400 x 3 =	$16,200
5 months of the 4th year		$ 2,250
Total Accumulated Depreciation		$18,450

(4) Record a realized gain or a loss for the difference in cash received and book value as follows:

Cash received	$12,000
- Book value ($35,000 - $18,450)	($16,550)
= The realized gain or (loss)	($ 4,550)

Capitalized Interest

The interest cost associated with financing the construction of a long-term asset is a cost to obtain the asset. Companies capitalize the cost of interest during the construction period.

The capitalized cost of construction includes the interest on the cost of the first expenditure through all costs to substantial completion. The amount capitalized is the cost of interest that could have been avoided if the construction of the long-term asset had not occurred. A company may not capitalize more interest than it actually incurred during the period. The company does not have to specifically borrow to pay for expenditures related to the long-term asset.

The weighted average accumulated expenditure is used to compute the associated capitalized interest cost.

Example 4 illustrates how companies determine the weighted average interest rate.

Long-term Debt Amount	Annual Interest Rate	Annual Interest Cost
$300,000	6%	$18,000
$500,000	9%	$45,000
$800,000		$63,000

$63,000 / $800,000 = 7.875% weighted average rate of interest

Example 5 illustrates how a company determines the weighted average accumulated expenditures. A company constructed a building from January 1 through June 30 at a total cost of $1,200,000. The company had general long-term debt in the amount of $800,000 at an average annual rate of 7.875%.

	Expenditure		**Time Months / 12**		**Weighted Average Cost**
1/1	$ 400,000	x	6/12	=	$200,000
2/1	$ 300,000	x	5/12	=	$125,000
5/1	$ 200,000	x	2/12	=	$ 33,333
6/1	$ 300,000	x	1/12	=	$ 25,000
Total	$1,200,000				$383,333 x 7.875% = $30,187

The journal entry to add the cost of interest to the cost of the building is:

	Debit	Credit
Building	$30,187	
Interest Expense		$30,187

The maximum amount the company can capitalize is limited to $800,000 at 7.875% for 6 months, or $31,500. The company cannot capitalize more interest costs than it actually incurs during a period.

26. Other Long-term Asset Issues

Changes to Estimates Used to Compute Depreciation Expense

The cost of using a long-term asset <u>for future periods</u> will change when the company:

- incurs additional costs related to the asset to increase the probable future economic benefit (increase the useful life or increase efficiencies).
- revises the estimated useful life.
- revises the estimated residual value.

The depreciation expense for each year after a change in cost or a revised estimate is calculated:

	Original historical cost
+	Added costs this period
-	Accumulated depreciation to date
=	Revised book value

and then:

$$\frac{\text{Revised book value - Revised residual value}}{\text{Revised useful life in future years}} = \text{Depreciation Expense for each future year}$$

Example 1 illustrates how a company's depreciation expense changes when the company adds costs and revises estimates. A company paid $200,000 for a machine at the beginning of the year. The company initially expected to use the machine for 10 years and then sell it for $20,000. At the beginning of the 4th year, the company rebuilt the key parts of the machine at a cost of $45,000 and extended the total expected life of the machine to 15 years. The company now expects $10,000 residual value. The company uses the straight-line method to estimate depreciation expense.

Depreciation expense for the first three years and accumulated depreciation at the end of three years is:

$$\frac{\$\ 200{,}000 - \$20{,}000}{10 \text{ years}} = \$18{,}000 \text{ depreciation expense each year}$$

Accumulated depreciation is $54,000 at the end of three years ($18,000 each year for 3 years).

Example 1 (continued):

The cost to rebuild the machine is capitalized at the beginning of year 4 because the increased life is expected to generate more total revenue (more probable economic future benefit).

The book value at the end of three years (also the beginning of the fourth year) is used to estimate the revised depreciable base of the machine.

Original cost	$200,000	
+ Rebuild cost	45,000	
= Revised total cost	245,000	
- Accumulated depreciation	(54,000)	
= Revised book value	191,000	at the beginning of year four
- Revised estimated residual value	(10,000)	
= Revised depreciable base	181,000	

Annual depreciation expense is revised to be $15,083.33 each year for the next 12 years.

$$\frac{\text{New Depreciable Base}}{\text{Revised useful life}} \qquad \frac{\$181{,}000}{\text{12 future years (15 total – 3 previous)}} = \$15{,}083.33 \text{ annual expense}$$

The total net cost of $235,000 ($200,000 + $45,000 - $10,000 RV) is reported as depreciation expense over the 15 years the company uses the machine:

3 years at $18,000	$ 54,000
+ 12 years at $15,083.33	$181,000
= Total depreciation expense	= $235,000

Impairment of LT Assets

Impairment is a **permanent loss of value** that occurs when the probable future economic benefit **(cash flows) generated from using the asset are expected to be less than net cost.**

Companies test for impairment annually or more frequently when circumstances indicate the future benefit of the asset may have significantly decreased due to:

- the company experiences substantial decreases in the price of goods or services
- cash flows generated from the use of the asset or the asset's physical condition changes.
- the business environment changes significantly.
- the company incurs current period losses and expects future losses.
- the useful life of the asset significantly decreases.

The income statement reports impairment losses as an operating expense because the loss is related to assets used for operations.

The impairment test is different for long-term assets with a finite useful life and an indefinite life.

Impairment Test for Long-term Assets with a Finite Useful Life

Accountants use a two-step process to evaluate long-term assets with a finite useful life for impairment. The first step determines if impairment is likely to have occurred and the second step determines the amount of the impairment.

Step 1)
Total estimated future cash flows
\- Book value of the asset
= if positive, no impairment loss
if negative, go to step 2

Step 2)
Book value of the asset
\- Fair market value of the asset
= Impairment loss

Fair market value is the estimated price of a current buy/sell transaction between two willing parties. Fair market value can be:

- A quoted market price
- An external appraisal
- The discounted present value of future estimated cash flows using a risk-free interest rate

Impairment Test for <u>Indefinite-Life Intangible Assets Other than Goodwill</u>
(Trademarks and Licenses without an end date)

A one step process is used to test indefinite life assets other than goodwill for impairment:

Book Value of the Asset

\- Fair Value of the Asset

= Impairment Loss

Impairment Test for <u>Goodwill</u>

Goodwill cannot be separated from a specific part of the business (reporting unit). A reporting unit is an operating segment or a component of an operating segment with separate financial information that is regularly reviewed by management. Therefore, the value of the reporting unit is used to test goodwill for impairment.

Fair market value of the reporting unit

\- Book value of the entire reporting unit (including goodwill)

= Impairment (only if it is negative)

Example 2 illustrates how the accountant determines and records impairment loss.

In 20Y1, Mailbox, Inc. purchased PostBox, Inc. for $1,000,000. Post Box, Inc. had 65 established locations at the time of purchase. Mailbox, Inc. earned $500,000 in 20Y0 and $750,000 in 20Y1. The economic recession and new competition caused the loss of significant customers and profits of Mailbox, Inc. decreased to a loss of $300,000 in 20Y2. The company does not expect to return to profitability in the future.

The Post Box, Inc. (reporting unit) has an estimated total fair market value of $320,000 **(A)** at the end of 20Y2. The book value of the Post Box Inc. at the end of 20Y2 is 400,000 **(A).** Equipment owned by Mailbox, Inc. that is not part of PostBox, Inc. has a book value of $380,000 **(B)** and total future estimated cash flows of $150,000 and the equipment can be sold for $120,000.

Mailbox, Inc. has new competitors that are driving down prices for services. The business environment has changed and Mailbox, Inc. must test their long-term assets for impairment at the end of 20Y2.

Impairment test of finite-lived assets: Equipment owned by Mailbox, Inc. end of 2025

1) Total estimated future cash flows	$150,000
- Book value of the asset	($380,000)
= if positive, no impairment loss	**($230,000)**

if negative, go to step 2

2) Book value of the asset	$380,000
- Fair market value of the asset	($120,000)
= **Impairment loss**	**$260,000**

Impairment test of Goodwill end of 2025:

Fair market value of the reporting unit	$320,000
- Book value of the entire reporting unit	($400,000)
= **Impairment, if negative**	**($ 80,000)**

The journal entry to record the impairment loss is:

Account	Debit	Credit
Impairment Loss	$340,000	
Equipment		$260,000
Goodwill		$ 80,000

Appendix A

In Class Exercises

Exercise 1.a: What Do These Financial Statements Tell You?

Below are personal financial statements for Professor Cobb (she wishes!). State what the balance sheet and income statement tell you about how Professor Cobb manages her business of life.

Assets:		Liabilities:	
Cash	89,000	Accounts payable (utilities, cable, phone)	350
Prepaid Insurance	600		
Supplies	100	Credit card payable	0
Food	200	Notes payable (auto loan)	0
ST Investments	100,000	S/T Mortgage payable	13,000
LT Investments	600,000		
Land	50,000		
Automobiles	60,000	L/T Mortgage payable	53,000
Buildings	200,000	Total Liabilities	66,350
Equipment	12,000		
Computer Equipment	1,500		
Furniture & Fixtures	12,500	Owners Equity:	
- Accumulated Deprec.	(176,200)		
PPE, net	159,800	Common Stock	1,000
		Retained Earnings	886,350
Copyrights	1,000	Total Owner's Equity	887,350
Other Assets	3,000		
Total Assets	953,700	Total Liabilities and Owner's Equity	953,700

Service Revenue (paycheck)	9,600
Income Tax Expense	(2,000)
Social Security Tax Expense	(750)
Interest Expense	(300)
Property & Health Insurance Expense	(1,500)
Food Expense	(700)
Utilities Expense	(600)
Maintenance Expense	(200)
Cable, phone, internet expense	(550)
Gasoline Expense	(500)
Depreciation Expense	(400)
Charities Expense	(1,000)
Net Income (Earnings)	1,100

Exercise 1.b: What Do These Financial Statements Tell You?

Below are personal financial statements for Janice Cobb. Read the line items and "between the lines" and determine what the balance sheet and statement of revenues and expenses tell you about her personality and how she manages her "business of life."

Assets:		Liabilities:	
Cash	7,000	Accounts payable (utilities, cable, phone)	600
Prepaid Insurance	600	Credit card payable	18,400
Supplies	100	CP Notes payable (auto loan)	11,000
Food	200	CP Mortgage payable	18,000
		LT notes payable (auto loan)	75,000
Automobiles	100,000	LT Mortgage payable	463,000
Building	500,000	Total Liabilities	586,000
Equipment	27,000		
Computer Equipment	10,500		
Furniture & Fixtures	32,500	Owners Equity:	
(Accum. Depreciation)	(41,500)		
PPE, Net	428,500	Common Stock	1,000
		Retained Earnings	49,400
		Total Owner's Equity	50,400
Total Assets	636,400	Total Liabilities and Owner's Equity	636,400

Service Revenue (paycheck)	9,600
Income Tax Expense	(2,000)
Social Security Tax Expense	(700)
Interest Expense	(1,200)
Insurance Expense	(1,500)
Food Expense	(1,100)
Utilities Expense	(450)
Maintenance Expense	(400)
Cable, phone, internet Expense	(400)
Gasoline Expense	(500)
Depreciation Expense	(1,600)
Net Income (Earnings)	(450)

Exercise 2: Reported on the Balance Sheet?

State the common name used to report each of the following on the balance sheet.

1. ______________________________ Items held only to sell to customers
2. ______________________________ The right to use a symbol
3. ______________________________ Cash value of life insurance policies
4. ______________________________ Amounts owed to a bank or financing company to be repaid in 2 years
5. ______________________________ Financial instruments for the purpose of earning money
6. ______________________________ Has physical qualities and is used long-term in the business to generate revenues
7. ______________________________ Amounts owed to investors that will be repaid in 10 years
8. ______________________________ The right to use technology
9. ______________________________ Amounts paid over and above the fair market value of assets when purchasing another company
10. ______________________________ Amounts paid in advance for service not yet provided to the company
11. ______________________________ Any instrument that the bank will accept on deposit
12. ______________________________ Amounts borrowed from investors that will be repaid in 10-90 days
13. ______________________________ Items used up in the day to day operation of the business
14. ______________________________ Amounts owed to the company; interest is charged
15. ______________________________ The right to publish
16. ______________________________ Amounts owed to suppliers for repeat purchases
17. ______________________________ Amounts that must be repaid this year for amounts owed to the bank the company must repay in equal monthly payments

Exercise 3: Read the Balance Sheets

Answer the following questions using the balance sheets for AMAZON for the most current year. Write the **account name and the amount** that answers the question.

1. How much cash does the company have in the bank or invested for less than 90 days with no risk of loss of principal?

2. How much does the company owe suppliers, normally paid in 30 days, to date?

3. How much does the company owe banks and financing institutions that is payable within the next year?

4. How much have stockholders contributed to date?

5. What is the company's cumulative profit or loss less dividends?

6. How much has the company spent to acquire its own stock they currently hold?

7. How much has the company paid for services the company has not yet received?

8. What is the cost of physical long-term assets currently used to produce revenues?

9. What is the cost of the assets the company uses in day-to-day operations?

Exercise 4: Revenue or Expense?

Swim School, Inc. (SSI) provides swim lessons to children between the ages of 2 and 6. Answer the 3 questions and determine if a **revenue or expense** occurred and will be reported on the income statement **for the month of February**. (Answer only for the one transaction stated. Do not assume other things occurred.

1. SSI provided swim classes in February. The customers paid for the classes in December and January.

a. Were goods or services provided to customers in February?________________
b. Was a service received in February?______________________
c. Was an asset used (up) in February to provide goods or services?_____________

2. SSI paid the utility bill received in February for the electricity received in January.

a. Were goods or services provided to customers in February?_______________
b. Was a service received in February?____________________
c. Was an asset used (up) in February to provide goods or services?___________

3. SSI employees worked in February. SSI paid the employees half the amount earned in February and the other half will be paid the first day of March.

a. Were goods or services provided to customers in February?_________________
b. Was a service received in February?______________________
c. Was an asset used (up) in February to provide goods or services?____________

4. SSI purchased pool cleaning equipment in February and began using the equipment in March.

a. Were goods or services provided to customers in February?_________________
b. Was a service received in February?______________________
c. Was an asset used (up) in February to provide goods or services?____________

5. SSI purchased toys in January that they provided to children in class in February.

a. Were goods or services provided to customers in February?_________________
b. Was a service received in February?______________________
c. Was an asset used (up) in February to provide goods or services?____________

Exercise 5: Prepare the Income Statement

Hansen Natural had the following transactions occur during the month of January:

1) Customers paid the company $10,000 for goods the company will provide in February.
2) The company provided $75,000 in goods to customers that cost the company $36,000
3) Employees worked and the company incurred $14,000 in salaries in January.
4) The company paid $12,000 for salaries to employees during January.
5) The company paid a December utility bills of $1,200 in January
6) The January utility bills of $2,500 was received but not paid. (used in January)
7) The company purchased office furniture for $15,000 in January that is expected to be used over a period of 5 years. The furniture was used during the month of January.
8) The company incurred $100 of interest expense in January that won't be paid until March.
9) The company paid $1,200 for liability insurance to cover the 1st six months of the year
10) The company paid $6,000 for rent for warehouse space for the 1st three months of the year.

Prepare an income statement using the accrual basis.

Hansen Natural
Income Statement
For the Month of January (In Thousands)

Sales	$ __________
Cost of Goods Sold	$ __________
Gross Profit	$ __________
Operating Expenses:	
__________________	$ __________
__________________	$ __________
__________________	$ __________
__________________	$ __________
__________________	$ __________
__________________	$ __________
Income / Earnings	$ __________

Exercise 6: Read the Income Statements

Answer the following questions using the Statement of Income for **AMAZON** for the most current year (far right column). Write the account name and the amount.

1. What is the cost of warehousing and shipping products?

2. How much did the company earn for each share of common stock outstanding?

3. How many total shares of ownership do investors own?

4. What is the cost of acquiring and supporting customers?

5. What is the value of the services the company received from the federal government?

6. What was the total price of services the company provided to customers?

7. What is the cost of using funds acquired through long-term debt?

Exercise 7: Cash is Different than Income Statement

State the line item or account that is reported on the balance sheet when cash is not received or paid in the same period for the following activities.

Activity	Balance Sheet Line Item / Account
1. Employees worked and have not been paid	______________
2. Provide goods to customers who will pay in the future	______________
3. Customers pay for gift cards that have not been used	______________
4. Pay for advertising that will be run next month	______________
5. Received utility services and the company will pay next month	______________
6. Borrowed and will pay the cost of using the funds in the future	______________
7. Received inventory and the invoice will come in the mail	______________
8. Received supplies and the invoice will come in the mail	______________

Exercise 8: Prepare Financial Statements

Sally Tipton opened a resale clothing shop on 6th Avenue that targets middle class families. Sally purchases goods from people who bring goods into the store and resells the goods at a target price of 50% over cost. Sally borrowed $12,000 from relatives to provide the funds to get the business started. The loan from relatives is expected to be repaid half at the end of the first year and half at the end of the second year. However, cash in the operating account was not sufficient to repay anything to relatives at the end of the first year.

Sally gives you the operating account information and asks you to prepare financial statements for the first year. The operating account was summarized as follows:

Loan from relatives	12,000
Sales of Goods	36,290
Payments to people for goods	15,925
Payments to part-time employees	7,650
Payments for rent	4,400
Payments for utilities & phone	1,154
Payments for insurance	964

Sally also tells you that she allowed customers to take goods on credit and these customers still owe the business $1,952. She gives you some December bills that have not been paid that include the utility bill for $138, the cell phone bill for $84, and insurance for the next year for $986. She has decided to pay herself $6,000 for working last year which has not yet been paid. The rent for the month of December in the amount of $400 has not yet been paid. Sally plans to give $1,000 to a local charity out of the earnings of the company in March of next year. Inventory on hand at year-end has a cost of $1,000.

Prepare the Income Statement and the Balance Sheet on the next page.

Prepare the income statement for the company for the first year of business.

Prepare the balance sheet for the company for the first year of business.

Exercise 9: Asset or Expense?

A product division of Monster Beverage had the following costs to operate the fruit drink product division of the company for the **month of March**:

1) Paid $320,000 for equipment to use for four years on various types of internal R & D. The equipment is used in March.
2) Paid $650,000 for salaries to employees who are working to develop new products expected to bring tremendous benefit to the company in the form of future profits.
3) Paid $ 478,000 for advertising run to promote products currently being sold.
4) Paid $280,000 to develop software that will be used internally for accounting and inventory control. 80% of the costs were incurred before the company determined the software would work. The software was not used in March.
5) Paid $32,000 to replace the roof on a warehouse expected to be used for another 40 years.
6) Paid $45,000 to an outside law firm to file for a patent related to drinks expected to be sold for 10 years.
7) Paid $225,000 for direct materials used to develop new flavors of products currently sold and expected to be sold for 5 years.
8) Paid $24,000 to install the equipment and $16,000 to train employees on equipment (see 1) before use.
9) Paid $129,000 in salaries to an attorney who works for the company on patents and trademarks
10) Purchased research and development that has achieved technological feasibility for $500,000. The R&D has not yet been incorporated in the company's products.
11) Paid $132,000 for salaries of employees working on contract R&D to be delivered in three years.
12) Incurred $5,000 interest related to the replacement of the roof on the warehouse.
13) Paid $100,000 for landscaping; $60,000 to be done each year and $40,000 to be done in 5 years.
14) Paid $22,000 for tires and $15,000 to replace an engine on delivery trucks used for 7 years.
15) Paid $25,000 to an outside firm to unsuccessfully defend a trademark.

Determining operating income for the company for the month of March.

Sales	$6,200,000
- Cost of Goods Sold	($2,500,000)
Gross Profit	$3,700,000)
Other Operating Expenses	($2,000,000)
______________	
______________	
______________	
______________	
______________	
______________	
______________	
______________	
______________	
Operating Income	

Exercise 10: Depreciation Expense

A company with a December 31 year end purchased a forklift on June 1, 20Y1 at a cost of $32,200 and also paid $1,500 for shipping. The manufacturer believes the forklift can be used for 20 years and then sold for $4,000. The company expects to use the forklift for 12 years (a total of 1,500,000 boxes moved) and then sell it for $8,000. The company downsized and sold the forklift on August 31, 20Y3 for $20,000.

The number of boxes moved by the forklift in the warehouse totaled:

20Y1: 68,000 20Y2: 142,000 20Y3: 54,000

A. Compute depreciation expense for 20Y1 and 20Y2 using

1. Straight-line

2. Double Declining Balance

3. Units of Production

B. State the accounts and amounts that will be reported on the balance sheet and income statement for the years-ended December 31, 20Y1, and 20Y2.

Straight-line:

Balance Sheet	20Y1	20Y2

Income Statement:	20Y1	20Y2

Double Declining Balance:

Balance Sheet	20Y1	20Y2

Income Statement:	20Y1	20Y2

Units of Production:

Balance Sheet	20Y1	20Y2

Income Statement:	20Y1	20Y2

C. Determine the gain or loss on the sale of the forklift given the company used the straight-line method.

Exercise 11: Cash Flow Statement Sections

State which section of the indirect cash flow statement will report the following transactions.
Operating Section (O), Investing Section (I), Financing Section (F)
Not on the Cash Flow Statement (N)

1. __________ Income earned during the year
2. __________ Depreciation expense
3. __________ Purchase of manufacturing equipment
4. __________ Dividends paid to shareholders
5. __________ Borrowing from the bank
6. __________ Interest Expense
7. __________ Cash received from the sale of long-term investments
8. __________ Repay loans
9. __________ Cash received from the sale of a building
10. __________ Change in accounts receivable
11. __________ Interest income
12. __________ Purchase an automobile and financed the entire amount with a note payable due in 3 years (no cash is paid)
13. __________ Change in current liabilities
14. __________ Purchase of treasury stock
15. __________ Acquisition of 100% of another Company

Exercise 12.A: Indirect Cash Flow Statement

	Income Statement	Cash	Difference (More or less cash than income)
Current period cash sales	$150,000	$______	$______
Current period sales on account, all collected this period	$750,000	$______	$______
Selling and Admin Expenses incurred and all paid this period	($300,000)	$______	$______
Depreciation Expense	($ 50,000)	$______	$______
Compensation Expense paid in stock	($ 75,000)	$______	$______
Gain on Sale of Equipment	$ 10,000	$______	$______
Income Tax incurred and paid this period	($200,000)	$______	$______
Net Income for the current period	$ 285,000		
Cash from Operations this period		$_______	

The Indirect Cash Flow Statement:

Net Income	$285,000
Cash from Operations	$________

Exercise 12.B: Indirect Cash Flow Statement

	Income Statement	Cash	Difference (More or less cash than income)
Current period cash sales	$150,000	$______	$______
Current period sales on account, 80% collected this period	$750,000	$______	$______
Selling and Admin Expenses incurred, 60% paid this period	($300,000)	$______	$______
Depreciation Expense	($ 50,000)	$______	$______
Compensation Expense paid in stock	($ 75,000)	$______	$______
Gain on Sale of Equipment	$ 10,000	$______	$______
Income Tax incurred, 75% paid this period	($200,000)	$______	$______
Net Income for the current period	$ 285,000		
Cash from Operations this period		$______	

The Indirect Cash Flow Statement:

Net Income	$285,000
Cash from Operations	$________

Exercise 13: Read the Cash Flow Statement

Read the cash flow statement for **AMAZON** and determine what the cash flow statement tells the investor about the company's strategy.

1)

2)

3)

4)

5)

6)

Read the cash flow statement for **APPLE. INC.** and determine what the cash flow statement tells the investor about the company's strategy.

1)

2)

3)

4)

5)

6)

Exercise 14: Read all Financial Statements

Answer the following questions using the 4 financial statements for **Johnson & Johnson** for the most current year.

A. How much does the company owe suppliers for items or services that the supplier sends an invoice for?

B. How much does the company owe to banks and financing institutions (cumulative) payable within the next year?

C. How much cash did the company pay to acquire its own stock during the year?

D. How much do customers owe the company?

E. How much cash does the company have in the bank or invested short-term with no risk of loss of principal?

F. How much did the company incur to acquire customers, ship products, and run the day to day operations of the business in the current year?

G. How much have stockholders contributed to the company for shares of stock since the company began?

H. How much total did the company pay for dividends during the current year?

I. How much does the company have in assets they use and replace in daily operations?

J. What is the company's profit or loss less dividends paid cumulative to date?

K. What is the value of services the company received from the federal government during the current year?

L. What is the total price of good and services the company provided to customers during the current year?

M. How much does the company owe for retirees at the end of the current year?

N. How much has the company paid for services the company has not yet received at the end of the current year?

O. How much cash did the company pay to reduce long term debt during the current year?

P. How much cash did the company pay to purchase property, plant, and equipment during the current year?

Q. How much did the company earn for each share of common stock outstanding during the current year?

Exercise 15: Journal Entries Tell a Story

Account	Debit	Credit
Cash	100,000	
Investments		100,000
Land	250,000	
Note payable		225,000
Cash		25,000
Land Improvement	8,000	
Cash		8,000
Equipment	22,000	
Notes Payable		22,000
Supplies	5,000	
Credit Card Payable		5,000
Contract Labor	12,500	
Accounts Payable		12,500
Gas & Diesel Expense	320	
Credit Card Payable		320
Meals & Entertainment	195	
Credit Card Payable		195
Accounts Payable	12,500	
Cash		12,500
Insurance Expense	1,500	
Accounts Payable		1,500
Building	18,000	
Notes Payable		18,000
Livestock	16,000	
Cash		16,000
Feed Expense	980	
Credit Card Payable		980
Credit Card Payable	6,495	
Cash		6,495
Cash	28,500	
Sales Revenue		28,500
Utilities and Phone	265	
Accounts Payable		265
Accounts Payable	1,765	
Cash		1,765

Exercise 16: Journal Entries

Hansen Natural, Inc. had the following transactions during the first year of business:
(All amounts are in thousands)

1) Received $20,000 from owners in return for stock in the company (No par)
2) Signed a note at the bank and received cash of $8,000 to be repaid plus interest in 18 months.
3) Paid $200 cash for desks, chairs, bookcases, and file cabinets.
4) Purchased company automobiles for $1,000, paid cash of $150 and financed the balance due to be paid in 3 years.
5) A customer purchased and Hansen delivered $2,200 of products that cost Hansen $1,300. The customer intends to pay within 30 days.
6) Purchased paper, pens, and toner for $24, to be paid in 30 days.
7) Purchased $3,500 of products to be sold to customers on account.
8) Paid $200 for advertising that was run on local radio stations across the country.
9) Gave samples of energy drinks (products) to college campuses at a cost of $18.
10) Paid $275 for rent for warehouses in January that is to be used for the entire year.
11) Received $1,800 from customers previously billed.
12) Paid $3,100 on account to suppliers.
13) Declared dividends to shareholders of $8 (not yet paid).

For the above transactions record the entry that is made at the time the initial transaction occurs. Do not record what occurs as time passes (interest, depreciation, use of assets, etc.)

1) 6)

2) 7)

3) 8)

4) 9)

5) 10)

11)

12)

13)

Prepare T accounts for the following accounts and balance the accounts

Cash		Accounts Receivable		Accounts Payable	

Exercise 17: Adjusting Entries

Following is an unadjusted trial balance and additional information for the company. Make adjusting entries, prepare an adjusted trial balance, prepare an income statement, record closing entries, and prepare the balance sheet for the year ended December 31st.

Unadjusted Trial Balance

Accounts	Debit	Credit
Cash	25,000	
Accounts Receivable	62,000	
Supplies	6,000	
Prepaid Insurance	10,000	
Equipment	70,000	
Accumulated Depreciation		10,000
Note Payable		20,000
Unearned Revenues		4,000
Capital Stock		1,000
Retained Earnings 1/1		90,000
Sales		92,000
Salary Expense	18,000	
Depreciation Expense	2,400	
Rent Expense	9,000	
Supplies Expense	10,600	
Insurance Expense	2,000	
Loss on Sale of Equipment	2,000	
Total	217,000	217,000

1) The company has $2,000 of supplies on hand at year end. 2) The cost of using property, plant, and equipment for the year is $7,000. 3) Employees earned $800 that was not paid by the end of the year. 4) The cost of rent used for the entire year totaled $10,000. 5) $1,500 of accounts receivable is not expected to be collected. 6) Interest expense for the year is $200. 7) The price of goods paid for in advance of shipment to customers that will be shipped next month totaled $1,800 on December 31st. 8) One year of insurance coverage was paid on September 1, for $12,000.

1) 5)

2) 6)

3) 7)

4) 8)

Prepare an adjusted trial balance

Adjusted Trial Balance

Accounts	Debit	Credit
Cash		
Accounts Receivable		
Supplies		
Prepaid Insurance		
Equipment		
Accumulated Depreciation		
Note Payable		
Unearned Revenues		
Capital Stock		
Retained Earnings 1/1		
Sales		
Salary Expense		
Rent Expense		
Supplies Expense		
Insurance Expense		
Loss on Sale of Equipment		
Total		

Exercise 18: Adjusting Entries 2

JLC2, Inc. had the following transactions during the first year of business:

The following occurred on January 1st of the first year.

A. On February 1, the company signed a note at the bank and received cash of $120,000 to be repaid plus interest in 18 months (8% annual interest expense paid at the beginning of the next year.)
B. Purchased company automobiles (5-year life) for $65,000 on June 1.
C. On October 31st, a customer paid $9,000 for goods to be shipped on December 11th. The goods were shipped on December 11th. The cost of goods shipped was $6,440.
D. Paid a full year annual insurance policy premium of $12,000 on May 1st.
E. Paid $7,200 for office rent for the next 12 months on August 1st.
F. On August 1st, loaned $100,000 to another company that agreed to pay annual interest at a rate of 5% each year on January 2nd.
G. JLC2, Inc. purchased $576,000 in inventory and sold inventory at a cost of $325,000. At year end, the warehouse workers counted $249,250 of inventory in the warehouse.
H. JLC2, Inc.'s accountant prepared the company's tax return for the first year. JLC2, Inc. owes $11,797 to the IRS.

Prepare the adjusting entries for the following transactions for the year ended December 31st

A. On February 1, the company signed a note at the bank and received cash of $120,000 to be repaid plus interest in 18 months (8% annual interest expense paid at the beginning of the next year.)

B. Purchased company automobiles (5-year life) for $65,000 on June 1.

C. On October 31st, a customer paid $9,000 for goods to be shipped on December 11th. The goods were shipped on December 11th. The cost of goods shipped was $6,440.

D. Paid a full year annual insurance policy premium of $12,000 on May 1st.

E. Paid $7,200 for office rent for the next 12 months on August 1st.

F. On August 1st, loaned $100,000 to another company that agreed to pay annual interest at a rate of 5% each year on January 2nd.

G. JLC2, Inc. purchased $576,000 in inventory and sold inventory at a cost of $325,000. At year end, the warehouse workers counted $249,250 of inventory in the warehouse.

H. JLC2, Inc.'s accountant prepared the company's tax return for the first year. JLC2, Inc. owes $11,797 to the IRS.

Exercise 19: Accounting Cycle

Listed below are business transactions for Emix, Inc. Record the transactions and complete the accounting cycle for the year. The transaction was done on January 2, unless otherwise stated.

1. Rented an office building. Paid $12,000 for the next two years. (initially recorded as an asset)
2. Purchased 3 desks and file cabinets for the office. This office furniture is expected to be used for 7 years. The cost of $2,600 was put on account.
3. Raised $100,000 from family and friends, in return for ownership in the company.
4. Purchased one year of insurance coverage on January 1, $2,000.
5. On January 15th, purchased inventory for a cost of $48,000, on account.
6. During the year, sold inventory that cost $33,000, for a sales price of $67,000, on account.
7. Paid salaries to part-time employees, $22,000, for the entire year.
8. Purchased office supplies at a cost of $500, paid cash. (asset) At the end of the year, $100 of office supplies is on hand.
9. Paid utility bills for the year, the total amount was $1,900.
10. Received $56,000 from customers who had purchased goods on account (6.)
11. The inventory team counted $13,850 of inventory in the warehouse at year end.

A. Record the initial transactions.

B. Prepare "T" accounts for each account. Balance each "T" accounts before the adjusting journal entries and after the adjusting journal entries.

C. Using the prior information, prepare adjusting journal entries for the year ended December 31st.

D. Post the adjusting journal entries in the T accounts above and get a final balance.

E. Prepare an adjusted trial balance from the "T" accounts.

F. Prepare an income statement from the adjusted trial balance.

G. Prepare closing journal entries from the adjusted trial balance.

H. Prepare a Balance sheet from the adjusted trial balance.

Exercise 19 Work Space

Exercise 19 Work Space

Exercise 19 Work Space

Exercise 19 Work Space

Exercise 20: Revenue - Hovercrafts R Us, Inc.

Hovercrafts R' Us Inc. (HRU) manufactures and sells Hovercrafts for both recreational and military use. The F-491 Tomahawk Hovercraft is one of its best-selling products. HRU works with 6 hovercraft dealers/representatives (including WHCC) that facilitate the sale of its hovercraft inventory. The dealers do not take title of the hovercrafts they sell for HRU.

Rocky Mountain Hovercraft Tours (RMHT) is one of the largest hovercraft tour operators in Arizona and Alaska. RMHT has purchased all its current Hovercraft fleet from HRU. The North American Hovercraft Tour Association (NAHTA) requires that all hover crafts used for public tours be replaced after 250,000 miles. RMHT believes that five of the hovercrafts in its fleet will reach 250,000 miles within three to six months.

On June 26, 20XX, RMHT signed a contract to purchase five new F-491 Hovercrafts for $1 million per hovercraft . RMHT received a 20% price discount that HRU only offered in the month of June. RMHT's purchase price included the cost of storage at WHCC with an estimated delivery date of October 1, 20XX. HRU is fully responsible for any damage to the hovercrafts while in storage at WHCC.

On June 27, 20XX, RMHT paid for and obtained the title to all 5 hovercrafts and HRU shipped the Hovercrafts to WHCC to store,

RMHT expedited the purchase of the hovercrafts to take advantage of the 20% discount on the price of each hovercraft. RMHT had no space to store the new hovercrafts at the time of the purchase. Per the contract, HRU will ship a hovercraft to RMHT's when RMHT's existing hovercraft reaches the 250,000 miles and is taken out of service. HRU will pay WHCC a market rate of $50,000 to store the hovercrafts for three to six months.

Determine the promises that HRU made to RMHT.

Determine HRU's separate performance obligations and support your answer.

Determine the revenue amount for each separate performance obligation.

State when HRU should report revenue for each performance obligation.

Exercise 21: Revenue Journal Entries

1. On June 1, CY Albia, Inc. signed a contract to provide a server (typical sales price of $13,000) and a three-year service contract (typical sales price of $5,000) to Amazon for a total price of $15,000. Amazon paid Albia, Inc. $15,000 on June 1, CY. The server was delivered on July 1, CY The three-year service contract began on July 1, CY.

A. Allocate the transaction price between the server and the service contract.

B. Record the revenue journal entries for Albia, Inc. for the CY.

2. TCU sold you 4 season football tickets for $2,400. The TCU football team will play 6 home games. You paid TCU the full price on May 6th, CY. TCU played 2 home games in September, 3 home games in October, and 1 home game in November. Record all revenue related entries for TCU for the CY.

May 6,

September: 2 Games

October: 3 Games

November: 1 Game

3. Agent or Principle

Amazon agreed to provide online marketing for NIKE, Inc. for a specific pair of shoes in return for 5% of the retail price of shoes sold. Shoes that cost NIKE $160,000 sold for a total price of $210,000.

A. Record the entry to record the revenue for Amazon given the goods are stored in NIKE's warehouse and **Amazon passes the orders on to NIKE to fill and ship.**

B. Record the revenue for Amazon given NIKE's goods **are stored in Amazon's warehouse on consignment and Amazon ships the order for NIKE** for an additional 2% of the total sales price.

C. Record the entry to record Amazon's sales for $210,000 given **Amazon first purchases the shoes (takes control) from NIKE** at a cost of $175,000 prior to shipment. NIKE ships the goods directly from NIKE's warehouse to the customer. NIKE charges Amazon a shipping fee of 2% of sales.

4. On February 1, CY, FitBit, Inc. signed an agreement with JP Morgan for a line of credit. JP Morgan agreed to make $500 million available to FitBit, Inc. for one year beginning on February 1, CY. FitBit, Inc. paid JP Morgan a fee of 0.1% of the total amount available on February 1, CY. Additionally, FitBit, Inc. agreed to pay JP Morgan an administrative fee of $2,000 on the first of each month beginning February 1, CY.

1st Step: Identify the performance obligations and the related price.

Performance Obligation	Price	Payment	Monthly Rev
Make funds available	$500M x 0.1% = $500,000 for the year	Feb 1, CY	$41,667 Starts 2/1/CY
Administrative Services	$2,000 each month	1st of each Month	$2,000

A. Record the revenue entries for JP Morgan on February 1, CY.

B. Record the revenue entries for the month of June, CY.

Exercise 22: Revenue Footnotes

Goldman Sachs

Revenue from Contracts with Clients. The firm recognizes revenue earned from contracts with clients for services, such as investment banking, investment management, and execution and clearing (contracts with clients), when the performance obligations related to the underlying transaction are completed.

Investment Banking Advisory. Fees from financial advisory assignments are recognized in revenues when the services related to the underlying transaction are completed under the terms of the assignment. Non-refundable deposits and milestone payments in connection with financial advisory assignments are recognized in revenues upon completion of the underlying transaction or when the assignment is otherwise concluded.

Underwriting. Fees from underwriting assignments are recognized in revenues upon completion of the underlying transaction based on the terms of the assignment. Expenses associated with underwriting assignments are generally deferred until the related revenue is recognized or the assignment is otherwise concluded. Such expenses are included in transaction-based expenses for completed assignments.

Incentive Fees. Incentive fees are calculated as a percentage of a fund's or separately managed account's return, or excess return above a specified benchmark or other performance target. Incentive fees are generally based on investment performance over a twelve-month period or over the life of a fund. Fees that are based on performance over a twelve-month period are subject to adjustment prior to the end of the measurement period. For fees that are based on investment performance over the life of the fund, future investment underperformance may require fees previously distributed to the firm to be returned to the fund. Incentive fees earned from a fund or separately managed account are recognized when it is probable that a significant reversal of such fees will not occur, which is generally when such fees are no longer subject to fluctuations in the market value of investments held by the fund or separately managed account. Therefore, incentive fees recognized during the period may relate to performance obligations satisfied in previous periods

Zoom Video Communications, Inc.

Revenue Recognition

We derive our revenue primarily from subscription agreements with customers for access to our unified communications platform and services. We also provide other services, which include professional services, consulting services, and online event hosting, which were immaterial to our consolidated financial statements. Revenue is recognized when a customer obtains control of promised services. The amount of revenue recognized reflects the consideration that we expect to receive in exchange for these services. We determine revenue recognition through the following steps:

Identification of the contract, or contracts, with the customer
We determine a contract with a customer to exist when the contract is approved, each party's rights regarding the services to be transferred can be identified, the payment terms for the services can be identified, the customer has the ability and intent to pay, and the contract has commercial substance.

Identification of the performance obligations in the contract
Performance obligations committed in a contract are identified based on the services that will be transferred to the customer that are both capable of being distinct, whereby the customer can benefit from the service either on its own or together with other resources that are readily available from third parties or from us, and are distinct in the context of the contract … Our performance obligations primarily relate to access to our unified communications platform, which consists of one or more software-based services. Our customers do not have the ability to take possession of our software, and through access to our platform, we provide a series of distinct software-based services that are satisfied over the term of the subscription.

Determination of the transaction price
The transaction price is determined based on the consideration to which we expect to be entitled in exchange for transferring services to the customer. Variable consideration is included in the transaction price if, in our judgment, it is probable that a significant future reversal of cumulative revenue recognized under the contract will not occur. …

Allocation of the transaction price to the performance obligations in the contract
Contracts that contain multiple performance obligations require an allocation of the transaction price to each performance obligation based on each performance obligation's relative standalone selling price. …

Recognition of the revenue when, or as, a performance obligation is satisfied
Revenue is recognized at the time the related performance obligation is satisfied by transferring the control of the promised service to a customer. Revenue is recognized in an amount that reflects the consideration that we expect to receive in exchange for those services. Fees for access to our unified communications platform and related services are subscription revenue and are considered one performance obligation, and the related revenue is recognized ratably over the subscription period as we satisfy the performance obligation. Professional services are time-based arrangements and revenue is recognized as these services are performed. Fees for services represent less than 2% of total revenue during the periods presented.

Amazon

Revenue is measured based on the amount of consideration that we expect to receive, reduced by estimates for return allowances, promotional discounts, and rebates. Revenue also excludes any amounts collected on behalf of third parties, including sales and indirect taxes. In arrangements where we have multiple performance obligations, the transaction price is allocated to each performance obligation using the relative stand-alone selling price. We generally determine stand-alone selling prices based on the prices charged to customers or using expected cost plus a margin.

A description of our principal revenue generating activities is as follows:

Retail sales - We offer consumer products through our online and physical stores. Revenue is recognized when control of the goods is transferred to the customer, which generally occurs upon our delivery to a third-party carrier or, in the case of an Amazon delivery, to the customer.

Third-party seller services - We offer programs that enable sellers to sell their products in our stores and fulfill orders through us. We are not the seller of record in these transactions. The commissions and any related fulfillment and shipping fees we earn from these arrangements are recognized when the services are rendered, which generally occurs upon delivery of the related products to a third-party carrier or, in the case of an Amazon delivery, to the customer.

Subscription services - Our subscription sales include fees associated with Amazon Prime memberships and access to content including digital video, audiobooks, digital music, e-books, and other non-AWS subscription services. Prime memberships provide our customers with access to an evolving suite of benefits that represent a single stand-ready obligation. Subscriptions are paid for at the time of or in advance of delivering the services. Revenue from such arrangements is recognized over the subscription period.

Advertising services - We provide advertising services to sellers, vendors, publishers, authors, and others, through programs such as sponsored ads, display, and video advertising. Revenue is recognized as ads are delivered based on the number of clicks or impressions.

AWS - Our AWS arrangements include global sales of compute, storage, database, and other services. Revenue is allocated to services using stand-alone selling prices and is primarily recognized when the customer uses these services, based on the quantity of services rendered, such as compute or storage capacity delivered on-demand. Certain services, including compute and database, are also offered as a fixed quantity over a specified term, for which revenue is recognized ratably. Sales commissions we pay in connection with contracts that exceed one year are capitalized and amortized over the contract term.

Unearned Revenue Unearned revenue is recorded when payments are received or due in advance of performing our service obligations and is recognized over the service period. Unearned revenue primarily relates to prepayments of AWS services and Amazon Prime memberships. Our total unearned revenue as of December 31, 20X0 was $xx.x billion, of which $x.x billion was recognized as revenue during the year ended December 31, 20X0 and our total unearned revenue as of December 31, 20X1 was $xx.x billion. Included in "Other long-term liabilities" on our consolidated balance sheets was $x.x billion and $x.x billion of unearned revenue as of December 31, 20X0 and 20X1.

In Class Exercise 23: Reporting Product Warranties

Samsung sells "Galaxy Earbuds" that cost them $110 for $250 each. Samsung provides a 3 month warranty that gives an immediate replacement the earbuds malfunction. Samsung also sells a separate 2-year extended warranty that covers unlimited repairs for $39. Samsung expects their cost of a quality warranty to be 4% of sales and their cost of the extended warranty to be $25 per warranty.

Samsung had sales of 100 and 120 earbuds in January and February, respectively.
Samsung paid quality warranty claims of $250 and $500 in January and February, respectively.
Samsung had sales of 20 and 22 extended warranties in January and February, respectively.
Samsung paid extended warranty claims of $12 and $18 in January and February, respectively.
Customers paid Samsung $8,000 and $26,000 in January and February, respectively.

Record the activity for sales of earbuds and quality warranty activity for January.

Sales of Earbuds ***Warranty Sales*** ***Cash Collections***

Estimated Warranty Expense ***Warranty Claims Paid***

Record the activity for sales of earbuds and quality warranty activity for February.

Sales of Earbuds ***Warranty Sales*** ***Cash Collections***

Estimated Warranty Expense ***Warranty Claims Paid***

Record the activity for extended warranty activity for January.

Sales of Warranty ***Revenue Earned***

Estimated Warranty Expense ***Warranty Claims Paid***

Record the activity for extended warranty activity for February.

Sales of Warranty ***Revenue Earned***

Estimated Warranty Expense ***Warranty Claims Paid***

Balance Sheet Liability T accounts:

Warranty Liability - Quality	

Warranty Liability - Extended	

Reported on February Balance Sheet? **Report on February Income Statement?**

Exercise 24: Estimating & Reporting BD Expense Example

XYZ Company began the current year with $530,000 in accounts receivable and had credit sales of $5,690,000 during the current year. The company began the current year with a credit balance of $56,000 in the allowance for uncollectible accounts. During the year, XYZ wrote off $17,000 of uncollectible accounts. Based on past history, the company estimates that customers will not pay 0.2% of sales and 4.1% of total accounts receivable.

XYZ Company reported the following accounts receivable aging as of the end of the current year:

	Amount	Estimated Uncollectible	
Current	$450,000	1 %	$ 4,500
Under 30 days past due	75,000	3 %	$ 2,250
31 to 60 days past due	16,000	10 %	$ 1,600
More than 60 days past due	39,000	60 %	$23,400
Total	$580,000		$31,750

The accountant at XYZ Company will record the following during the year:

A. Record credit sales for the current year.

Account	Debit	Credit
Accounts Receivable	$5,690,000	
Sales		$5,690,000

B. Record collections from customers for the current year.

Account	Debit	Credit
Cash	$5,623,000	
Accounts Receivable		$5,623,000

Accounts Receivable	
530,000	
5,690,000	17,000
	5,623,000
580,000	

C. Record the write-off during the current year.

Account	Debit	Credit
Allowance for Uncoll. Accts.	$17,000	
Accounts Receivable		$17,000

D. Record the entry (in total) that XYZ Company will record bad debt expense during each month using <u>only the percent of sales method</u>. The entry is made at the end of each month based on monthly sales. However, the example does not provide monthly sales and therefore, one entry is made for the total sales for the year.

Sales	$5,690,000
x Historical %	0.2%
= Bad Debt Expense	$ 11,380

Bad Debt Expense	$11,380	
Allowance for Uncoll. Accts.		$11,380

E. Estimate and record bad debt expense only at the end of the year using <u>only the percent of accounts receivable (aging) method</u>.

Allow for Uncoll. Accts.	$7,250	
Bad Debt Expense		$7,250

Allowance for U. Accts

Debit	Credit
	56,000
17,000	
Unadj. Bal.	39,000
7,250	
	31,750

F. Now, assume the Company uses the percent of sales method at the end of each month during the year and uses the percent of accounts receivable aging method at the end of the year to determine the estimated uncollectible amount (by far the most common approach).

Record the entry to adjust bad debt expense at the end of the year.

Allow for Uncoll. Acct.	$18,630	
Bad Debt Expense		$18,630

Allowance for U. Accts

Debit	Credit
	56,000
17,000	11,380
Unadj. Bal.	50,380
18,630	
	31,750

G. Determine the lines items and amount the company will report on the balance sheet and income statement for using 1) only % sales, 2) only % total A/R, or 3) both % sales and % A/R aging.

Balance Sheet:	***% Sales***	***% A/R Aging***	***% Sales + Aging***
Accounts Receivable	$580,000	$580,000	$580,000
-Allowance for Uncoll. Accts.	($ 50,380)	($ 31,750)	($31,750)
Accounts Receivable, Net	$529,620	$548,250	$548,250

Income Statement: Bad Debt Expense

% Sales	***% Total A/R***	***Both % Sales & % A/R aging***
$11,380	($7,250)	$11,380
		($18,630)
	Overestimated in Prior Year Take Exp Back	$ (7,250)

Exercise 25: Accounts Receivable 1

XYZ Company began the current year with $2,800,000 in accounts receivable and had credit sales of $18,100,000 during the current year. Customers paid the company $17,994,000 during the current year. The company began the current year with a credit balance of $115,000 in the allowance for uncollectible accounts. The company estimates that customers will not pay 0.4% of sales.

XYZ Company reported the following accounts receivable aging as of the end of the current year:

	Amount	Estimated Uncollectible
Current	$1,950,000	0.4%
Under 30 days past due	425,000	1 %
31 to 60 days past due	210,000	6 %
More than 60 days past due	182,000	10 %

The accountant at XYZ Company will record the following during the year:

A. Record credit sales for the current year.

B. Record collections from customers for the current year.

C. Record the write-off during the current year.

D. Record the entry (in total) that XYZ Company will record bad debt expense during each month using only the percent of sales method. The entry is made at the end of each month based on monthly sales. However, the example does not provide monthly sales and therefore, one entry is made for the total sales for the year.

E. Estimate and record bad debt expense only at the end of the year using only the percent of accounts receivable (aging) method.

F. Now, assume the Company uses the percent of sales method at the end of each month during the year and uses the percent of accounts receivable aging method at the end of the year to determine the estimated uncollectible amount (by far the most common approach).

Record the entry to adjust bad debt expense at the end of the year.

G. Given F., Determine the amount the company will report for bad debt expense on the income statement

Exercise 26: AR Bad Debt Expense 2

XYZ Company began the current year with $325,000 in accounts receivable and had credit sales of $3,190,000 during the current year. The company began the current year with a credit balance of $36,000 in the allowance for uncollectible accounts. During the year, XYZ wrote off $12,000 of uncollectible accounts. Based on past history, the company estimates that customers will not pay 1% of sales.

XYZ Company reported the following accounts receivable aging as of the end of the current year:

	Amount	Estimated Uncollectible
Current	$250,000	1 %
Under 30 days past due	25,000	3 %
31 to 60 days past due	10,000	10 %
More than 60 days past due	34,000	30 %
Total	$319,000	

The accountant at XYZ Company will record the following during the year:

A. Record credit sales for the current year.

B. Record collections from customers for the current year.

C. Record the write-off during the current year.

D. Record the entry (in total) that XYZ Company will record bad debt expense during each month using <u>only the percent of sales method</u>. The entry is made at the end of each month based on monthly sales. However, the example does not provide monthly sales and therefore, one entry is made for the total sales for the year.

E. Estimate and record bad debt expense only at the end of the year using <u>only the percent of accounts receivable (aging) method</u>.

F. Now, assume the Company uses the percent of sales method at the end of each month during the year and uses the percent of accounts receivable aging method at the end of the year to determine the estimated uncollectible amount (by far the most common approach). Record the entry to adjust bad debt expense at the end of the year.

G. Determine the lines items and amounts the company will report on the balance sheet and income statement for using 1) only % sales, 2) only % total A/R, or 3) both % sales and % A/R aging.

Exercise 27. Monster Beverage extends 30 day terms with no discount offered to customers. The company's aging report of accounts receivables showed the following on December 31st for the company's largest customers and all other customers. (Not real numbers; however, represents what the company may experience).

Customer Total Owed	Current	Past Due 0-30 Days	Past Due 31-60 days	Past Due 61-90 days	Past Due 90+ days	Past Due 1 Year +
Cadbury Swepps Bottling						
13,039,521	5,833,672	5,829,562	632,943	181,248	520,080	42,016
Walmart						
10,220,560	4,547,984	3,936,394	563,976	132,076	824,074	216,056
CostCo						
4,583,056	2,240,985	2,135,066	133,656	18,035	28,902	26,412
Kalil Bottling Group						
4,137,012	2,467,209	1,562,675	102,356	2,462	2,310	0
Pepsi Canada						
2,837,012	1,189,312	1,537,067	42,965	3,462	0	64,206
Safeway						
1,136,934	693,045	239,453	142,643	24,045	37,748	0
Kroger						
856,239	459,241	342,056	22,783	20,114	12,045	0
Albertsons						
709,521	222,573	199,452	227,652	21,357	32,045	6,442
Florida Distributors						
567,368	0	0	0	0	0	567,368
Swire Coca Cola						
551,120	368,186	63,670	0	0	0	119,264
Other Customers						
72,396,657	55,984,179	14,213,495	788,595	351,528	242,532	816,328
Total						
111,035,000	74,006,386	30,058,890	2,657,569	754,327	1,699,736	1,858,092

Customers pay Monster Beverage after a document proving receipt has been matched to the invoice received from Monster Beverage. Amounts on the aging report consist of thousands of individual shipments and invoices to customers. "Other Customers" consists of approximately 1,750 customers. **Determine the most appropriate value of uncollectible accounts receivable as of Dec 31st.**

Exercise 28: Sales Returns

During February 20Y1 (1st month of business), Drive, Inc. sold a new model of motorized chairs for the mobility challenged. Total sales in February and March were $250,000 and $320,000 (cost of $100,000 and 128,000), respectively. Returned inventory is restocked and sold again. Customers pay on credit card at the time of purchase and the company records a refund liability for returns. Bad debt expense is typically 1 % of sales. Customers paid $55,000 and $406,000 on account in February and March, respectively. Drive's past experience indicates that 6% of new model motorized chairs will be returned due to some customers find it difficult to operate. Customers actually returned $12,000 and $16,000 (sales price) in February and March, respectively.

Record the entries related to the sales of motorized chairs in February 20Y1.

Sales

Returns

Cash collections

Claims

B/D Expense

Record the entries related to the sales of motorized chairs in March 20Y1.

Sales

Returns

Cash collections

Claims

B/D Expense

What will Drive, Inc. report on the balance sheet and income statement for March 20Y1 related to the new motorized chair.

Balance Sheet

Income Statement

Accounts Receivable	Allow for U. A	Allowance for S. Returns

Exercise 29: Factoring Accounts Receivable

Salley Trucking Company has $400,000 of accounts receivable and they need cash within the next 3 days of the end of March.

A. What will be reported on Salley's balance sheet and income statement if Salley gets a $300,000 (8% annual interest) collateralized loan against the accounts receivable with an estimated uncollectible of 3%

Balance Sheet		**Income Statement**	
Accounts Receivable	$400,000	Bad Debt Expense	$12,000
-Allowance for U. A	($12,000)		
Accounts Receivable, net	$388,000	Interest Expense	$2,000
		(300,000 x 8% = 24,000 / 12 mo)	
Notes Payable	$300,000		

B. What will be reported on Salley's balance sheet and income statement if Salley factors $400,000 **without recourse** at a fee of 5% and estimated bad debt expense of 4%.

Balance Sheet		**Income Statement**	
Accounts Receivable	$0	Loss on Sale of A/R	$36,000 (9% total)
Cash	$364,000		

C. What will be reported on Salley's balance sheet and income statement if Salley factors $400,000 with recourse at a fee of 5% and estimated uncollectible accounts of 3%.

Balance Sheet		**Income Statement**	
Accounts Receivable	$0	Loss on Sale of A/R	$32,000 (8% total)
Cash	$380,000		
Factoring Liaility	$12,000		

Exercise 30: Periodic Inventory Methods

Hansen Natural purchases it products from contract manufacturers in units of 24 cans or bottles of product. The company sold 3,700 units during May. The company uses the **periodic method** of accounting for inventory. Inventory on hand on May 1st and the cost to purchase a unit follows for each week during the month of May follows:

	Quantity in thousands of units	Cost per unit of 24	Total Cost (in thousands)
Beginning Inventory	3,100	$10.65	$33,015
Week 1	900	$11.45	$10,305
Week 2	700	$11.64	$ 8,148
Week 3	1,500	$12.21	$18,315
Week 4	1,800	$12.79	$23,022

Calculate the value of ending inventory and cost of goods sold to be reported on the financial statements using the following methods.

FIFO:

LIFO:

Average:

Prepare the income statement for Hansen Natural given the various methods of inventory for the month of May (in thousands). The company sold 3,700 units at a sales price of $20 per unit.

	FIFO	LIFO	Average
Sales	74,000	74,000	74,000
Cost of Goods Sold	_______	_______	_______
Gross Profit	_______	_______	_______
Operating Expense	(32,000) _______	(32,000) _______	(32,000) _______
Income From Operations	_______	_______	_______

Compute the total amount of assets for each method given the following information:

	FIFO	LIFO	Average
Assets not including Inventory:	430,000	430,000	430,000
Add Inventory	_______	_______	_______
Total assets to be reported on the Balance Sheet	_______	_______	_______

In Class Exercise 31:
Record Inventory – Perpetual and Periodic Method

1. ABC, Inc. began March with 100 items at a cost of $10 each. On March 5th, the company purchased 1,000 items for $10 each. On March 10th, 200 items of the March 5th purchase were returned. On March 18th, 250 items were sold to a customer at a price of $20 each. At the end of March, inventory was counted and it was determined that 629 units were in the warehouse. All sales and purchases are on account.

Make all required journal entries for the month of March using the **perpetual method** of accounting for inventory.

3/5

3/10

3/18

End of period adjustment

Total CGS reported on the income statement is: ____________________

2. ABC, Inc. began March with 100 items at a cost of $10 each. On March 5th, the company purchased 1,000 items for $10 each. On March 10th, 200 items of the March 5th purchase were returned. On March 18th, 250 items were sold to a customer at a price of $20 each. At the end of March, inventory was counted and it was determined that 629 units were in the warehouse. All sales and purchases are on account.

Make all required journal entries for the month of March using the **periodic method** of accounting for inventory.

3/5

3/10

3/18

End of period adjustment

Total CGS reported on the income statement is: ____________________

Exercise 32: Periodic and Perpetual Value Inventory

The Company had the following transactions during the first quarter of the current year:

		Units	Cost-per-unit
January 1	Beginning Balance	700	$6.00
January 15	Purchased	500	$6.50
February 5	Purchased	400	$7.00
March 15	Purchased	400	$7.50
January 29	Sold	400	
February 2	Sold	400	
March 19	Sold	600	

Units are sold for $15 each. Compute the reported cost of goods sold and ending inventory for the quarter ended March 31st using

1. Periodic:

A. FIFO
B. LIFO
C. Average cost (round to dollars and cents)

2. Perpetual:

A. FIFO
B. LIFO
C. Average cost

1st: Establish the order of purchase and the total dollars available:

1. Periodic:

A. FIFO

CGS: ____________________

Inventory: ________________

1. Periodic:

B. LIFO

CGS: ____________________

Inventory: ________________

1. Periodic:

C. Average cost (round to dollars and cents)

CGS: ____________________

Inventory: ________________

2. Perpetual:

A. FIFO

CGS: ____________________

Inventory: ________________

2. Perpetual:

B. LIFO

CGS: ______________________

Inventory: __________________

2. Perpetual:

C. Moving Average (round to dollars and cents)

CGS: ______________________

Inventory: __________________

Exercise 33: Which Inventory Method?

As of December 31, 20Y1: Inventory Report

	Item #	Item Description	Quantity	Cost for 1	Total Cost
1	126	Natural Hair Oil			
	9-Jan		250	$12.65	$3,162.50
	8-Feb		150	$13.25	$1,987.50
	17-Mar		120	$13.10	$1,572.00
	30-Apr		375	$13.29	$4,983.75
	31-May		450	$13.74	$6,183.00
	30-Jun		240	$13.89	$3,333.60
	31-Jul		285	$13.96	$3,978.60
	31-Aug		330	$14.25	$4,702.50
	30-Sep		225	$13.64	$3,069.00
	31-Oct		180	$13.12	$2,361.60
	30-Nov		225	$13.52	$3,042.00
	Dec	Online Sales			
	5-Dec	WK ended	150	$17.50	$2,625.00
	12-Dec	WK ended	75	$17.79	$1,334.25
	19-Dec	WK ended	80	$17.25	$1,380.00
	31-Dec	12/20-12/31	125	$17.10	$2,137.50
			3260		$45,852.80

	Item #	Item Description	Quantity	Cost for 1	Total Cost
2	410	Hair Conditioner			
	9-Jan		200	$8.74	$1,748.00
	8-Feb		150	$8.54	$1,281.00
	17-Mar		150	$8.10	$1,215.00
	30-Apr		300	$8.25	$2,475.00
	31-May		275	$8.36	$2,299.00
	30-Jun		300	$8.19	$2,457.00
	31-Jul		350	$7.95	$2,782.50
	31-Aug		350	$8.12	$2,842.00
	30-Sep		325	$7.78	$2,528.50
	31-Oct		325	$8.52	$2,769.00
	30-Nov		285	$8.55	$2,436.75
	Dec	Online Sales			
	5-Dec	Wk	100	$10.25	$1,025.00
	12-Dec	Wk	80	$10.32	$825.60
	19-Dec	Wk	75	$10.49	$786.75
	31-Dec	Wk	75	$10.10	$757.50
			3,340		$28,228.60

			Quantity	Cost for 1	Total Cost
3	196	Rose Anti-wrinkle Cream			
	9-Jan		80	$22.75	$1,820.00
	8-Feb		75	$22.50	$1,687.50
	17-Mar		150	$22.64	$3,396.00
	30-Apr		125	$22.32	$2,790.00
	31-May		125	$22.68	$2,835.00
	30-Jun		125	$21.94	$2,742.50
	31-Jul		125	$21.84	$2,730.00
	31-Aug		150	$21.67	$3,250.50
	30-Sep		175	$22.01	$3,851.75
	31-Oct		175	$22.08	$3,864.00
	30-Nov		150	$21.84	$3,276.00
	Dec	Online Sales			
	5-Dec	Wk	100	$24.60	$2,460.00
	12-Dec	Wk	75	$24.90	$1,867.50
	19-Dec	Wk	40	$24.40	$976.00
	31-Dec	Wk	50	$24.96	$1,248.00
			1,720		$38,794.75

			Quantity	Cost for 1	Total Cost
4	221	Acai Orchard	Moisturizer		
	9-Jan		175	$16.79	$2,938.25
	8-Feb		150	$16.95	$2,542.50
	17-Mar		125	$17.10	$2,137.50
	30-Apr		100	$17.35	$1,735.00
	31-May		180	$17.32	$3,117.60
	30-Jun		180	$17.42	$3,135.60
	31-Jul		180	$17.59	$3,166.20
	31-Aug		180	$17.10	$3,078.00
	30-Sep		225	$16.78	$3,775.50
	31-Oct		225	$16.89	$3,800.25
	30-Nov		250	$16.64	$4,160.00
	Dec	Online Sales			
	5-Dec	Wk	200	$19.50	$3,900.00
	12-Dec	Wk	150	$19.82	$2,973.00
	19-Dec	Wk	50	$20.10	$1,005.00
	31-Dec	Wk	85	$19.65	$1,670.25
			2,455		$43,134.65

			Quantity	Cost for 1	Total Cost
5	81	Tooth Paste			
	9-Jan		300	$3.25	$975.00
	8-Feb		300	$3.34	$1,002.00
	17-Mar		300	$3.49	$1,047.00
	30-Apr		300	$3.55	$1,065.00
	31-May		325	$3.46	$1,124.50
	30-Jun		330	$3.12	$1,029.60
	31-Jul		350	$3.23	$1,130.50
	31-Aug		350	$3.45	$1,207.50
	30-Sep		350	$3.50	$1,225.00
	31-Oct		350	$3.60	$1,260.00
	30-Nov		400	$3.37	$1,348.00
	Dec	Online Sales			
	5-Dec	Wk	200	$5.29	$1,058.00
	12-Dec	Wk	100	$5.51	$ 551.00
	19-Dec	Wk	75	$5.42	$ 406.50
	31-Dec	Wk	75	$5.34	$ 400.50
			4,105		$14,830.10

Total Available	$170,840.90
Total Ending Inventory	$12,733.43
Total Cost of Goods Sold	$158,107.47

Which method should the company use to:

A) Minize Income Taxes

B) Reduce Cash Paid for Inventory?

C) Maximize Net Income

D) Best match Revenues to Costs

Exercise 34: LCM and LCNRV

1. Information related inventory held at Jizzie's Inc. is provided below.

Product	Qty	Selling Price	Cost	Cost to Sell	Normal Gross Profit
A	400	150	200	30	(50)
B	250	680	490	68	190
C	60	720	510	72	210
D	325	200	260	48	(60)

Replacement cost is currently 10% higher than the purchase cost.

A. Determine the value of inventory reported on the balance sheet using **Lower of Cost or Net Realizable Value** by individual product. Record any necessary adjustment to inventory.

A. LCNRV by individual product

Product	Selling Price	Cost to Sell	NRV	Cost	LCNRV
A	150	30	120	200	120
B	680	68	612	490	490
C	720	72	648	510	510
D	200	48	152	260	152
				1460	1272

	Cost	Qty	Total Cost	LNCRV	Qty	Total LCNRV
A	$200	400	$ 80,000	$ 120	400	$ 48,000
B	$490	250	$ 122,500	$ 490	250	$ 122,500
C	$510	60	$ 30,600	$ 510	60	$ 30,600
D	$260	325	$ 84,500	$ 152	325	$ 49,400
			$ 317,600			**$ 250,500**

Difference: LCM is lower $ 67,100

	Debit	Credit
CGS	$67,100	
Inventory		$67,100

B. Determine the value inventory will be reported on the balance sheet using **Lower of Cost or Market** by individual product. Record any necessary adjustment to inventory.

B. LCM by individual product

Replace Cost	NRV	NRV - GP	Market	Cost	LCM
220	120	170	170	200	170
539	612	422	539	490	490
561	648	438	561	510	510
286	152	212	212	260	212
				1460	1382

	Cost	Qty	Total Cost	LCM	Qty	Total LCM
A	$200	400	$ 80,000	$ 170	400	$ 68,000
B	$490	250	$ 122,500	$ 490	250	$ 122,500
C	$510	60	$ 30,600	$ 510	60	$ 30,600
	$260	325	$ 84,500	$ 212	325	$ 68,900
			$ 317,600			**$ 290,000**

Difference: LCM is lower $ 27,600

	Debit	Credit
CGS	$27,600	
Inventory		$27,600

2. After performing LCM, the sales manager notified the CFO that the sale price for Product B was dropping to $450. Do the analysis and make the entry to adjust for the new information.

Prior Price	$680
Revised Price	$450
Value Drop	$230
X Quantity	250 units
Total Value Drop	$57,500

	Debit	Credit
CGS	$57,500	
Inventory		$57,500

Exercise 35: Change Estimate

On January 1, 20Y1, Peanuts, Inc. purchased equipment for $130,000 that was expected to be used for 6 years and then be sold for $13,000. At the beginning of 20Y3, the company incurred costs of $28,000 for improvements to extend the useful life to a total of 10 years. Residual value at the end of use was revised to be $15,000 after the improvements. On May 31, 20Y4, the company sold the equipment for $49,000. The company incurred costs for maintenance and repairs of $3,500 each year the machine was used.

Prepare required journal entries for all years the equipment is used given the company used the straight-line method.

Exercise 36: Statement of Cash Flows 1

A company had the following information available:

	Current Year	Prior Year
Cash	22	16
Accounts Receivable	200	250
Inventory	125	95
Prepaid Expenses	18	10
Plant Assets	1,019	1,000
Accumulated depreciation	527	587
Accounts Payable	75	50
Interest Payable	10	8
Income Tax Payable	90	107
Bonds Payable	117	77
Common Stock	338	300
Retained Earnings	227	242

	Current Year
Sales	1,300
CGS	880
Depreciation Exp	70
S,G,A Exp	240
Interest Exp	15
Income Tax Exp	35
Net Income	60

Plant assets were sold for cash for their book value of $200 during the year. The assets had an original cost of $330.

Prepare an indirect cash flow statement for the current year.

Exercise 37: Cash Flow Statement 2

	20Y1	20Y0
Cash	$ 47,000	$ 28,000
Accounts receivable	$ 67,000	$ 74,000
Inventory	$ 52,000	$ 68,000
Prepaid Insurance	$ 2,500	$ 11,000
Supplies	$ 800	$ 950
Long-term Investments	$ 50,000	$ 75,000
Property & Equipment	$ 148,000	$ 109,000
Accumulated Depreciation	$ (47,300)	$ (36,200)
Patents	$ 16,000	$ 14,600
Accumulated Amortization	$ (2,400)	$ (1,600)
Total Assets	$ 333,600	$ 342,750
Accounts Payable	$ 25,400	$ 28,600
Accrued Expenses	$ 14,200	$ 12,800
Line of Credit	$ 50,000	$ 40,000
Income Taxes Payable	$ 23,950	$ 21,750
Long-term Debt	$ 90,000	$ 135,000
Total Liabilities	$ 203,550	$ 238,150
Common Stock	$ 1,000	$ 500
Paid in Capital	$ 143,000	$ 99,500
Treasury Stock	$ (40,000)	$ (25,000)
Retained Earnings	$ 26,050	$ 29,600
Total Stockholders Equity	$ 130,050	$ 104,600
Total Liabilities & S/E	$ 333,600	$ 342,750

	20Y1
Sales	$ 582,000
Cost of Goods Sold	$ (384,000)
Gross Profit	$ 198,000
Depreciation Expense	$ 16,800
Amortization Expense	$ 800
Salary Expense	$ 98,000
Other Operating Expense	$ 28,900
Insurance Expense	$ 18,000
Operating Income	$ 35,500
Gains / Losses, Net	$ (19,400)
Interest Expense	$ (10,000)
Income Before Tax	$ 6,100
Tax Expense	$ (2,200)

During 20Y1, the company:

- paid cash to purchased equipment with a cost of $55,000.
- sold equipment and recorded a gain of $6,000.
- purchased investments for cash in the amount of $50,000.
- borrowed $125,000 under the line of credit
- made payments of $45,000 on long-term debt

Prepare the cash flow statement for 20Y1 using the Indirect Method

<u>Journal Entries for Additional Information:</u>

Long term Investments	
75,000	
50,000	

Property Plant Equipment	
109,000	
148,000	

Accum Depreciation	
	36,200
	47,300

Patents	
14,600	
16,000	

Accumulated Amortization	
	1,600
	2,400

Line of Credit	
	40,000
	50,000

Long-term Debt	
	135,000
	90,000

Common Stock	
	500
	1,000

Paid In Capital	
	99,500
	143,000

Treasury Stock	
25,000	
40,000	

Retained Earnings	
	29,600
	26,050

Indirect Cash Flow Statement:

Net Income

Changes in Current Assets & Current Liabilities:

Cash from Operating Activities

Cash from Investing Activities

Cash from Financing Activities

Total Change in Cash

Exercise 38: Cash Flow Statement 3

	20Y1	20Y0	Difference
Cash	$ 176,400	$ 58,000	$ 118,400
Accounts receivable	$ 32,000	$ 26,600	$ (5,400)
Inventory	$ 21,000	$ 25,400	$ 4,400
Prepaid Insurance	$ 5,600	$ 4,000	$ (1,600)
Long-term Investments	$ 6,000	$ 16,800	
Property & Equipment	$ 80,000	$ 66,000	
Accumulated Depreciation	$ (19,000)	$ (18,000)	
Total Assets	$ 302,000	$ 178,800	
Accounts Payable	$ 7,000	$ 11,200	$ (4,200)
Interest Payable	$ 1,000	$ 2,000	$ (1,000)
Income Taxes Payable	$ 12,000	$ 8,000	$ 4,000
Long-term Notes Payable	$ 16,000	$ 24,000	
Total Liabilities	$ 36,000	$ 45,200	
Common Stock	$ 110,000	$ 100,000	
Paid in Capital	$ 32,000	$ 30,000	
Treasury Stock	$ (10,000)	$ (20,000)	
Retained Earnings	$ 134,000	$ 23,600	
Total Stockholders Equity	$ 266,000	$ 133,600	
Total Liabilities & S/E	$ 302,000	$ 178,800	

	20Y1
Sales	$ 704,000
Cost of Goods Sold	$ (368,000)
Gross Profit	$ 336,000
Operating Expenses	$ (185,000)
Operating Income	$ 151,000
Interest Expense	$ (800)
Gain on sale of LT Investment	$ 2,000
Loss on Sale Equipment	$ (1,000)
Income Before Tax	$ 151,200
Tax Expense	$ (37,600)
Net Income	$ 113,600

Additional Information for 20Y1:

- Purchased equipment with a cost of $75,000 and paid cash of $15,000 and financed the difference over 5 years.
- Sold Equipment for cash of $57,500
- Purchased Investments for $35,000 Cash

Long-term Investments	
$ 16,800	
$ 6,000	

Long-term Notes Payable	
	$ 24,000
	$ 16,000

Property & Equipment	
$ 66,000	
$ 80,000	

Common Stock & Capital	
	$ 130,000
	$ 142,000

Accumulated Depreciation	
	$ 18,000
	$ 19,000

Treasury Stock	
$ 20,000	
$ 10,000	

Retained Earnings	
	$ 23,600
	$ 134,000

Net Income

Changes in Current Assets & Current Liabilities:

Cash from Operating Activities

Cash from Investing Activities

Cash from Financing Activities

Total Change in Cash

Exercise 39: Tesla Cash Flows

As Tesla's car sales and share price plummet in response to Elon Musk's political and physical stances, we would like to draw readers' attention to something puzzling in the group's accounts. Compare Tesla's capital expenditure in the last six months of 2024 to its valuation of the assets that money was spent on, and $1.4bn appears to have gone astray.

The sum is big enough to matter even at Tesla, and comes at a moment when attention is returning to the group's underlying numbers, now that its fully diluted stock market valuation has crashed from $1.7tn to below $800bn.

A closer look at Tesla's cash flow statement may also prompt investors to ask other questions, such as why a business with a $37bn cash pile raised $6bn of new debt last year?

First, consider the apparent anomaly. Tesla is investing heavily, particularly in AI infrastructure. It intends to spend at least $11bn in each of the next few years, aiming to take advantage of opportunities in robots, computing and batteries. Looking at last year, in the third and fourth quarter combined, Tesla spent $6.3bn on "purchases of property and equipment excluding finance leases, net of sales" according to its cashflow statements. Over on the balance sheet, however, the gross value of property, plant and equipment rose by only $4.9bn in that period, to $51bn. Note seven to the financial statements has the breakdown:

We'd expect the numbers to tally. General Motors, for instance, spent $30bn on capex over the past three years, disposed of $14bn of assets, and so reported a $16bn rise in the gross value of property, plant & equipment to $88.7bn at the end of last year.

Luzi Hail, professor of accounting at the Wharton School, told us:
The reasons for why the reported numbers will not fully add up in most cases is that we only see the net changes in these accounts (i.e., PP&E and the associated Accumulated Depreciation accounts) but do not have all the detailed transactions that were going on. Maybe they sold off some PP&E and we do not know what the net book value (the respective gross amounts) were. Other things that will make an exact reconciliation impossible are M&A transactions and foreign currency transactions. So, in most cases, the capex number will give you a good approximation for the increase in gross PP&E but there could be other reasons going on for why in a particular case this might not be the case.

Tesla reports the gross figures and the accumulated depreciation, so we can see how the net figure is arrived at. It didn't disclose any sales or "material" asset impairments that would account for the missing $1.4bn, and we're sure auditors PWC would be alive to the important signal such declarations of mal-investment would send.

Foreign exchange seems unlikely to explain the gap either. Tesla makes cars in the US, China, and Germany, and while the euro did weaken against the dollar in the periods, four-fifths of Tesla's "long-lived assets" are in America. See note 17, for those reading along:

Tesla's gap is also unusual by its own standards. Here's a chart of capital expenditure on PP&E vs the change in gross value of those assets for every quarter since the start of 2019:

A positive number indicates that the balance sheet value of assets rose by more than capex. Aside from 2021, when there was a $1.3bn rise in the value of the assets, the variance has tended to even out and has not approached the scale of the last quarter.

Such anomalies can be red flags, potentially indicative of weak internal controls. Aggressive classification of operating expenses as investment can be used to artificially boost reported profits.

Tesla did not respond to requests for comment.

Perhaps the assets will show up next quarter. It's also possible the recent presidential endorsement will boost sales, and that some would-be buyers are waiting for an updated Model Y to hit showrooms. If not, the question of what Tesla is doing with its cash, and where the money is held, may become more pertinent.

Last year the group generated $15bn of operating cashflow. It invested $11bn into its businesses, and didn't pay a dividend or buy back shares with its large cash pile (putting Tesla in a very select club of large companies that do not, along with mysterious Temu owner PDD).

Yet Tesla also raised a net $3.9bn in new finance, on top of the $2.6bn raised in 2023.

A combination of excess cash flow and ongoing capital raising is another red flag that can signal accounting misstatements. Jacek Welc, professor of corporate finance at the SRH Berlin University of Applied Sciences, has examined 17 such examples including Germany's Wirecard, the US-listed but Chinese-based Longtop Financial Technologies, and the FTSE-listed hospital chain NMC Health.

He says in those cases "allegedly healthy (but in reality inflated) operating cash flows tend to be matched by significantly positive financing cash flows (and a seeming "cash cow" appears to require large amounts of new debt and/or new equity financing)."

Tesla may of course be opportunistically managing its balance sheet, given its plans for substantial further capital investment. The group sometimes has to manage short-term cash needs. Last year rising inventories soaked up $1.5bn in the first quarter. With thieves now targeting car parks holding spare vehicles and dealerships attracting protests, this year's figure could be significantly higher.

Tesla Cash Flows - March 25, 2025 1 Week later

Mea culpa. Having last week got rather excited by the minutiae of Tesla's accounting, it's time to row back on the apparent $1.4bn gap between capital investment and asset values.

The question of why a cash-rich company raised new debt in both of the last two years still stands, as does the trajectory of that cash balance if car sales continue to crater. But Tesla's balance-sheet mismatch may have a benign explanation. Lessons below, including kind words from one of the expert correspondents who got in touch to say that "reconciling accrual-based accounts with cash accounts (especially with the cash flow statement in its indirect form) is always difficult." Indeed.

At issue was the difference between Tesla's $6.3bn of capital investment in the second half of last year, and the smaller $4.9bn rise in the value of the gross assets it reported.

Two things help to reconcile the numbers: payments for assets already purchased, and the possible disposal of depreciated property. The first is found at the bottom of the cash flow statement, where Tesla notes a balance sheet detail:

1) Supplemental Non-Cash Investing and Financing Activities
2) Acquisitions of property and equipment included in liabilities

The line, explained in moderately simple terms here, represents the balance of property plant and equipment purchased on credit. During the six months in question, Tesla paid down $689mn of those liabilities, shrinking the apparent gap to $733mn.

Asset disposals reduce the gap by another $270mn, to $463mn. While Tesla didn't disclose any material asset sales or impairments, its capital investment figure is reported on a net basis. Comparing the depreciation expense with the change in accumulated depreciation indicates that assets depreciated by $270mn were disposed of.

The crack we're left with at Tesla is now small enough — just under half a billion dollars — to be filled with some combination of foreign exchange movements, non-material asset write-offs, or the sale of machinery or equipment close to its not-fully depreciated value.

Working capital movements are such an example. Last year, changes in "accounts payable, accrued and other liabilities" contributed $3.6bn to Tesla's operating cash flow.

The line suggests that even though Tesla sales shrank last year, it improved its cash position in part by taking longer to pay suppliers.

Like other large listed companies, the link to the balance sheet figures is not immediately apparent. The total for "accounts payable" plus "accrued liabilities and other" fell by $300mn, to $23.5bn, which might suggest a small cash outflow overall. There was also a $2bn rise in long-term other liabilities, which are mainly composed of lease liabilities and warranty commitments.

The likely explanation, our new accountant friends tell us, is in the allocation of flows to the operations, investing or financing parts of the cash flow statement, which would require insider knowledge or documentation to reconcile.

If Tesla, which does not often respond to media requests, does come back with comments we'll update this post.

In the meantime, those fascinated by accounting minutiae still have plenty to hold their interest, as Tesla invests heavily in AI infrastructure and has almost $7bn worth of assets under construction. Cash generation and debt issuance remain areas of interest.

US investors may be interested to learn that under international accounting standards, no-such sleuthing is required because a reconciliation of these factors is published. For instance, here's VW:

CHANGES IN PROPERTY, PLANT AND EQUIPMENT IN THE PERIOD JANUARY 1 TO DECEMBER 31, 2024

€ million	Land, land rights and buildings, including buildings on third-party land	Technical equipment and machinery	Other equipment, operating and office equipment	Payments on account and assets under construction	Total
Cost					
Balance at Jan. 1, 2024	**52,814**	**54,271**	**95,537**	**11,001**	**213,622**
Foreign exchange differences	267	183	292	129	872
Changes in consolidated Group	159	22	30	5	215
Additions	2,524	1,450	4,731	8,004	16,710
Transfers	1,068	2,006	2,561	-5,882	-247
Disposals	897	1,862	2,971	249	5,978
Balance at Dec. 31, 2024	**55,935**	**56,070**	**100,181**	**13,007**	**225,194**
Amortization and impairment					
Balance at Jan. 1, 2024	**24,627**	**42,857**	**79,243**	**15**	**146,742**
Foreign exchange differences	112	165	249	0	526
Changes in consolidated Group	35	12	12	-	59
Additions to cumulative amortization	2,439	3,027	5,437	-	10,903
Additions to cumulative impairment losses	139	132	62	92	424
Transfers	-23	11	17	-3	1
Disposals	643	1,798	2,447	-	4,887
Reversal of impairment losses	7	5	5	9	26
Balance at Dec. 31, 2024	**26,680**	**44,401**	**82,567**	**95**	**153,742**
Carrying amount at Dec. 31, 2024	**29,256**	**11,670**	**17,614**	**12,912**	**71,452**

Exercise 40: Prepare Financial Statements

ElectroDis, Inc. (EI) is a start up electronics distributor that just completed the first year of operations. The company issued 1,000 shares of stock to the 5 founders in exchange for $1,000,000 and borrowed $500,000 from Citibank to get the initial capital to fund the business.

EDI provided the following summary of the **Citibank operating cash** account:

Stock Issuance	1,000,000
Loan from Citibank	500,000
Payment for Warehouse Equipment	(160,000)
Transfer to Short-term Investment	(700,000)
Sales of Goods – cash collected	1,050,000
Payment for goods purchased	(850,000)
Payments to employees	(225,000)
Payments for rent	(132,,000)
Payments for utilities & phone	(39,000)
Payments for insurance	(24,000)
Payments for shipping to customers	(49,000)
Three quarters of tax payments	(30,000)
Total Cash on 12/31/20Y1	341,000

Additional information EI has not yet received or paid.

Customers owe EI $189,000 with payment terms of 45 days. EI has December bills that have not been paid that include: utility and phone for $4,200, inventory purchases of $108,000, shipping $9,000, and insurance coverage for 2026 for $26,000. The board of directors authorized a $50,000 total bonus for the EI management team for this first year that has not yet been paid. EI's rent for the month of December in the amount of $12,000 has not yet been paid. EI plans to give $10,000 to a local charity in March of next year. Inventory on hand at year end has a net cost of $422,000. EI expects to pay an estimated $20,000 discount to customers who met 2025 sales targets. EI expects to use the warehouse equipment for 10 years and did use the equipment for the entire first year. EI's estimated tax rate is 35%.

Prepare financial statements for EI for the first year of operations (on the next page).

EI: Balance Sheet as of December 31, 20Y1:

EI: Income Statement for the Year Ended December 31, 20Y1

EI: Cash Flow Statement for the Year Ended December 31, 20Y1

www.ingramcontent.com/pod-product-compliance
Lightning Source LLC
LaVergne TN
LVHW080032210926
848481LV00011B/3167
* 9 7 9 8 3 1 9 7 1 1 6 4 9 *